Hitler's Command

Hitler's Command

Luftwaffe, Kriegsmarine, V Weapons, Jets and the A Bomb

Rex Bashford

Pen & Sword
MILITARY

First published in Great Britain in 2024 by
Pen & Sword Military
An imprint of Pen & Sword Books Limited
Yorkshire – Philadelphia

Copyright © Rex Bashford 2024

ISBN 978 1 39907 036 2

The right of Rex Bashford to be identified as
Author of this Work has been asserted by him in accordance
with the Copyright, Designs and Patents Act 1988.

A CIP catalogue record for this book is
available from the British Library

The Author has taken reasonable steps to trace the copyright holders
to obtain permissions for use of images and quotations but, despite his
best endeavours, has been unable to do so. The copyright holders, or the
late copyright holders' estates, are advised to make themselves known to
the Publishers.

All rights reserved. No part of this book may be reproduced or
transmitted in any form or by any means, electronic or mechanical
including photocopying, recording or by any information storage and
retrieval system, without permission from the Publisher in writing.

Typeset by Mac Style
Printed in the UK by CPI Group (UK) Ltd, Croydon, CR0 4YY.

Pen & Sword Books Limited incorporates the imprints of After the
Battle, Atlas, Archaeology, Aviation, Discovery, Family History, Fiction,
History, Maritime, Military, Military Classics, Politics, Select, Transport,
True Crime, Air World, Frontline Publishing, Leo Cooper, Remember
When, Seaforth Publishing, The Praetorian Press, Wharncliffe
Local History, Wharncliffe Transport, Wharncliffe True Crime and
White Owl.

For a complete list of Pen & Sword titles please contact

PEN & SWORD BOOKS LIMITED
47 Church Street, Barnsley, South Yorkshire, S70 2AS, England
E-mail: enquiries@pen-and-sword.co.uk
Website: www.pen-and-sword.co.uk
or
PEN AND SWORD BOOKS
1950 Lawrence Rd, Havertown, PA 19083, USA
E-mail: uspen-and-sword@casematepublishers.com
Website: www.penandswordbooks.com

To my dear Mother, and the memory of my Father and Brother.

Contents

Glossary		viii
Introduction		x
Chapter 1	Hitler and the Kriegsmarine	1
Chapter 2	Hitler and the Luftwaffe	57
Chapter 3	Hitler's Involvement in Weapons Development Programmes and Production Priorities	109
Chapter 4	The Generals' View of Hitler as Commander-in-Chief	135
Chapter 5	The Effect on German Military Operations of the Attempted Assassination and Coup of 20 July 1944	164
Chapter 6	Hitler As Warlord – Final Conclusions	172
A Note on Sources and Further Reading		208
Epilogue		214
Appendix I: Text of the Memorandum of 3 July 1944 from Field Marshal Rommel to Hitler		220
Appendix II: Senior German Military Personnel and their Fate		224
Notes		225
Index		234

Glossary

Abwehr	The German military intelligence and secret service. The head of the service was Admiral Wilhelm Canaris, who was opposed to the Nazi regime. Canaris came into conflict with Reichsfuhrer-SS Heinrich Himmler, who suspected him of playing a double game with the enemy Western powers and convinced Hitler this was true. The Abwehr was abolished in February 1944 and its operations subsumed with those of the SS intelligence services. After the attempt on Hitler's life on 20 July 1944, Canaris was arrested by the Gestapo; although there was no direct evidence against him, he was executed on 9 April 1945.
AGp	Army Group. In the German context, usually a group of three corps of three or four divisions each. However, these groupings could be much larger; for example, Army Group Centre on the Eastern Front comprised over seventy divisions for Operation *Typhoon*, the attempt to take Moscow in October 1941.
Kriegsmarine	The name given to the naval forces of the Third Reich. It was the weakest of the three branches of the Wehrmacht, but had the crucial role of attempting to sink the merchant ships of Great Britain in sufficient numbers to compel it to surrender or cause starvation to its people. The U-boat fleet that the Germans possessed did not inflict anywhere near enough damage to achieve this, but did cause a great deal of anxiety in the Allied leadership.
Luftwaffe	The name given to the German air force during the Second World War. It was formed in 1935 when Hitler appointed Hermann Goering to be its commander-in-chief, a role he retained until the very last days of the Nazi regime.
NAZI Party	The National Socialist German Workers' Party (Nationalsozialistische Deutsche Arbeiterpartei/NSDAP).
ObDH	Oberfehlshaber des Heeres, the commander-in-chief of the army. Prior to Hitler taking over this role, it was held by Field Marshal von Brauchitsch.

Glossary

Ob West	Oberfehlshaber West. Commander-in-chief of the western group of armies in France, Holland and Belgium.
OKH	Oberkommando des Heeres, the High Command of the Army.
OKL	Oberkommando der Luftwaffe, the High Command of the Luftwaffe.
OKM	Oberkommando der Kriegsmarine, the High Command of the Navy.
OKW	Oberkommando des Wehrmacht, High Command of the Armed Forces. Hitler's personal military staff.
PzKpfw	Abbreviation of the German term for tank types, Panzerkampfwagen.
SA	The semi-military arm of the Nazi Party initially formed by Hitler to guard speakers at their meetings and to disrupt those of other political parties. At its height in 1933, it had an estimated membership of 2 million, which made it potentially more powerful than the army, which was limited to 100,000 troops by the Versailles Treaty. Hitler accused the leadership of the SA of plotting to overthrow the government, and on 30 June 1934 ('The Night of The Long Knives') used the SS to murder the leadership of the SA, even though it was comprised of some of his longest-standing and most devoted followers.
Waffen-SS	The military branch of the SS. It did not have any duties guarding concentration camps. Its units were used in conjunction with normal army units in the field and were under the direction of the army's commanders when they were employed in battle. However, they were not under the jurisdiction of the army command in any other respect, remaining under the control of the Reichsfuhrer-SS, Heinrich Himmler. The divisions of the SS conducted themselves very brutally on the battlefield, frequently not taking prisoners but murdering enemy soldiers when they had surrendered. There are well-evidenced accounts of this occurring on the Eastern and Western Fronts, which frequently led to opposing forces using the same tactics in retaliation.
Wehrmacht	The name given by Hitler to the armed forces of Nazi Germany. It encompassed four branches: the army, air force, navy and Waffen-SS.

Introduction

Hitler sent his armies to invade Poland on 1 September 1939 in what was to be the first act of his long-meditated war to create the *Lebensraum* required for his German Aryan 'master race'. The space needed by the master race was to be taken from the *untermensch*[1] who occupied the territories of the USSR, as he had so clearly stated in his Bible of Nazism, *Mein Kampf*:[2]

> 'We terminate the endless German drive to the South and West of Europe and direct our drive to the land of the East. We finally terminate the colonial and trade policy of the pre-war period and proceed to the territorial policy of the future. But if we talk about new soil and territory in Europe today we can think primarily only of Russia and its vassal border states.'

This was the war which Hitler wanted, not the war with the Western powers which resulted from his unnecessary brinkmanship with them over the issues he fabricated against Poland. Consequently, the war which the Fuhrer had to confront found Nazi Germany woefully unprepared for any conflict except a very short-term one against Poland. Hitler's diplomatic miscalculations which resulted in this situation were the most fundamental of all those he made before and during the war and are beyond rational understanding given the clarity of the repeated warnings addressed to him by the British and French governments.

The timing of his war meant that the Luftwaffe had no strategic bombers, while the Kriegsmarine had nowhere near the number of U-boats he had accepted as being necessary for any war against the Western powers and the German Army's tanks were not as powerful as those of the Allies. These were exactly the weapons Germany needed for the long-term war he had so unnecessarily provoked and now had to prosecute.

The chances of immediate success depended on superior strategy and a new combination of the weapons the Luftwaffe and the German Army possessed. Hitler believed he could rely on the leadership of the Luftwaffe, but he considered the Army's leaders reactionary and not committed to the Nazi regime, or to him. The early victories achieved did not convince the Fuhrer of their loyalty, but did convince him of his own infallibility. Victory in the West in 1940 put the doubts relating to his generals in abeyance; or did it? Hitler wasn't sure, so he continued to treat them with marked reserve bordering on contempt.[3]

Because Hitler had achieved total domination of the sources of power in the Nazi state, its economy had been virtually geared to a war footing since 1936. There was rationing and wage and price fixing before the war commenced. The most resistance Hitler had experienced in his determination to expand the military without counting the cost had come from the President of the Reichsbank and Finance Minister, Hjalmar Schacht, whom Hitler had appointed. Schacht resigned in 1937 in protest at the continued level of military spending, which he knew was unsustainable. The Fuhrer avoided this problem in the future by changing the legal status of the Reichsbank, requiring it to provide unlimited credit to the Nazi government. There had also been resistance to the scale of the expansion from the Generals,[4] which Hitler took very badly and never forgot.

The emphasis upon medium- to long-term planning regarding military operations and weapons programmes for the Wehrmacht, and the manufacturing priorities assigned to them because of the war Hitler did not want, became of the utmost importance to Germany's war effort. As he had arrogated to himself the central power relating to all matters concerning the armed forces, these matters became some of the most crucial of those which Hitler personally managed. The undisputed authority which he exercised and the decisions which he made therefore determined overall German war strategy, the operational deployment of the armed forces – and especially the Army – the types of weapons developed for all branches of the Wehrmacht and the production priorities assigned to them, together with every other major decision regarding the German war effort.

The previous two volumes of my trilogy have dealt with the structure of Hitler's military command and the effect of his decisions on the major campaigns Germany was committed to by his concepts of military strategy, political ideology and diplomacy. This concluding volume deals in detail with his relationship with the command of the Luftwaffe and Kriegsmarine, and how those arms of the Wehrmacht were affected by his strategic and operational decisions. It also investigates the effect of Hitler's involvement in the development of new weapons for the German armed forces and his decisions relating to the priority the various programmes and weapons were accorded for production.

The most important and resource-intensive projects affecting the front-line fighting power of the Wehrmacht were those relating to tanks, U-boats and aircraft, so I have analysed these in detail. Because of their relative importance to the Fuhrer's view of how they could affect the war, I have also included information regarding the V-1 and V-2, to which Hitler accorded the highest priority in the war programmes because he saw them as potentially war-winning weapons.

This volume also includes a chapter looking at the views expressed by the most senior commanders of the Army with respect to Hitler's competence as the military warlord of Germany, so far as those perceptions can be determined. In this regard, the recorded views of the three most senior commanders of the OKW,[5] who were the same for the duration of the war, have been included, along with those of the three Chiefs of the General Staff,[6] five field marshals,[7] who were also the most senior field commanders of the German armed forces during the Second World War, and the senior-most Waffen-SS commander.[8] These have been ascertained from comments they made in interviews or from material published soon after the end of the war. In this regard, I have also included material from Hermann Goering, as he was the most senior military officer in the Wehrmacht,[9] Commander-in-Chief of the Luftwaffe and Hitler's designated political successor until the very last days of the war, together with his views on some of the most important campaigns that Hitler committed the Wehrmacht to undertake. The views of General Hasso von Manteuffel have been included too, as he was one of Hitler's most favoured generals, commanded the Fifth Panzer Army during the Ardennes offensive and was exposed to the Fuhrer's decision-making during most of the war. I have also frequently referred to the views expressed by Grand Admiral Doenitz as he was in command of the U-boat fleet and was at the highest levels of the Nazi state throughout the conflict. I have not included material from other more junior commanders because they did not play a large part in the general strategy of the war.

The Kriegsmarine was the weakest of the arms of the Wehrmacht at the commencement of the war when viewed in comparison with the strength of the navies of other major nations, especially that of Great Britain. In order to succeed in its role, the strategy for its use had to be exceptionally well defined and executed, and the means for achieving that strategy had to be identified and procured with the utmost speed. Plan Z, which was developed by Grand Admiral Raeder, involved the construction of a surface fleet of battleships, aircraft carriers and other conventional ship types that were intended to be constructed by 1944–45, which was the time Hitler had specified as being likely for a major war. The plan was based around a strategy of commerce raiding to disperse the elements of the Royal Navy so that the Kriegsmarine would be able to deal with isolated units of it, but such ideas were out of date by the time the war occurred because it was no longer possible for naval raiders to 'disappear' – as had been the case in previous conflicts – because of the use of aircraft and other technical developments. The plan also envisaged that aircraft carriers would be used to provide long-range reconnaissance for the surface ships of the German fleet, which would then destroy the enemy fleet through its main heavy units rather than through carrier-borne aircraft. This approach would have been extremely difficult to achieve given the enormous superiority of the Royal Navy in all classes of combat ships, including aircraft carriers. However, the ships of Plan Z would have presented a real threat to Britain had it been completed, not because the intended strategy was the best possible use of the ships, but because the plan called for the construction of 229 U-boats, which would have caused great difficulties for the British in the protection of their oceanic trade. As events turned out, at the beginning of the war, the Germans only had fifty-seven U-boats, and yet with this very modest force they were able to cause the greatest difficulty to the British in defending their trade arteries. The losses which the Germans inflicted were spectacular given the small number of U-boats they had and the almost complete absence of co-operation from the Luftwaffe, which was supposed to provide reconnaissance capabilities for the U-boats. Admiral Doenitz, who was the officer in charge of the German submarine fleet, recognized before the war that the only chance the Germans had to inflict meaningful damage on British maritime trade was to use an unrestricted U-boat campaign as soon as possible and with the greatest number of boats possible. To this end, Doenitz attempted to have the construction of U-boats given the highest priority in the German war production programme as soon as hostilities broke out. Nevertheless, it was not until April 1943 that Hitler assigned the highest priority to U-boat construction, which proved too late because of Allied technological countermeasures and the more efficient management and use of their air force and naval resources.

In dealing with Hitler's involvement with the Luftwaffe, its creation and deployment, it is vital to determine the effect of his decisions on its ability to carry out a strategic bombing campaign and to defend Germany against the Allied strategic bombing offensive. The virtual non-existence of a strategic bombing fleet was the main reason for Germany's inability to inflict serious damage on British industry during the Blitz in 1940 and 1941. While this lack of heavy bombers was the result of a decision by Goering, the timing of the war against Britain was entirely due to Hitler's miscalculations. The Fuhrer's decisions regarding the deployment of the Luftwaffe were also directly responsible for the defence of the Reich and the damage which occurred to German industry and population. Analysis of the findings of the United States Strategic Bombing Survey show just how damaging the Allied strategic bombing offensive was to German industry. The effects on German society were also certainly very significant, perhaps even more than the effect on manufacturing. The Allied strategic bombing offensive was the single most important factor in the demise of the Luftwaffe through the battles which occurred for air supremacy over Germany. However, the air offensive also caused major resources to be diverted to the defence of Germany through the need for radar systems, anti-aircraft artillery, munitions and thousands of personnel moved away from other war-related activities. These diversions caused a significant reduction in the defensive and offensive power of the German Army, markedly lowering the number of tanks and anti-tank weapons which could be put in the field together with the number of recruits available. These reductions materially assisted the Soviet offensives from 1943 onwards, as the Germans lacked the defensive armament to defeat them. Not only was it unable to combat the Allied bomber offensive, but the Wehrmacht was starved of other vital equipment and supplies such as petrol because of the damage caused to the manufacturing infrastructure and related resources of the Reich. Hitler's decisions concerning the defence of the Reich by the Luftwaffe were therefore existential for Germany, as were those relating to the development and production of new aircraft and other weapons systems to defeat the enemy bombers. In this context, the decisions the Fuhrer made with respect to the Me 262 project are extremely instructive.

The V-1 and V-2 weapons could not have been produced but for Hitler's enthusiastic support. While they are primitive by today's standards, they represented a radical departure from any weapons system which had previously existed. They were also the most expensive of the German new weapons development programmes, consuming some five billion Reichsmarks between them. The comparison of the damage they caused and their cost with that of conventional four-engine bomber has been included in my analysis, and is extremely interesting and important in understanding why the Allies won the war.

The German capacity to create the atom bomb has caused much discussion since the war, much of it speculative and based on hypotheses which convey an incorrect and misleading view of the true situation. Albert Speer, the Minister of Armaments, co-ordinated all aspects of German weapons production, and his view of the situation is clear and conclusive. It is interesting to note that Hitler's racial views also played an important part in the potential development of these weapons.

The Fuhrer's views and decisions also determined the type of tanks produced by German industry, the number of them and their operational availability. These decisions were therefore extremely important to the day-to-day front-line fighting power of the German Army. There is little doubt that their impact was detrimental to the power and mobility of the panzer forces Germany could field during the war. That he initially created the panzer forces which made such a difference to the 1940 campaign, only to impair their fighting ability by his decisions, is another irony associated with Hitler's methods of discharging the roles he assigned to himself.

The attempted putsch known as Operation *Valkyrie* was the most significant act of resistance against the Nazi regime, and was ultimately the result of Hitler's mistrust of the German Army's leadership during the war. One of its most important results was the final and complete erosion of the relationship between Hitler and the command of the Army. Hitler imposed his version of command on the Army which was totally anathema to the tenets previously inculcated by the German General Staff. Hitler's methods completely stifled all initiative in the lower levels of the command structure and were entirely consistent with his view of his own infallibility.

The chapter of this book titled 'Hitler as Warlord – Final Conclusions', based on all the available information regarding the Fuhrer's performance of the numerous roles he attempted to fulfil, leaves little doubt that his exercise of command over the German war effort and Wehrmacht was disastrous for Germany. The tragedy of his rule is that it took so many lives to destroy him despite the numerous manifestations of this incompetence.

Chapter 1

Hitler and the Kriegsmarine

When Adolf Hitler became Chancellor in January 1933, Germany was bound by the terms of the Treaty of Versailles regarding the composition and size of its naval forces. The treaty imposed a limit of 15,000 personnel for the navy, which effectively meant that it could perform little more than coastal defence. There were also limits on the size and types of ships which Germany could build and an absolute ban on U-boats in its fleet. These limits were intentional, as the High Seas Fleet which Germany had possessed during the First World War was a major cause of international tension and a real threat to the commerce of the rest of the world. The restrictions caused much resentment and bitterness in German nationalist circles, the armed forces and much of the community.

The German Navy had been under the command of Admiral Erich Raeder since 1928. Raeder, a product of the Imperial Navy, had been on the staff of Grand Admiral von Tirpitz during the First World War, which inevitably influenced his views on the type of ships and war strategy which the Kriegsmarine should adopt.

The Kriegsmarine was formally created on 21 May 1935 by the passing of the Law for the Reconstruction of the National Defence Forces. This law also reconstituted the German Army, with a peacetime strength of thirty-six divisions, and created the air force (Luftwaffe), which had been banned under the terms of the Versailles Treaty. The three services were collectively termed the Wehrmacht (Defence Force), which was the name used for them during the whole of the Second World War.

The Anglo-German Naval Agreement of 1935

Hitler's avowed policy with respect to naval rearmament was to avoid any conflict with Great Britain, or to give any cause for tension relating to the speed and level of German naval rearmament. To this end, the Nazi Foreign Minister, Joachim von Ribbentrop, was given the task of negotiating a limit on naval rearmament with Britain which would enable Germany to rearm but cause no undue concern. By doing so, the Fuhrer also hoped to create an issue that would potentially cause friction between Britain and its allies from the First World War. The German proposals were in clear violation of the Versailles Treaty, but the British National government of Ramsay MacDonald seemed to be unconcerned with this obvious problem.

The terms of the Anglo-German Naval Agreement, which was signed on 18 June 1935, limited the size of the German fleet to 35 per cent that of the British Royal Navy and allowed Germany to build up to 100 per cent of the submarines that Britain possessed within that limit, although the Germans stated that they would not build more than 40 per cent without first giving notice to the British. The size of new German capital ships was limited to 35,000 tons. It is difficult to understand the reasoning behind the British acceptance of these terms. At that time, there was no prospect of Germany being able to match the size of the British fleet, which was still the largest in the world. German shipyards had not built any major ships since during the First World War, and their capacity to do so was very limited compared to the programmes which culminated in the powerful German High Seas fleet of 1914–18. It was also obvious that the successful negotiation of such an agreement would enhance Hitler's prestige within Germany and internationally and had the potential to cause friction with other naval powers, particularly France, which was not included under its terms or consulted with respect to them, whereas it was included in the Washington Treaty regarding naval limitations and also the Treaty of Versailles. Subsequent to the naval agreement, France commenced the construction of two new battleships which were larger and more heavily armed than the new British King George V class, which led to a protest from Britain. The French merely stated that the new ships were being constructed to counter the Italian Littorio-class ships being built, and contended that the new British agreement was a breach of Versailles, which was entirely reasonable and foreseeable.

During the course of an answer relating to the new agreement given in the House of Commons debate relating to its contents, the First Lord of the Admiralty, Sir Bolton Eyres Monsell, stated:[1]

> 'We have to deal with the essentially practical problem that Germany is already constructing a fleet which is outside the limits laid down in the Versailles Treaty.'

This statement is not entirely correct, as before the Anglo-German Agreement the Germans built only ships which were stated to be in conformity with the restrictions of the Treaty of Versailles. The so-called pocket battleships of the Deutschland class were stated to be within the 10,000-ton limit in the treaty and had various innovations which made them lighter than other ships with equivalent armament. However, these ships weighed approximately 16,000 tons fully loaded, but because of differences in the way that the displacement of ships was calculated, the Germans were able to argue that the ships did not infringe the limits set by the treaty. Nevertheless, although these ships were a clear violation of the treaty, they were not a threat to either the British or French navies and could not have stood up to any serious combat. The battlecruiser *Scharnhorst*, which was the first capital ship said to be constructed under the terms of the Anglo-German Naval Agreement, was clearly contrary to the terms of the Versailles Treaty but was not commenced until 15 June 1935, by which time the terms of the new agreement with Britain were known. Since these ships conformed to the new agreement, however, Britain could hardly complain of the breach of the Treaty of Versailles. Acceptance of the German proposal seems to have been motivated by a well-intentioned but naïve belief that the Nazis would adhere to its terms, leading to the likelihood of other similar agreements to control naval armaments. Neither result ensued.

The Anglo-German Agreement was amended in 1938 to increase the displacement of new capital ships to 45,000 tons, which both governments agreed was necessary to take into account the new French and Italian construction, and the Germans gave the required notice that they would increase the size of their U-boat fleet up to that of the British submarine fleet. The result of the agreement was therefore entirely negative for Britain, especially with respect to its diplomatic relations with France, and wholly positive for Germany. It can only be regarded as a self-inflicted wound of the first magnitude for Britain.

When Britain gave a guarantee of Poland's territorial integrity in March 1939, Hitler cited this as one of the reasons for denouncing the naval agreement, which he did on 28 April 1939. Thus, the terms of the agreement were only operative for less than four years.

Plan Z

Plan Z was developed by Admiral Raeder to reconstitute the German Navy, which Hitler had redesignated as the Kriegsmarine, within the limits of the Anglo-German Naval Agreement as a balanced force intended to be built and in place by 1944–45. This was the date that Hitler had specified to Raeder by which tensions between Great Britain and Germany might lead to war.

The new ships which were intended to be built by the end of 1944 had Plan Z been achieved were as follows:[2]

eight battleships;
five battlecruisers;
three pocket battleships;
two aircraft carriers;
five heavy cruisers;
four light cruisers;
nine scout cruisers;
fifty destroyers;
fifty-four torpedo boats; and
229 U-boats.

However, the fleet which actually existed on 1 September 1939 when Hitler decided to invade Poland was as follows:[3]

two battleships (*Scharnhorst* and *Gneisenau*);
two battleships nearing completion (*Bismarck* and *Tirpitz*);
three pocket battleships (*Graf Spee*, *Scheer* and *Deutschland*);
three heavy cruisers (*Admiral Hipper*, *Blucher* and *Prinz Eugen*, the latter awaiting completion);
five light cruisers (*Koenigsberg*, *Nuernberg*, *Leipzig*, *Koeln* and *Karlsruhe*);
22 Destroyers;
20 Torpedo boats and small destroyers and
fifty-seven U-boats.

Added to this were several obsolescent ships from the First World War era which had no significant combat value. It can thus be seen that the outbreak of war in 1939 left the Kriegsmarine in a position of total inferiority to the Royal Navy, which then comprised fifteen battleships (with an additional nine being built or intended), six aircraft carriers (plus six being built or intended), 15 heavy cruisers, 40 light cruisers (with an additional eight being built), six anti-aircraft cruisers (with sixteen more being built), 113 modern destroyers (with an additional twenty-four being built), sixty-eight older destroyers, fifty-four escort destroyers (with 80 more being built), forty-seven modern submarines (plus twelve being built) and forty-two fleet minesweepers (with an additional ten being built).[4] The Royal Navy was justified in believing that with such superiority there was no realistic chance that the Germans would be able to effectively dispute control of the Atlantic shipping lanes which were so vital to Britain's survival.

In a document entitled 'Reflections of the C.-in-C., Navy, on the Outbreak of War, September 3, 1939', contained in the 'Fuhrer Conferences on Naval Affairs 1939–1945', Admiral Raeder stated:[5]

> 'Today the war against France and England broke out, the war which, according to the Fuhrer's previous assertions, we had no need to expect before about 1944.'

His frustration is palpable. That same day, Raeder added:[6]

> 'The surface forces, moreover, are so inferior in number and strength to those of the British Fleet that, even at full strength, they can do no more than show that they know how to die gallantly and thus are willing to create the foundations for later reconstruction.'

Attempting to complete Plan Z would have presented at least three formidable practical problems for the Nazi state. Firstly, there was not enough capacity at shipyards to construct the projected fleet within the timeframe required or the skilled labour available to achieve it. The British Admiralty commentary on the situation in *Brassey's Naval Annual 1948* states:[7]

> 'The development of the German Navy under the Nazi regime was governed by the amount of ship-building German yards could undertake and the type of warfare to be waged. The first factor limited German naval expansion far more than anything else. The London Treaty of 1935 allowed Germany to have a navy of 35 per cent of British surface warships and 100 per cent of British submarines, but in spite of this the limitations of the German shipbuilding yards did not permit a navy of such a size to be completed before 1944/45. The beginning of British naval rearmament on December 31, 1936, caused Hitler to issue an order for German naval construction to be speeded up with particular emphasis on U-boats, but though this order did improve matters slightly, the physical difficulties of insufficient yards and factories could not be quickly overcome.

Secondly, the fuel needed by the ships envisaged was more than the entire fuel consumption of the Reich during 1938.[8] The total available was 6 million tons for the whole of Germany, but the estimated consumption of the ships of Plan Z would have exceeded this level in war conditions. Although crucial to the whole viability of the plan, neither Hitler nor Raeder ever addressed this basic problem,[9] which surely shows the almost total absence and chaotic state of strategic planning in Nazi Germany.

Thirdly, the finances of the Reich were stretched to the limit by the already existing rearmament programme. Hitler had appointed Horace Greely

Schacht, who was an internationally recognized expert economist, as President of the Reichsbank and Finance Minister. Schacht resigned both positions in 1937 because he disagreed with the Fuhrer's continuing acceleration of the rearmament programme. In his evidence before the Nuremberg Tribunal, Schacht stated that as President of the Reichsbank,[10] 'I blocked Hitler's credits', which meant that the rearmament programme could not be further expanded. After sidelining Schacht, Hitler changed the law and the Reichsbank provided unlimited funding for his rearmament plans. Schacht was suspected (correctly) of being peripherally involved in the 20 July 1944 attempted assassination of Hitler and was imprisoned by the Nazis. Nevertheless, he survived the war and ironically was also a defendant at the Nuremberg trials, where he was charged with having co-operated in Hitler's conspiracy to wage aggressive war by financing the rearmament programme but was found not guilty.

It is hard to see how the plan could have been achieved within the limitations imposed by the resources available to Germany in 1939. Perhaps Hitler already saw the resources of his Eastern empire as being available for the realization of his dreams.

The Surface Ships of Plan Z

The emphasis of Plan Z on battleships and battlecruisers reveals Raeder's belief that these ships would still be crucial in naval warfare, which was certainly still the prevalent view in all the navies of the major powers during the 1920s and 1930s. There were two types of battleships proposed in the plan, of which only one was ever built, the Bismarck class (*Bismarck* and *Tirpitz*). The other type, known as the H class, were to be larger and armed with eight 16in guns. Three of the latter were commenced but were scrapped immediately after the war commenced. During the planning of the H-class ships, Hitler expressed the view that they should be armed with 800mm main guns, which is equal to 31½in. These would have been the largest guns by far ever mounted on any battleship, the largest actually fitted to an operational battleship being the 18.1in guns of the Japanese Yamato class. During the design estimates for the H class, it was established that a ship capable of mounting the 800mm weapons would have a displacement approaching 110,000 tons, making them unable to dock in any German port. Furthermore, with the limited German steel manufacturing capacity, they would have absorbed far too much steel to be practically possible. Consequently, the H-class ships were reduced to 16in main armament with a displacement of over 65,000 tons,[11] which would still have made them larger than any battleships built except for the Japanese Yamato class.

The Bismarck class were built within the limits set by the 1935 Anglo-German Naval Agreement as amended in 1938, but were a clear violation of the Versailles Treaty. They were very well constructed and were very stable gun platforms. Their optical ranging system was excellent, but in other respects their design was not in keeping with the most advanced contemporary naval thinking. Firstly, the main armament consisted of eight 15in guns in four double turrets. All other new capital ship designs around the world used either triple or quadruple gun turrets for their main armament, which permitted more guns at a lower total weight per gun. A crucial reason for using this configuration was that by having fewer turrets, the ship's armour could be concentrated more effectively in protecting the turret and ammunition supply system and magazines. Secondly, the Bismarck class's secondary armament consisted of four different types of guns, which meant that its endurance in battle was limited by having so many different types of ammunition. In the latest British and US ships, the main secondary armament for anti-aircraft and anti-ship purposes were of one type, so more ammunition could be provided for each gun.

The radar used by the Germans was not as advanced as that of contemporary Allied vessels. The *Bismarck* was fitted with a Funkmessortung 25 and 26 Seetakt Gema set, which was standard equipment on Kriegsmarine ships at the time. But this equipment could not be used for gun control; it was the excellent Zeiss optical range-finding equipment that meant the *Bismarck*'s accurate fire was able to quickly destroy HMS *Hood*.[12] The *Bismarck*'s sinking of the British battlecruiser was not a true test of the German ship's strength and power, as the *Hood* was a battlecruiser with comparatively light armour and should never have been committed against a battleship in any combat situation.

The Scharnhorst class were referred to by the Germans as battleships, being very strongly built with good armour protection, but the British and other navies always called them battlecruisers. Indeed, for a ship of their size, they were lightly armed, having only nine 11in guns as main armament. This limit was imposed by the Fuhrer, who was concerned that any larger armament would prevent the British from agreeing to the Naval Agreement he was intending to propose,[13] as set out above. In comparison, the battlecruisers of the Royal Navy had 15in main guns and the Dunkirk-class French battlecruisers had 13½in armament. There were plans for the Scharnhorst class to be retrofitted with six 15in guns, but this could not be accomplished during the war years. The Scharnhorst class were not good sea-keeping ships, being so wet that the bows had to be completely redesigned and replaced after construction was completed to reduce the amount of sea water shipped at high speed or during anything but moderate seas. They also had a very similar configuration of secondary armament types as the Bismarck class, and therefore the same deficiencies. Their engines were of a new design and not yet reliable. On 3 September 1939, Raeder described them as follows:[14]

> 'The *Scharnhorst* and the *Gneisenau*, which are still by no means ready for action or reliable in operation.

One of the German aircraft carriers had been commenced, the *Graf Zeppelin*, but its construction was halted when the war began; although recommenced in 1942, it was stopped for good in 1943. The aircraft for the ship had been designed and prototypes were produced, which were variants on the Messerschmitt Me 109 and the Junkers Ju 87 Stuka. These planes would probably have been quite effective in action, although the Me 109 may have been difficult to land aboard ship because of its undercarriage design. The ships would have displaced approximately 33,000 tons and were designed to carry only forty-two aircraft, so were not likely to be as effective as the latest contemporary designs which carried more aircraft.[15]

The Deutschland-class Panzerschiffe (the pocket battleships) were intended for commerce raiding and were very well designed for that purpose. They had a main battery of six 11in guns, a secondary armament of eight 5.9in guns and a top speed of 26 knots. They were diesel-powered, which gave them a cruising range of over 30,000km, making them well suited to commerce raiding. Their armament was sufficient to overpower most convoy escorts, but they were not heavily armoured; the Battle of the River Plate, where the *Graf Spee* was attacked by two light and one heavy British cruisers off the coast of Uruguay and Argentina, gave clear evidence that these ships could not absorb much punishment. Although their armament was completely outclassed by the *Graf Spee*, the British cruisers raced in to attack at very close ranges, from which even their armament could inflict damage. Although the British ships were heavily damaged themselves, the *Graf Spee* was too and had to seek harbour to make repairs to be seaworthy. Raeder reported to Hitler on 16 December 1939:[16]

> 'The C.-in-C, Navy, reports that at least two weeks are needed to make the *Graf Spee* seaworthy, and that the Government of Uruguay has granted only 72 hours.'

The 72-hour limit was the time specified by international agreements for ships of states at war being permitted to stay in neutral harbours. Another problem exposed was that the ammunition available was almost exhausted by the engagement, which was a problem that could only be dealt with by replenishment at sea. The *Graf Spee* was thus scuttled, while its supply ships were found and destroyed. The threat to merchant shipping from these commerce raiders did not develop to anywhere near the degree which Plan Z had intended.

The Hipper-class heavy cruisers were once again very well constructed, and with a main armament of eight 8in guns were formidable. But they too were not comparable with the latest similar US ships, which had nine 9in guns, and their propulsion system was not reliable, causing them to cut short several missions. Their range of 6,750 miles was also very limited, which meant that these ships would have to be refuelled at sea to fulfil their role as commerce raiders.

The German destroyers were not good sea-keeping ships, which was mainly caused by them being 'over gunned' with 5.9in guns which were too heavy. This caused them to retire from missions before they had been accomplished due to their poor stability in even moderately heavy seas.

The lack of experience of the designers of the new German ships thus meant that they suffered significant limitations in operational situations. Furthermore, the ships which had been completed did not by any means create a balanced force which could have any effect on the supremacy of the Royal Navy.

Plan Z and U-Boats

Karl Doenitz was appointed by Raeder as commander of the U-boat arm of the Kriegsmarine, with the title Fuehrer der U-Boote and rank of captain, on 1 October 1936. He had experience in the U-boat service, having been the commander of a submarine in the Mediterranean during the First World War. He claimed that he always had a strategy for the use of U-boats that dated from his experience in the Great War, which he called 'wolfpacks'. He outlined this strategy in a paper he wrote on 23 November 1937, entitled 'The Employment of U-boats in the Framework of the Fleet'. Simply put, this tactic, which had not been used by either side during the First World War, involved as many U-boats as possible acting together to hunt and sink merchant ships sailing in convoys. Convoys had been adopted as a very successful means of protecting merchant shipping, for although they may be large, they were still difficult to locate on the vast oceans. Concentrating the ships also allowed the defending navy vessels to optimise their defensive capacity. By using U-boats in wolfpacks, these advantages could be largely negated. In his memoirs, Doenitz comments:[17]

'The tactics of U-boats operating in unison were tried out for the first time in large-scale exercises at the "German Armed Forces Manoeuvres" in the autumn of 1937. As Officer Commanding U-boats, I was aboard a submarine depot ship in Kiel, from which by wireless I directed the operations being conducted by U-boats in the Baltic. Their task was to locate, concentrate and attack an enemy formation and convoy somewhere on the high seas to the north of the coasts of Pomerania and West and East Prussia. The operation of bringing the concentrated submarines into contact with their objective was carried out with complete and impressive success. After further large-scale exercises in the North Sea, in May 1939 the U-boats carried out an exercise in "group tactics" in the Atlantic to the west of the Iberian peninsula and the Bay of Biscay. ... All these exercises showed that we had evolved the right principles in our solution of the problem and that the tactical details were also perfectly clear, in so far as it was possible to clarify tactical details in peace time.'

This was the strategy which Doenitz put in place and used throughout the war against Allied shipping.

Once he had realized the full offensive potential of the U-boat as the commander of the German submarine arm, Doenitz strove to have the largest number of them possible produced as part of the expansion of the Kriegsmarine. This was a very logical step for Germany to take, as U-boats were faster to construct, required far fewer resources and were therefore a much lesser strain on the already stretched Nazi economy. As a result of his representations to Raeder, the number of U-boats in the final Plan Z was 229, to be ready by 1944, as set out above. If these had been built, it would have presented a major problem for the Royal Navy, which did not have anywhere near enough destroyers and other anti-submarine ships to contain such a large number of U-boats. However, at the outbreak of war, the number which had been built was only fifty-seven. During his defence at the trial of the Nazi war criminals in Nuremberg, Doenitz was cross-examined on the matter:[18]

Flottenrichter Kranzbuhler: 'In the year 1939, then, was the German U-boat service prepared technically and tactically for a naval war against England?'

Doenitz: 'No. The German U-boat service, in the fall of 1939, consisted of about thirty to forty operational boats. That meant that at any time about one-third could be used for operations. In view of the harsh reality the situation seemed much worse later. There was one month, for instance, when we had only two boats out at sea. With this small number of U-boats it was, of course, only possible to give pinpricks to a great naval power such as England. That we were not prepared for war against England in the Navy is, in my opinion, best and most clearly to be seen from the fact that the armament of the Navy had to be radically changed at the beginning of the war. It had been the intention to create a homogeneous fleet which, of course, since it was in proportion much smaller than the British fleet, was not capable of waging a war against England. This programme for building a homogeneous fleet had to be discontinued when the war with England started; only these large ships which were close to completion were finished. Everything else was abandoned or scrapped. That was necessary in order to free the building capacity for building U-boats. And that, also, explains why the German U-boat war, in this last war, actually only started in the year 1942, that is to say, when the U-boats which had been ordered for building at the beginning of the war were ready for action. Since peacetime, that is in 1940, the replacement of U-boats hardly covered the losses.

There is no doubt that this statement is correct, and that the U-boat arm of the Kriegsmarine did not have anywhere near the number of craft needed to present a major problem to British trade from the beginning of the war. This was, however, not because of any lack of effort or intent on Doenitz's part.

It is of great importance to note that Hitler did not give the highest priority to the construction of U-boats until April 1943, although he had been pressed to do so by Doenitz. Albert Speer, the German Armaments Minister, commented on the situation as follows:[19]

'Without consulting me, after hearing a report from Doenitz, Hitler raised all naval armament to the highest priority. This happened in the middle of April, but only three months before, on January 22, 1943, he had already classified the expanded tank programme as the task of highest priority. The upshot was that the two programmes would be competing. It was unnecessary for me to appeal to Hitler again. Before any controversy developed, Doenitz had already realized that co-operation with the massive apparatus of army procurement would be more useful than Hitler's favoritism. We soon agreed to transfer naval armaments to my organization. In taking this on, I pledged myself to carry out the naval programme Doenitz had envisaged. This meant instead of the previous monthly production of twenty submarines of the smaller type totalling sixteen thousand tons displacement, producing forty U-boats per month with a displacement totalling more than fifty thousand tons.'

This illustrates in microcosm the confusion which reigned at the top of the Nazi war effort, which Speer states to be one of the primary problems the Germans had during the war, and which is dealt with in detail later in this volume. It also highlights that Hitler did not properly appreciate the importance of U-boats in the maritime war against Great Britain or the full potential in it of submarines, or he would have made U-boat construction the highest priority long before he did.

Plan Z and Naval Aviation

Plan Z envisaged that the role of naval aviation would be an extremely important element of the total naval strategy, and included the development of land- and carrier-based aircraft capability which would be organic elements of the Kriegsmarine. However, naval aviation was conceived as having essentially a limited role, which concentrated on using aircraft as a means of reconnaissance and target finding for other units of the fleet. The aircraft carriers were seen primarily within this role, with the range of their aircraft being an extension of reconnaissance enabling the surface ships to attack worthwhile targets. How the role would have developed in practice may have been substantially different, as happened during the war with other navies in the light of battle experience.

The biggest problem which the Kriegsmarine had to deal with for the development of its own air power was the concentration of all responsibility for it and related matters of the Nazi state in the person of Reichsmarschall Hermann Goering. He was not only commander-in-chief of the Luftwaffe, but also Minister for Aviation and in charge of the Four-Year Plan, in which role he co-ordinated all aspects of the German economy. These offices gave Goering complete control over the allocation of all raw materials and all aspects of production relating to the Wehrmacht, unless his decisions were overridden by Hitler. He was determined to keep the development of air power firmly under his own control and was in a much more powerful position to do so than the commander-in-chief of the Kriegsmarine, who had no other government positions from which to dispute anything Goering decided. A similar problem relating to the development of aircraft for the Royal Navy had pertained in Britain during the 1920s and 1930s, in that the RAF was allocated responsibility for the development of naval aircraft. The result was that the Royal Navy entered the Second World War with obsolescent aircraft because naval air arm requirements were seen as a secondary priority by the RAF, which concentrated on its needs.

This situation applied during the entire war for the Kriegsmarine and meant that all maritime and naval aviation matters had to be organized through Luftwaffe co-operation channels, which were less than efficient on many occasions. In a chapter entitled 'Luftwaffe Support of the German Navy' in the book *The Battle of The Atlantic 1939–1945*, author Horst Boog[20] comments upon the situation regarding air power for the Kriegsmarine:[21]

> 'Germany's failure in the Battle of the Atlantic was to a large extent also the failure of Luftwaffe air support for the Kriegsmarine.'

On 3 June 1943, Doenitz made a presentation to the senior members of the U-boat command in which he addressed the crisis which had arisen in the North Atlantic due to the success of Allied defensive measures against the U-boat campaign. He said:[22]

> '*Counter measures*. **Remove forces from the main operating area** [author's emphasis] in the North Atlantic to concentrate on areas that are not so closely watched. It is imperative that I make the U-boats more powerful. Although this development could have been foreseen, few weapons have been developed.
> **This crisis originated in our air force** [author's emphasis]. This is our fault, since we built a strong U-boat force, but not an air force to support it. In spite of this, we have to make up for it now.'

There are two important aspects of this extract. The first is that Doenitz decided that the U-boats must leave the North Atlantic. This admission of failure on the part of the Kriegsmarine was of vital importance because it meant that the lend-lease convoys on which Great Britain and the USSR largely depended would not be intercepted and sunk by German submarines, although the Luftwaffe did continue to attack the convoys. The depredations of the U-boats had caused the utmost concern to the Allies, so the retirement of the U-boat fleet from the North Atlantic was a significant blow against the German war effort. Although it was still possible for the U-boats to achieve sinkings in other areas of the ocean, the main convoy routes were all in the North Atlantic; moving the U-boats from there meant that the Allies' supply position was markedly improved.

The second important aspect to note is that Doenitz specifically refers to the failure of the Luftwaffe and the lack of aircraft to fulfil the necessary convoy detection role, which was vital for the U-boats to achieve maximum effect. The lack of these types of aircraft was directly attributable to decisions made by Hitler and Goering to concentrate on the development of all aircraft in the Luftwaffe, which meant that aircraft manufacturing programmes did not take into account the special needs of the Kriegsmarine. This was also a consequence of the failure of the Fuhrer's diplomatic efforts to avoid a general war at this time following the German attack on Poland.

The inevitable conclusion from these facts is that the internal politics of the Nazi state curtailed the development of a force capable of providing the necessary reconnaissance capability for the Kriegsmarine, which materially lessened the effectiveness of the U-boat campaign.

German Naval War Strategy

Admiral Raeder and the other senior officers of the Kriegsmarine realized that even had the ships of Plan Z been constructed, they would not be able to directly challenge the dominance of the Royal Navy because the British had already commenced a new capital ship construction programme to ensure that they retained their advantage, as previously outlined. The British programme commenced with construction of five King George V-class battleships, which were each armed with ten 14in guns as their main armament and were a match for the Bismarck class. These were to be followed by six Lion-class battleships armed with nine 16in guns. The Lion-class vessels would therefore be more powerfully armed than the planned German H-class ships, and furthermore the new British ships were more numerous than the German ones. The British had also commenced the building of new aircraft carriers and the other classes of vessel needed for the support of their capital ships, which would have significantly overpowered the German construction programme. Additionally, the British had a very large margin of advantage with respect to submarines, which they could have increased by new construction at any time. This British augmentation would have resulted in the Royal Navy at least maintaining its dominant position over the Kriegsmarine, even if all the ships proposed in Plan Z were constructed.

The German maritime war strategy was therefore designed around the need to disperse the British fleet so that the Kriegsmarine could deal with it in separate parts. This was intended to be accomplished by using commerce raiders to attack British merchant shipping, which would in turn force the British to use some of the main units of the Royal Navy to protect convoys; when this occurred, the opportunity would arise for the Germans to attack the remaining British units with a stronger grouping of the Kriegsmarine. The internal staff study embodying this strategy, entitled 'Sea Warfare Against England', was carried out at Raeder's instruction and produced by Admiral Hellmuth Heye, dated 25 October 1938.[23]

Some conclusions of the study make curious reading in retrospect. First of these was the expectation that the role of the U-boat would not be as significant as it had been in the First World War. It was believed this would be the result of the technological advance made with Asdic (Anti-Submarine Detection Investigation Committee) towards the end of the Great War, which enabled the detection of U-boats while underwater and was a precursor of the much more powerful and efficient Sonar (Sound Navigation and Ranging) system. Asdic had been one of the main weapons the British had used to defeat the German U-boat campaign in the First World War, and it was expected that this would be the case again. It is hard to believe, however, that the study came to this conclusion when it is considered how close the Germans came to success in the U-boat war against Britain in the Great War. Doenitz recounted in his memoirs:[24]

> 'After the First World War the British had written and published a great deal about a new British apparatus for the detection of a submerged submarine – the ASDIC which, it was claimed, could locate and pinpoint the position of a submarine at a range of many thousands of yards, by means of echoes produced with the help of sound waves. The submarine, therefore, could be regarded, in British official opinion as a more or less obsolete weapon, and it was not thought by the British that other nations would find it worthwhile to continue to build them.
>
> 'For these reasons there existed in the German Navy, too, in 1935, considerable doubts about the real value of the new U-boats, even though the obviously enhanced dangers of service in a submarine, the greater measure of independence enjoyed by the arm and the undimmed glory of the German U-boats in the First World War still made the new arm attractive in the eyes of young and zealous officers, petty officers and men.'

The result of this appreciation was that Doenitz, as head of the U-boat arm of the Kriegsmarine, had a significant battle to incorporate the number of submarines he considered necessary in Plan Z to give a real chance for the U-boat war against Britain to succeed. Even then, however, because of the relatively low priority assigned to U-boat construction, the number of them that were available upon the commencement of war was nowhere near the level he deemed necessary to starve Britain. Indeed, the results which were achieved are amazing given the small number of U-boats in service at that time.

The study resulted in Plan Z, which was presented by Raeder to Hitler and adopted by him on 27 January 1939. The British Admiralty commented in *Brassey's Naval Annual 1948*:[25]

'The type of naval warfare that Germany should wage was the subject of considerable controversy. Goering believed implicitly in the Luftwaffe which he boasted would be more than a match for any ship, and Hitler was to some extent swayed by his opinion. The High Command was also "land-minded" and was ignorant of the importance of sea power. Nevertheless, Hitler supported Raeder's plans during the pre-war years and encouraged the building of a surface fleet as well as the development of the U-boat arm. In deciding what ships to build Raeder was guided by Hitler's early contentions that war would not take place with England until at least 1944 or 1945, though trouble with France, Poland, or Russia might be expected sooner. Raeder therefore decided that he had time to build a small balanced fleet which, though not as big as the British fleet, would still be big enough to wage a successful war against Britain's long sea communications. This plan was based on the practical capabilities of German shipbuilding firms, and was modified from time to time in the pre-war years.'

This strategy was made redundant by Hitler' pressing for his resolution to the Polish crisis and the firm stand then taken by Great Britain and France.

In his memoirs, Doenitz commented on Plan Z and its strategic implications:[26]

The Z Plan, I thought, contained the following weaknesses:

1. It would take at least 6 years to complete; and throughout those years – years most likely of political tension – the navy would remain unequipped for a war with Great Britain.
2. If we began to build battleships, cruisers and aircraft carriers in large numbers, our adversary would undoubtedly follow suit, and in the ensuing arms race we should certainly be left behind, particularly as at the very start we were a very long way from having taken up, in the capital ship category, the 35 per cent to which we were entitled under the Naval Agreement.
3. As a result of the air menace which had developed since the First World War, the German battle groups would be exposed to the danger of air attack by the British as they lay at anchor in their home ports and dockyards, where they were well within the range of the British Air Force, and from which they could not seek refuge elsewhere. For the U-boats we could build concrete shelters, but not for the big surface ships. The British fleet, on the other hand, could withdraw to northern ports well out of reach of the German air arm.

4. The plan did not give due consideration to our geographical position vis-à-vis Britain. Britain's vital arteries, which had to be attacked, lay to the west of the British Isles on the high seas of the Atlantic. *And it was essential that German naval forces should be able to break out into these areas and maintain themselves there, if they were to have the slightest effect. It was then absolutely essential that the naval forces we proposed to create should be capable of adequately fulfilling these vital prerequisites* [emphasis in original].'

These observations were very well founded and proved to be all too accurate with respect to the weaknesses apparent in the Kriegsmarine from the very start of the war. The German naval rearmament programme suffered more than the other services because of the timing of Hitler's war and there was no effective means of addressing the construction shortfall to make the Kriegsmarine a viable force. The only possible avenue to ameliorate the situation was to dramatically increase the construction of U-boats, but Hitler did not do this until April 1943 after the U-boat campaign had been lost because of technological advances made by the Allies which Germany could not counter.

In the meantime, the only alternative which existed was to try to carry out the commerce raiding strategy without the means to do so effectively.

To this end, the pocket battleships were sent to war stations in the weeks prior to the outbreak of war with the intention of commencing raiding activities immediately upon the start of hostilities. The most successful of these raiders was the *Graf Spee*, which was sent to the South Atlantic and raided British sea lanes until it was caught by a group of three British cruisers and scuttled in December 1939.

The orders given to the *Graf Spee* upon the outbreak of war stressed that the primary mission of the ship was commerce raiding and included the following:[27]

'Disruption and destruction of enemy merchant shipping by all possible means.
   'For this the following is ordered:

(a) Merchant warfare is, in the beginning, to be waged according to Prize Law.
(b) If in the beginning or during the course of the war Germany declares "danger zones" then unrestricted warfare is permitted in these areas. To avoid attacks from our own U-boats due to mistaken identity,

pocket-battleships are to keep out of "danger zones" unless special areas are named.

'(c) Enemy naval forces, even if inferior, are only to be engaged if it should further the principal task (i.e. war on merchant shipping).

'(d) Frequent changes of position in the operational areas will create uncertainty and will restrict enemy merchant shipping, even without tangible results. A temporary departure into distant areas will also add to the uncertainty of the enemy.

'(e) If the enemy should protect his shipping with superior forces so that direct successes cannot be obtained, then the mere fact that his shipping is so restricted means that we have greatly impaired his supply situation. Valuable results will also be obtained if the pocket-battleships continue to remain in the convoy area.

'(f) The enemy is not in a position to carry his complete import requirements in escorted convoys. Independent ships can therefore be expected.'

The scuttling of the *Graf Spee* showed how difficult it would be for the Kriegsmarine to achieve its intended strategy in the face of the overwhelming superiority the Royal Navy enjoyed.

One of Germany's biggest problems with respect to waging maritime warfare was its lack of overseas bases. This was aggravated by its geographic position in relation to Great Britain, whose location blocked almost all access from the German coast to the North Sea, which led to the German need to obtain outlets from the Dutch and French coasts to the Atlantic. These had proven to be of limited value in the First World War and were not desired by Raeder in the Second World War. He did, however, realize the value of Norway, with its many harbours and fjords, and mentioned to Hitler during the pre-war and early war period that Norway would be a very useful area from which to launch Germany's strategic maritime warfare. The conquest of Norway thus enhanced the power of the U-boats, but unfortunately for the Germans they were not able to capitalize on this accretion before Allied countermeasures became effective.

Germany's Non-Aggression Pact with the USSR in the summer of 1939 had an unexpected benefit, as recorded in the Fuhrer Naval Conferences:[28]

'The Navy reports that the Russians have placed at our disposal a well-situated base west of Murmansk. A repair ship is to be stationed there.'

This was not known at the time by the British or French governments, which could hardly have seen it as the act of a genuinely neutral power.

The Kriegsmarine's inability to implement its wartime strategy was the direct result of its weakness flowing from the timing of the outbreak of the war, which Hitler had indicated to Raeder would not be likely to involve Great Britain until 1944.

Main Surface Fleet Operations

There were five occasions during the war when the Kriegsmarine was involved in operations which required the major commitment of the surface fleet.

1) Invasion of Norway

The most significant surface fleet operation of the Kriegsmarine during the Second World War was the invasion of Norway in April 1940, which was dealt with in detail in Volume 1 of this work. The decision to invade Norway was Hitler's, who correctly stated at the beginning of the operation that it was 'the most impudent operation of the new military history'.[29]

The invasion involved virtually all the Kriegsmarine's surface ships in the eleven groups that were transporting troops and supporting the landings of the Army. The heaviest ships committed were the only two capital vessels the Kriegsmarine possessed at that time, the battlecruisers *Scharnhorst* and *Gneisenau*. The other main ships involved included the *Lutzow*, which had previously been known as the pocket battleship *Deutschland* but was reclassified as a heavy cruiser by the Germans when it was renamed (at Hitler's insistence, as he was concerned at the loss of prestige which would occur if a ship of that name was sunk), and which mounted a main battery of six 11in guns. Also committed were the two Hipper-class heavy cruisers *Admiral Hipper* and *Blucher*. The rest of the naval commitment consisted of five light cruisers and fourteen destroyers. In total, these ships comprised virtually all the surface units available to the Kriegsmarine at that time. There were also thirty-one U-boats committed to cover the main landing sites and the approaches from which British ships could be expected.[30]

During the invasion, the *Scharnhorst* and *Gneisenau* were engaged by the British battlecruiser *Renown*, which had a main armament of six 15in guns. Both the *Scharnhorst* and *Gneisenau* were hit, and were lucky not to have been significantly damaged. However, they had the speed to outrun the *Renown* and retired from the action. Although the invasion was a success, the surface fleet was almost destroyed by battle losses, being reduced to an active strength of one heavy cruiser, two light cruisers and four destroyers,[31] a far worse position compared to the Allied navies than when the war had begun. As the battleship *Bismarck* did not become available until April 1941, these losses left the Germans without any capital ships until the *Scharnhorst* and *Gneisenau* were repaired. This is further evidence of how ill-equipped the Germans were to embark on war at the time Hitler chose. The Fuhrer was concerned that the losses involved in supporting the invasion would be worse, but stated that he would have been willing to lose the entire Kriegsmarine to achieve victory in Norway.

The result of the campaign was one of the few German strategic victories during the war and obviated the primary threat to Germany's iron ore imports from Sweden during the winter months, which had to be sent via Norway when the normal sea routes were blocked by ice. Victory enhanced the stature of Raeder and the Kriegsmarine with Hitler at the time, and was probably the reason that Hitler did not interfere in the operation of the Kriegsmarine as much as he did with the other services until relatively late in the war, when it became necessary to destroy the lend-lease convoys to the USSR.

The victory also gave the ships of the Kriegsmarine – both surface vessels and U-boats – invaluable access routes to the Atlantic, which were used during the war to great effect until the reconnaissance and anti-U-boat technologies of the Allies became fully operational during 1943. That the Germans were not able to capitalize on the strategic value of the Norwegian bases to carry on the war at sea more vigorously was another direct consequence of the weakness of the Kriegsmarine and entirely due to the timing of the outbreak of hostilities. Had the Germans possessed the 229 U-boats as contemplated by Plan Z at the outbreak of war, Great Britain's position would have been in great peril.

2) Operation *Berlin*

Operation *Berlin* was the sortie by the *Scharnhorst* and *Gneisenau* to disrupt merchant shipping between North America and Britain. The Scharnhorst-class ships were not very well adapted for commerce raiding, mainly because their range was only 9,020 miles, which meant that they needed refuelling at sea to fulfil their purpose. They were, however, more heavily armed than the ships usually used as convoy escorts, and were fast and heavily armoured.

On 22 January 1941, the ships sailed on their mission from Kiel. They broke into the Atlantic sea lanes after eluding the Royal Navy by approaching through the Denmark Strait between Iceland and Greenland. The operation was only moderately successful, sinking 116,000 tons of shipping. The ships returned to Brest on 22 March 1941. They did not, however, find any peace there, being repeatedly bombed and damaged by the RAF.

The attempt to disrupt the trade routes had not been successful. The British had diverted some older battleships to reinforce the escort of some of the Atlantic convoys, and standing orders from Raeder meant the German ships were forbidden from fighting them, but were to concentrate on sinking the merchant ships. The *Scharnhorst* and *Gneisenau* met with convoys escorted by the British battleships *Malaya* and *Ramillies*, which although older ships carried a main battery of eight 15in guns, which would have caused heavy damage to sink the German ships if they had engaged. However, the ageing British battleships only had a top speed of approximately 23 knots and were not able to force an engagement with the German pair, which broke away from the convoys at high speed. Capital ships of the Royal Navy Home Fleet were sent to intercept the German raiders, and very nearly did so on several occasions, but were not successful in bringing them to battle before they came under the protection of Luftwaffe air cover from France.

This sortie showed the basic problem of the German strategy, which was that the British Fleet was strong enough to divert formidable units to negate the potential for even the most powerful German ships to raid the convoys.

Both the *Scharnhorst* and *Gneisenau* had developed engine trouble and were also damaged by storms during the sortie. These mechanical problems were a major flaw in their design and limited their potential use for long-range commerce raiding, which was the main role for which they were intended.

After the sinking of the *Bismarck*, the pair were joined at Brest by the heavy cruiser *Prinz Eugen* on 1 June 1941. The *Prinz Eugen* had been released by the *Bismarck* to continue its commerce raiding mission but had to retire due to engine trouble, once again showing the unreliability of the German ships for the role they were expected to fulfil.

3) Operation *Rheinubung*

Probably the most famous operation involving German surface fleet units during the war was the first and only sortie by the *Bismarck*, Operation *Rheinubung* ('Rhine Exercise') during May 1941. The operation was an attempt by the *Bismarck*, in company with the heavy cruiser *Prinz Eugen*, to break into the Atlantic trade routes and disrupt the convoys between the USA and UK.

Neither the *Bismarck* nor the *Prinz Eugen* were particularly well suited to commerce raiding, as their range of operations was not great; the *Bismarck*'s being 8,870 miles at cruising speed and that of the *Prinz Eugen* only 6,750 miles, which made them dependent on being refuelled while at sea.

A report by Raeder to Hitler on 6 June 1941 outlined the mission statement for the operation:[32]

'Enemy supply traffic in the Atlantic north of the equator was to be attacked. The operation was to last as long as the situation permitted.

The route out to the Atlantic was through the Great Belt, the Skagerrak, and the Norwegian Sea. The ships were to attempt to break through unobserved. Even if the break-through into the Atlantic were observed, the mission remained as defined in the operational directive. It was left to the discretion of the Fleet Commander to shorten or break off the operation as the situation developed. According to the Group's directive the main aim throughout the entire operation was the destruction of enemy shipping. As far as possible, they were to shun risks which would jeopardise the operation. Hence they were to avoid encounters with ships of equal strength. If an encounter were inevitable then it should be an *all-out* [emphasis in original] engagement.'

Famously, however, the *Bismarck* was sunk after first sinking the Royal Navy battlecruiser *Hood*. *Bismarck* led a group of pursuing British ships on a long and tortuous chase, to be eventually crippled by naval aircraft and then sunk by the combined gunfire of the battleships *King George V* and *Rodney*. The *Prinz Eugen* escaped but had engine problems and had to return to Brest, where it joined the *Scharnhorst* and *Gneisenau* on 1 June.

Hitler quizzed Raeder about the loss of the *Bismarck* at their meeting on 6 June:[33]

'The Fuhrer inquires why the Fleet Commander did not return to port after the engagement with the *Hood*. The C-in-C, Navy, replies that a break through the northern straits would have been a far more dangerous undertaking than a withdrawal to the Atlantic. The Fleet Commander was doubtless trying to achieve this as long as his fuel supplies permitted, in the hope of shaking off shadowers and finally making for St Nazaire. Tankers were available in the Atlantic. A return break-through to the north would have incurred great risk of attack from numerous aircraft and light naval forces …

'… The Fuhrer inquires further why the *Bismarck* did not rely on her fighting strength and attack the *Prince of Wales* again in order to destroy her after the *Hood* had been sunk, even if it meant an all-out fight. **Even if this had led to the loss of the *Bismarck*, the final score would have been two British losses against one German one** [author's emphasis]. The C-in-C, Navy, replies that the *Bismarck* re-engaged the *Prince of Wales* on May 24 in order to make the withdrawal of the *Prinz Eugen* possible. After the *Hood* sank, however, the *Prince of Wales* carefully retired out of effective firing range, just as the other heavy enemy ships evidently did later. **(The *Bismarck*'s speed is only 28 knots.)** [Author's emphasis] Furthermore, the Fleet Commander had to keep his main object in view, that of "damaging enemy merchant shipping," as long as the *Bismarck* and *Prinz Eugen* were in a position to do so.'

Hitler's remarks to Raeder emphasized his ignorance of the factors important in naval warfare. For example, if the *Bismarck* had forced another engagement with the *Prince of Wales*, and was sunk in the process, it may have been 'two for one', but that result would not have improved the Kriegsmarine's position against the Royal Navy. Doing so would not have necessarily resulted in a German victory in any event, as the *Prince of Wales*' main armament was undamaged from the previous engagement, although it was still experiencing problems because it had not had time to properly 'work up' its main armament systems. In addition, if the *Bismarck* had been further damaged, there were the two British cruisers shadowing the German vessel which could have attacked it with torpedoes.

Hitler's comments also illustrate that his predilection for fighting to the last, which was so evident in his discussions with army leaders, was also present in his talks with the commanders of the Kriegsmarine. They were equally inappropriate in each case. Raeder knew that if the *Bismarck* was lost, for any reason, it would leave the Kriegsmarine with no battleship as the *Tirpitz* had not yet been commissioned, and this would mean there was no chance of accomplishing Germany's naval strategy of commerce raiding, slight as that chance already was.

The result of the sortie was therefore completely negative for the Germans, despite the sinking of the *Hood*. It is noteworthy that there was no further attempt to use any of Germany's major surface ships in such a venture into the Atlantic during the rest of the war.

4) Operation *Cerberus*

Operation *Cerberus*, also known as 'The Channel Dash', was the operation during February 1942 by which the Kriegsmarine withdrew its surface forces from the French Atlantic coast. It did this for two reasons: firstly, because Hitler feared that the Western Allies were about to invade Norway and he wished to use the ships to reinforce the defences there; and secondly, because the ships had been repeatedly bombed while they were at Brest, and although they were not sunk, they were damaged and repeatedly required to be repaired.

Three of the most important units of the Kriegsmarine were at Brest after having been on missions to raid convoys in the Atlantic: the battlecruisers *Scharnhorst* and *Gneisenau* and the heavy cruiser *Prinz Eugen*. They were thus perfectly placed to carry out further raids – either by themselves or in co-operation with U-boats – on the vital shipping from North America to Britain, upon which the British war effort largely depended. However, their proximity to Britain also meant that the British were able to use all the means at their disposal to bomb the ships and prevent them returning to offensive operations in the Atlantic. While the ships therefore presented a danger for the British if they sortied again, they were also at risk themselves if they did so from superior Royal Navy forces, and if they stayed in harbour they faced being bombed and disabled by the RAF. So although they represented a significant potential threat, from a practical point of view they were bottled up in Brest in various states of repair and were unable to carry out any offensive operations.

Raeder did not agree with Hitler's view that the Allies were about to invade Norway in early 1942, but the Fuhrer insisted that this was the case and ordered the reinforcement of naval and Luftwaffe defences of Norway. The Fuhrer Naval Conferences recorded Hitler's fears on this matter:[34]

> 'Latest reports have thoroughly convinced the Fuhrer that Britain and the United States intend to make every effort to influence the course of the war by an attack on northern Norway. Several places along the coast from Trondheim to Kirkenes will probably be occupied shortly.'

This recurring line of thought in Hitler's strategic vision was entirely incorrect. The Allies had no plans to make any landing in Norway, and it is almost farcical that at this stage of the war Hitler apparently believed this to be the situation. Indeed, the Allies never had any intention of invading Norway after the German occupation of the country in 1940; although it was discussed at the highest levels of the British command, it was never seriously considered as an operation. The forces which Hitler committed to the defence of Norway against this imagined threat were far above the actual requirements and served only to materially lessen those available for the fronts that actually were threatened, another example of his amateurish approach to strategy by attempting to be strong everywhere.

Because the ships in Brest were also under constant attack by the RAF and the Royal Navy's Fleet Air Arm, Hitler decided they should make a dash for safer ports in Norway:[35]

> 'Finally the Fuhrer emphasises once more that nothing can be gained by leaving the ships at Brest. Should the Brest Group manage to escape through the Channel, however, there is a chance that it might be employed to good advantage at a later date. If, on the other hand, the ships remain at Brest, their "flypaper effect," i.e. their ability to tie up

enemy air forces, may not continue for long. As long as the ships remain in battleworthy condition they will constitute worthwhile targets, which the enemy will feel obliged to attack. But the moment they are seriously damaged – and this may happen any day – the enemy will discontinue his attacks. Such a development will nullify the one and only advantage derived from leaving the ships at Brest. In view of all this the Fuhrer in accordance with the suggestions of the C-in-C, Navy, finally decides that the operation is to be prepared for as proposed.'

The withdrawal of the ships from Brest actually marked the end of any possibility of Raeder's strategy of commerce raiding by surface ships being implemented. However, the operation itself was successful, probably the single most humiliating episode in home waters for the Royal Navy during the Second World War. The German ships left Brest at night, then passed through the English Channel during daylight right under the noses of the Royal Air Force and Royal Navy on 11 February 1942. Through a series of bungles committed by both the RAF and Royal Navy, the ships were able to escape and seemed at the time not to have been seriously damaged in doing so. However, both the *Scharnhorst* and *Gneisenau* struck mines. The *Scharnhorst* was under repair for approximately a year because of the damage, and the *Gneisenau* was bombed on the night of 26 February while in dry dock undergoing repairs and never put to sea again.

The withdrawal plan was conceived by the Naval Operations Staff of the Kriegsmarine and personally approved by Hitler, and was unquestionably one of the most audacious naval undertakings of the war. This is recorded in the Fuhrer Naval Conferences as follows:[36]

> '(b) The necessity of leaving Brest under cover of darkness, taking maximum advantage of the element of surprise, and of passing through the Straits of Dover in the daytime, thus making the most effective use of the means of defence at our disposal. The Fuhrer likewise expresses approval, emphasising particularly the surprise to be achieved by having the ships leave after dark.'

The naval operation was synchronized with Luftwaffe air cover consisting of over 250 aircraft,[37] which was able to successfully shield the ships during their passage through the Channel. The Germans succeeded far beyond their hopes. *The Times* wrote on 13 February:

'Vice-Admiral Ciliax has succeeded where the Duke of Medina Sidonia [the commander of the Spanish Armada] failed … Nothing more mortifying to the pride of sea power has happened in home waters since the 17th century.'

The operation was undoubtedly a tactical victory for Germany, but at the cost of a strategic defeat because it resulted in the withdrawal of the surface ships of the Kriegsmarine from its bases in France, ultimately meaning that there was no chance of the pre-war commerce raiding strategy put forward in Plan Z being carried out.

However, there was one potential advantage to the relocation of the surface ships in that, by moving the ships to Norway, they were closer to the lend-lease convoys which had to pass to the north of Norwegian waters on their journey to the ports of the USSR. If the Germans could have taken advantage of this proximity, the redeployment of the ships would have created some compensating strategic value even if it was unintended at the time.

5) Operation *Sea Lion*

Operation *Sea Lion* is important as an example of how Hitler determined which strategy to follow of those available when France had been defeated and Britain was almost unprotected following the evacuation of the British Expeditionary Force from Dunkirk. It is therefore more important than a study of actual events may otherwise indicate, especially as it was not the option which the Fuhrer eventually decided to pursue. Hitler's 'Directive 16' of 16 July 1940 relating to Operation *Sea Lion* had the following specific provision relating to the role of the German Navy:[38]

> **'Directive No. 16 PREPARATIONS FOR THE INVASION OF ENGLAND**
>
> 'As England, in spite of the hopelessness of her military position, has so far shown herself unwilling to come to any compromise, I have therefore decided to begin to prepare for, and if necessary to carry out, an invasion of England. This operation is dictated by the necessity of eliminating Great Britain as a basis from which the war against Germany can be fought, and if necessary, the island will be occupied.
>
> …
>
> '(b) Navy – Will provide and safeguard the invasion fleet and direct it to the individual points of embarkation. As far as possible, ships belonging to defeated nations are to be used. Together with aircraft

patrols, the Navy will provide adequate protection on both flanks during the entire Channel crossing. An order on the allocation of the commands during the crossing will follow in due course. The Navy will further supervise the establishment of coastal batteries, and will be responsible for the organisation of all coastal guns.'

On 19 July, Raeder sent Hitler a long memorandum explaining the difficulties of the operation from the naval point of view:[39]

'The task allotted to the Navy in operation "Sea Lion" is out of all proportion to the Navy's strength and bears no relation to the tasks that are set to the Army and the Air Force ... The principal difficulties confronting the Navy are as follows:-

'(a) The transport of Army troops must take place from a coast whose harbour and installations and adjacent inland water-ways have been extensively damaged through the fighting in the campaign against France, or are of limited capacity.

'(b) The transport routes lie in a sea area in which weather, fog, current, tides, and the state of the sea may present the greatest difficulties. ...

'(c) Owing to the strong defence of the enemy harbours, the landings cannot take place there, but the first wave, at least, must take place on the open coast ... The great navigational difficulties (rise and fall of tide, currents, sea and swell) are obvious.

'(d) At present there is no information whatever as to the position of mines in the eastern portion of the Channel, through which the transports will have to pass. An adequate safety margin as regards mines will not be obtainable, in spite of the use of all resources. It must be appreciated that the enemy is in a position, at least near his own coast, to lay protective minefields at short notice and at the last moment.

'(e) The gaining of air supremacy is vital to the possibility of assembling the requisite Naval Forces and shipping in the relatively restricted area of embarkation.

'(f) So far the enemy has not needed to use his Fleet fully, as a matter of life and death, but the landing operations on the English Coast will find him resolved to throw in fully and decisively all his Naval forces. It cannot be assumed that the Luftwaffe alone will succeed in keeping the enemy Naval forces clear of our shipping, as its operations are very dependent on weather conditions. The task of the German Navy must therefore be to strengthen the effect of Luftwaffe operations by the following measures: Minefields, use of light naval forces on the flanks of the transport area, operations for creating diversions. In this connection it must be taken into consideration that the minefields will not afford absolute safe protection in the face of a determined opponent. Thus the possibility must be envisaged that, even if the first wave has been successfully transported, the enemy will still be able to penetrate with resolute Naval forces so as to place himself between the first wave, already landed, and the succeeding transports …

'(g) The great effect of air attacks on defensive installations is undeniable, as shown by the Western campaign. The nature of anti-invasion defences on the enemy coast, however, and the detailed preparations against invasion, which he has been making for a considerable time, cause doubt as to whether the Luftwaffe will succeed in eliminating defensive troops on the coast sufficiently to allow a landing to take place, and without any effective artillery support from seawards.

'These reflections cause the Naval Staff to see exceptional difficulties that cannot be assessed individually until a detailed examination of the transport problem has been made.'

The tasks given to the Kriegsmarine in Directive 16 must be viewed in the context that Operation *Sea Lion* was to be launched after the Norwegian campaign. The losses in that campaign, as outlined above, left the Kriegsmarine's surface fleet practically powerless. This threw onto the Luftwaffe almost the entire weight of destroying the defences of Great Britain in preparation for the landings. The only arm of the Kriegsmarine which could have attempted to make any contribution was the U-boat fleet, but this was at a much lower level than the irreducible minimum which Admirals Raeder and Doenitz had specified as being required at the beginning of any war with Great Britain. A further problem was that the effectiveness of the U-boats in any operation to support the invasion would have been significantly influenced by the unsuitable nature of the Channel, because of its shallowness and the currents in which the U-boats would have had to operate to oppose any Royal Navy forces attacking the invasion fleet.

On 19 July, the following intelligence report was quoted in the German Admiralty War Diary relating to Britain's defensive measures:[40]

'English defence measures. Coastal defence by the Army. Defence is based on mobility and concentration of all available fire-power. No defence line with built-in defences. The task of the Fleet and the RAF would be to render impossible the landing of armoured units or surprise landing by troops. The RAF is so organised that strong units can be quickly concentrated at any danger spot, and also to attack the new German bases in Northern France and Holland and to search for indications of German activity, such as the assembly of ships and barges.'

On 21 July, Raeder met with Hitler and made the following record of the Fuhrer's observations relating to *Sea Lion*:[41]

'The invasion of Britain is an exceptionally daring undertaking, because even if the way is short, this is not just a river crossing, but the crossing of a sea which is dominated by the enemy. This is not a case of a single crossing operation as in Norway; operational surprise cannot be expected; a defensively prepared and utterly determined enemy faces us and dominates the sea area which we must use. For the Army operation **40 divisions will be required** [author's emphasis]; the most difficult part will be the continued reinforcement of material and stores. We cannot count on supplies of any kind being available to us in England. The prerequisites are complete mastery of the air, the operational use of powerful artillery in the Dover Straits, and protection by minefields. The time of year is an important factor, since the weather in the North Sea and in the Channel during the second half of September is very bad and the fogs begin in the middle of October. The main operation would therefore have to be completed by September 15; after this date co-operation between the Luftwaffe and the heavy weapons becomes too unreliable. But as air co-operation is decisive, it must be regarded as the principal factor in fixing the date. The following must be established:

'(1) How long does the Navy require for its technical preparations?
'(2) How soon can the guns be in place?
'(3) To what extent can the Navy safeguard the crossing?

'If it is not certain that preparations can be completed by the beginning of September, other plans must be considered.'

It is now known that the 'other plans' concerned the invasion of the USSR.

Raeder records that the following was discussed during a further meeting with the Fuhrer on 25 July:[42]

'Operation "Sea Lion" – The C-in-C, Navy, describes forcefully once again the effects of these preparations on the German economy: cessation of inland shipping and a great part of maritime shipping, strain on shipyards, etc. The C-in-C, Navy, requests that an order be issued that these preparations be given preference over anything else. The Fuhrer and the Chief of Staff, OKW agree. There follows a report on the state of preparations on July 25, 1940. The C-in-C, Navy, again stresses the necessity of establishing air superiority soon in order to carry out preparations. At the present time, the following can be said. Every effort is being made to complete preparations by the end of August. Provided that there are no special difficulties and that air superiority is established soon, it will be possible to do the following:

'(1) Provide and convert barges.
'(2) Make available the necessary personnel.
'(3) Prepare ports for embarkation.
'(4) Reconnoitre the enemy coast.
'(5) Clear the invasion area of mines.
'(6) Lay protecting minefields.
'(7) Set up the organisation.

'It is still very uncertain whether a sufficient number of ships can be obtained along the Belgian-French coast and how long it will take to convert them. The C-in-C, Navy, will try to give a clear picture by the middle of next week. The Fuhrer orders a conference for the middle of next week.

Raeder's confidence that these tasks could be achieved, provided that air superiority was attained, states in a very restrained fashion the total dependence of the Kriegsmarine's operations on the victory of the Luftwaffe's campaign against the RAF. It is also apparent that there was a very narrow window available for the campaign by the Luftwaffe to achieve air supremacy.

The Army's requirements were made clear in the next meeting[43] which occurred on 29 July, as noted in the German Admiralty's War Diary:

'(a) The Army requires the transport of 13 landing divisions (about 260,000 men). In view of their anticipated tasks, the Army High

Command regards this as the minimum number, from which no departure can be permitted, even if there are difficulties in transport. This is a considerable reduction compared with the original requirement of the Fuhrer (on July 21) of 40 divisions.

'(b) These 13 divisions must attack the English coast on the widest front (from Ramsgate to Lyme Bay); which means that they must leave the French coast as far as possible simultaneously, and on the widest front.

'(c) The landing divisions must be ready for operations in England within the shortest time, that is, within 2 to 3 days. A period of 10 days for the transport as provided by the timetable for the second wave, is unacceptable to the Army.

'(d) The landing divisions must include sufficient heavy artillery (for own use and for setting up along the English coast) and AA [anti-aircraft] batteries (for AA protections and for anti-tank defence).

'(e) The Army General Staff requires the landing to take place at dawn.'

These requirements were quite obviously beyond the strength of the Kriegsmarine.

The British Admiralty commented in Brassey's edition of the Fuhrer Naval Conferences on the German Army's requirements as follows:[44]

'These demands of the Army began a series of acrimonious disputes with the Navy on the question of landing on a broad or narrow front. From the point of view of the German Navy full security for the landing could only be guaranteed if the landing took place on a narrow strip near Dover and near Beachy Head. The Army demand for a landing area stretching from Ramsgate to Lyme Regis was regarded as quite impracticable by the Navy.'

Bearing in mind that the first-wave divisions of the Normandy invasion in 1944 comprised five divisions on a much narrower front, the very large scale of the German Army's plan for *Sea Lion* is apparent. It is also apparent that this estimate of the forces required was made having regard to German intelligence reports which considerably overstated the strength of the British Army, as is referenced later in this chapter.

Raeder's note relating to the Fuhrer Conference on Naval Affairs of 31 July 1940 is extremely important:[45]

'(b) The Army has requested that the landing should cover a wide front, from the Straits of Dover to Lyme Bay. Transports from Le Havre and

Cherbourg will proceed virtually unescorted into the immediate vicinity of the main British bases of Portsmouth and Plymouth, from which, even if British naval forces are considerably weakened by air attacks, motor boats and destroyers can come out in great numbers. The unloading of the steamers at the two western landing points will last thirty-six hours, during which time they will be lying off that coast. This is unjustifiable. Full operational readiness of the British Fleet must be reckoned with on this occasion. It would be irresponsible to do otherwise. The C-in-C, Navy, is therefore of the opinion that the crossing should be concentrated at first entirely on the Straits of Dover as far as Eastbourne, and that this route should be protected as strongly as possible by guns, mines, and the available naval forces. The demand of the Navy for the most favourable time, i.e. two hours after high tide by day, must also be met. It is clear that the operation will thus be rendered more difficult for the Army. The main thing, however, is to get the Army across in the first place. The Air Force will also not be able to protect the landing effectively at three landing points extending over about 100 kilometers, but will have to concentrate on operating in one area. The C-in-C, Navy, is of the opinion that the Army and Navy should co-operate in making careful preparations for the operation in this form, and the Straits of Dover route should be prepared accordingly. The best time for the operation, all things considered, would be May, 1941.

'The Fuhrer decides as follows – An attempt must be made to prepare the operation for September 15, 1940. The Army should be ready for action by then. The decision as to whether the operation is to take place in September or is to be delayed until May 1941 will be made after the Air Force has made concentrated attacks on southern England for one week. The Air Force is to report at once when these attacks will commence. If the effect of the air attacks is such that the enemy air force, harbours, and naval forces, etc., are heavily damaged, operation "*Sea Lion*" will be carried out in 1940. Otherwise it is to be postponed until May 1941.

'2. The Fuehrer inquires about reinforcements for the Navy during the winter months until May 1941. Reply – *Prinz Eugen*, *Bismarck*, and *Tirpitz* will be available, although training will leave a lot to be desired; possibly eight destroyers, six torpedo boats, and a number of motor boats and submarines will be ready. It is doubtful whether the *Seydlitz* will be finished, since there have been delays.

'3. The Fuhrer considers other actions in the meantime. **The C-in-C, Army, advocates supporting the Italian attack on the Suez Canal with** two Panzer divisions. **The Fuehrer is planning an attack on Gibraltar** [author's emphasis].

'4. The C-in-C, Navy, requests permission for a more extensive submarine programme. More steel and other metals are needed, and in particular the manpower shortage which already hampers the present reduced submarine programme must be relieved. The Fuhrer gives his permission.

'5. The C-in-C, Navy, emphasises the fact that all matters having to do with operation "*Sea Lion*" must be given precedence over the top priority programme. The Chief of Staff, OKW, promises an order to this effect.'

This note clearly shows that Hitler was actively considering options to carry out the attack on Great Britain. He had apparently not at this point made up his mind to concentrate on the USSR. Thereafter, the questions surrounding the implementation of *Sea Lion* bounced back and forth between the Army and Navy commands, with the Fuhrer making decisions as required relating to the plan. Ultimately, Hitler decided that the view of the Kriegsmarine was the most practical and made the following order:[46]

> 'Main crossing to be on narrow front, simultaneous landing of four to five thousand troops at Brighton by motor boats and the same number of airborne troops at Deal–Ramsgate. In addition on D-1 day, the Luftwaffe is to make a strong attack on London, which would cause the population to flee from the city and block the roads.'

There thus appears no doubt that if the Luftwaffe had been able to attain air supremacy, Operation *Sea Lion* would have been carried out. It is therefore of great interest that on 27 August, Hitler decided that the attack could only be made on the basis of the submissions of the C-in-C of the Kriegsmarine, that is on a narrow front, and final decisions were made on this basis. Landings were to take place in four main areas: Folkestone–Dungeness, Dungeness–Cliff's End, Bexhill–Beachy Head and Brighton–Selsey Bill. The first operational objective of the Army was a line from Southampton to the mouth of the Thames.[47]

At the beginning of September, the German estimate of the British Army forces which would be used to defend Britain in the event of an invasion were as follows:[48]

'Intelligence reports in fact assessed the available strength in England as:

'320,000 trained troops
'100,000 reserves
'900,000 recruits
'320,000 others (Home Guard, etc.).
'Total   1,640,000

'Unconfirmed reports placed the number of divisions in England as 39, of which 20 were regarded as completely operational, but whose artillery was believed to be at only half the normal strength. These reports worried the German High Command, and in addition the preparation of barges was behind schedule. It was nevertheless decided to continue with the operation.'

This estimate was way above the mark. The number of operational forces available to the British Army on 15 September 1940 was actually much lower, according to the then Lieutenant General Alan Brooke, commander-in-chief, Home Forces:[49]

'we have 22 divisions of which only about ½ can be looked upon as in any way fit for any form of mobile operation!'

It can thus be seen that if the Germans had carried out the invasion landing successfully, even with the considerably reduced forces that Raeder was suggesting, the British would have had great difficulty in defeating them. This is especially so because of the very high level of operational efficiency and *élan* which the German panzer and mechanized divisions had attained during the victory in France. This gross overestimate of the forces available to the British therefore assumes significant importance.

On 10 September, the day before Hitler was to have given the executive order for *Sea Lion*, the German Naval Staff reported on the situation regarding the feasibility of an invasion:[50]

'The weather conditions which for the time of year are completely abnormal and unstable, greatly impair transport movements and minesweeping activities for "*Sea Lion*." It is of decisive importance for the judgment of the situation, that no claim can be made to the destruction of the enemy air force over Southern England and the Channel area. The preparatory attacks of the Luftwaffe have achieved a perceptible weakening of enemy fighter defence, so that it can be taken for granted that the German forces have a considerable fighter superiority over the English area.

'The English bombers, however, and the minelaying forces of the British Air Force, as the experiences of the last few days show, are still at full operational strength, and it must be confirmed, that the activity of the British forces has undoubtedly been successful, even if no decisive hindrance has yet been caused to German transport movements. In spite of interruptions and delays the timely conclusion of the preparations – the earliest D Day (21.9.40) – is provisionally guaranteed, but is endangered by further difficulties and stoppages resulting from weather conditions and enemy action. The operational state, which the Naval War Staff, as opposed to the High Command, gave as the most important prerequisite for the operation, has so far not been achieved, i.e. clear air superiority in the Channel area and the extinction of all possibilities of enemy Air Force action m the assembly areas of the Naval Forces, auxiliary vessels, and transports.

'**It would be more in the sense of the planned preparation for operation *Sea Lion*, if the Luftwaffe would now concentrate less on London and more on Portsmouth and Dover, and on the naval forces in and near the operation area, in order to wipe out any possible threat from the enemy** [author's emphasis]. The Naval War Staff, however, does not consider it suitable to approach the Luftwaffe or the Fuhrer now with such demands, because the Fuhrer looks upon a large-scale attack on London as possibly being decisive, and because a systematic and long drawn-out bombardment of London might produce an attitude in the enemy which will make the *Sea Lion* operation completely unnecessary. The Naval War Staff therefore does not consider it necessary to make such a demand.'

These comments clearly show that the Kriegsmarine's operational view was more sound than that of either the Luftwaffe or Hitler, who had initiated the attacks on London. Plainly, the Luftwaffe's operational plan did not concentrate its forces on the decisive targets, which were not London but the Royal Air Force and its airfields, the ports of south-eastern England and the Royal Navy's infrastructure.

The British Admiralty commented that Hitler postponed his decision for three days, i.e. until 14 September. However:[51]

'On September 13, the RAF sank 80 barges at Ostend. Ships of the Royal Navy bombarded Calais, Boulogne, Ostend, and Cherbourg, while light coastal forces attacked minesweepers and barges and, on the same day as the RAF attacked Ostend capital ships of the Home Fleet moved south to Rosyth [a port on the Firth of Forth in Scotland], in readiness to dash at full speed to the invasion area. The Luftwaffe attacks continued, but weather hampered their activities. On September 14 Hitler called his commanders together.

'Raeder, before the meeting began, presented a short memorandum[:]

'(a) The present air situation does not provide conditions for carrying out the operation, as the risk is still too great.
'(b) If the "*Sea Lion*" operation fails, this will mean great gain in prestige for the British; the powerful effect of our attacks will thus be annulled.
'(c) Air attacks on England, particularly on London, must continue without interruption. If the weather is favourable attacks should be intensified, without regard to "*Sea Lion.*" The attacks may have a decisive outcome.
'(d) "*Sea Lion,*" however, must not yet be cancelled, as the anxiety of the British must be kept up; if cancellation became known to the outside world, this would be a great relief to the British.'

So, while the British air attacks on the embarkation ports and transport fleet were not decisive in delaying *Sea Lion*, they certainly caused the Germans to realize that the Luftwaffe attacks had not achieved the degree of air supremacy necessary and that the conditions for the invasion in that regard had not been attained.

At a conference of the commanders-in-chief of the Wehrmacht on 14 September, the Fuhrer announced that *Sea Lion* was being delayed and the bombing of London would continue:[52]

'(1) Sea Lion:

'(a) The start of the operation is again postponed. A new order follows on September 17. All preparations are to be continued.
'(b) As soon as preparations are complete, the Luftwaffe is to carry out attacks against the British long-range batteries.
'(c) The measures planned for the evacuation of the coastal area are not to be set in motion to the full extent. Counter-espionage and deception measures are, however, to be increased.

'(2) Air attacks against London. The air attacks against London are to be continued and the target area is to be expanded against military and other vital installations (e.g. railway stations).

'Terror attacks against purely residential areas are reserved for use as an ultimate means of pressure, and are therefore not to be employed at present.'

Although there was still a possibility of invading in October, shipping was dispersed to prevent further losses. By 21 September, the state of the invasion armada was as follows:[53]

	Shipping previously available	*Lost or damaged*
Transports	168	21 (= 12.5 per cent)
Barges	1,697	214 (= 12.6 per cent)
Tugs	360	5 (= 1.4 per cent)

Troops and ships were kept in readiness until October 12, when the operation was postponed until the spring of 1941.

It can therefore be seen that the weakness of the Kriegsmarine was a major cause of the postponement and eventual abandonment of the invasion of England at the time of its greatest weakness. It should have been easy to deduce that this would probably be the only chance that the Germans would have to invade during the war, when Britain was so weak, having just lost most of its army's equipment at Dunkirk and while making frantic efforts to reconstitute it with imports from the USA and increased production at home. Any time granted for this to occur would result in appreciable increases in Britain's defensive power, which would make any subsequent invasion more difficult; and the longer the respite granted, the more difficult it would become.

The Kriegsmarine's Appreciation of German War Strategy – Britain or *Barbarossa*?

The question which inevitably arose with the postponement of *Sea Lion* was whether the defeat of Great Britain or the invasion of the USSR was the paramount strategic war aim for Nazi Germany to adopt in 1941. The Kriegsmarine had no doubt that the defeat of Britain was the correct course to take. This concept was put to Hitler by Raeder during a meeting on 26 September 1940, which was noted in the Fuhrer Conferences as being 'without witnesses':[54]

'The C-in-C, Navy, begs leave to state to the Fuhrer his views on the progress of the war, including also matters outside his province. The British have always considered the Mediterranean the pivot of their world empire. Even now eight of the thirteen battleships are there; strong positions are held in the Eastern Mediterranean; troop transports from Australia were sent to Egypt and East Africa. While the air and submarine war is being fought out between Germany and Britain, Italy, surrounded by British power, is fast becoming the main target of attack. Britain always attempts to strangle the weaker. The Italians have not yet realised the danger when they refuse our help. **Germany, however, must wage war against Great Britain with all the means at her disposal and without delay, before the United States are able to intervene effectively** [author's emphasis]. For this reason the Mediterranean question must be cleared up during the winter months.

'(a) Gibraltar must be taken. The Canary Islands must be secured beforehand by the Air Force.

'The Suez Canal must be taken. It is doubtful whether the Italians can accomplish this alone; support by German troops will be needed. An advance from Suez through Palestine and Syria as far as Turkey is necessary. If we reach that point, Turkey will be in our power. The Russian problem will then appear in a different light. Fundamentally, Russia is afraid of Germany. It is doubtful whether an advance against Russia from the north will be necessary. There is also the question of the Dardanelles. It will be easier to supply Italy and Spain if we control the Mediterranean. Protection of East Africa is assured. The Italians can wage naval warfare in the Indian Ocean. An operation against India could be feigned.

'(b) **The question of North-west Africa is also of decisive importance. All indications are that Britain with the help of Gaullist France, and possibly also of the USA, wants to make this region a centre of resistance and to set up air bases for attack against Italy** [author's emphasis]. Britain will try to prevent us from gaining a foothold in the African colonies. In this way Italy would be defeated.

'Therefore action must be taken against Dakar. The USA already has a consul there, the Italians two representatives, and we are not represented at all. The economic situation will quickly deteriorate, but the attitude toward the British is still hostile. In spite of demobilisation there are still about 25,000 troops left in this area; in the neighbouring British territory on the other hand there are only about six to eight battalions.

The possibility of action on the part of France against the British is therefore very promising [author's emphasis]. It is very desirable that support be given to the French, possibly by permitting the use of the *Strasbourg* [a new French battlecruiser].

'It would be expedient to station air forces in Casablanca in the near future. In general, it appears important to co-operate with France in order to protect North-west Africa – after certain concessions have been made to Germany and Italy. The occupation of France makes it possible to compel her to maintain and defend the frontiers advantageous to us.

'The Fuhrer agrees with the general trend of thought. Upon completion of the alliance with Japan he will immediately confer with the Duce, and possibly also with France. He will have to decide whether co-operation with France or with Spain is more profitable; probably with France, since Spain demands a great deal (French Morocco) but offers little. France must guarantee beforehand to fulfil certain German and Italian demands; an agreement could then be reached regarding the African colonies. Britain and the USA must be excluded from North-west Africa. If Spain were to co-operate, the Canary Islands, and possibly also the Azores and the Cape Verde Islands would have to be seized beforehand by the Air Force.

'An advance through Syria would also depend on the attitude taken by France; it would be quite possible, however. Italy will be against the cession of the Dardanelles to Russia. Russia should be encouraged to advance toward the south, or against Persia and India, in order to gain an outlet to the Indian Ocean which would be more important to Russia than the positions in the Baltic Sea. The Fuhrer is also of the opinion that Russia is afraid of Germany's strength; he believes, for instance, that Russia will not attack Finland this year.

'The Fuhrer is obviously hesitant about releasing additional French forces at Toulon; he feels himself bound by previous decisions. He wishes to discuss this matter with the Duce before deciding.

'Operation "*Sea Lion*" – The C-in-C, Navy, states that the Navy will be unable to maintain readiness for operation "*Sea Lion*" after the middle of October. The entire Navy has been reorganised on its account; the manning of battleships and the execution of the submarine training programme have been affected, and this cannot be continued after the middle of October. The C-in-C, Navy, requests a decision by October 15.

'Aerial-mine warfare. At present numerous aerial mines are being dropped on London by the 6th Air Division. They have a decided effect, to be sure; however, the time has come for large-scale mine operations, since the new type of fuse is now available in sufficient quantities (approximately 780; and a weekly increase of 200). If such operations are delayed, there is a danger that this new weapon will become as ineffective as the magnetic mine did some time ago when the C-in-C, Air, stopped its use off the Thames, etc. The Fuhrer is in complete agreement and will give the necessary order.

'Russian Navy – According to a report from our Naval Attache the Russians are building three battleships in Leningrad, one of which is about 45,000 tons. Several submarines of about 2,800 tons are available.

Further Questions – **The C-in-C, Navy, points out that the probable course of the war, i.e. the entrance of the USA** [author's emphasis], makes it necessary for Germany to build up her fleet to the highest possible degree now, in order to be prepared for the future. Unfortunately this is impossible today; as Germany's capacity for ship construction is barely sufficient to carry out the submarine programme, to complete the large ships under construction, and to build a few light naval vessels. The Fuhrer agrees entirely.

'The C-in-C, Navy, remarks that the lack of an adequate fleet will constitute a continual drawback in the case of further extension of warfare, e.g. with regard to the occupation of the Canary Islands, the Cape Verde Islands, the Azores, Dakar, Iceland, etc. The Fuhrer agrees that islands taken by the Air Force in surprise attacks can be held only by troops and material transported with the assistance of the Navy.

'The Fuhrer volunteers the information that the C-in-C, Air, declared some time ago that he could substitute aircraft for submarines, which would have jeopardised the submarine programme. However, the Fuhrer himself had clearly recognised that the Air Force is partially dependent on the weather, and that its transport facilities are limited. Enemy shipping is best reduced by submarines; harbours can be destroyed by the Air Force. All branches of the Armed Forces must co-operate. It is the combined effect which is decisive.'

I have quoted this document at length because it gives an entirely rational and very strong case for an alternative strategy which had a very good chance of neutralizing Great Britain or winning the war for Germany. There is no question that this assessment by Raeder represents a very rational view of the possibilities for the Germans after the conquest of France and the appropriate course to follow with respect to defeating Britain, which he indicates should be regarded as the main enemy and defeated before any other operations are undertaken. His remarks concerning the entry into the war of the USA are based on the view that the Americans would become involved at some point, something which was not at all certain given the strength at that time of the isolationist movement in the US Congress and wider community. Raeder's comments relating to the best course of action in the Mediterranean are prescient and accurate, especially with regard to North Africa and Syria, and exactly what the British dreaded most. In both cases, the Vichy French government could have assisted Hitler to secure those areas with the resources they had in place, which, together with the Italians and a modest German contribution, would have made the British position untenable. It must be remembered that in 1940, the Vichy government came close to declaring war on Great Britain because of the Royal Navy's attack on the French naval base at Mers-el-Kebir in July that year, when approximately 1,300 French sailors were killed. Consequently, it is quite likely that Hitler could have come to an understanding with them to attack the British position in the Mediterranean if he had been willing to give the undertaking priority and put sufficient pressure on the Italians to adapt to the situation as may have been necessary. The Axis offensive with the meagre forces allocated to Rommel revealed just how exposed the British position was, especially after the defeats in Greece and Crete, so any additional German force could well have forced the defeat of Britain in the Mediterranean.

On 14 November 1940, Raeder once again urged concerted action in the Mediterranean and North Africa:[55]

> 'The Naval Staff is of the opinion that the recognition that Britain and the USA are constantly moving closer together forces us not only to form a European union, but also to fight for the African area as the foremost strategic objective of German warfare as a whole. If we could secure control of the economic block of Europe and Africa in our hands, it would mean that we would possess the decisive bases for raw materials (cotton, copper, and oil) and foodstuffs. For this purpose the first task is to drive the British Fleet from the Mediterranean Sea in order to gain control of the Mediterranean.'

It is hard to fault this logic. The added incentive and benefit for the Germans were that a campaign in North Africa would have required a much more modest level of forces to be effective and would have placed Germany in a far better economic position to attack the USSR subsequently. Germany would also have been far less dependent on the USSR, even if there was no war between the two totalitarian states, which would surely have been a preferable position than applied under the German-Soviet Pact.

On 27 December 1940, Raeder met with Hitler again, returning to the strategic issues and the correct course for Germany to follow:[56]

'Concentration against Britain – It is absolutely necessary to recognise that the greatest task of the hour is concentration of all our power against Britain. In other words, the means necessary for the defeat of Britain must be produced with the utmost energy and speed. All demands not absolutely essential for warfare against Britain must deliberately be set aside. There are serious doubts as to the advisability of operation "*Barbarossa*" before the overthrow of Britain. **The fight against Britain is carried on primarily by the Air Force and the Navy. There is therefore the greatest need to produce the weapons used by these two services and to concentrate these weapons on the British supply lines** [author's emphasis], which are taking on increased significance, in view of the fact that the entire armament industry, particularly aircraft and ship construction, is being shifted to America. Britain's ability to maintain her supply lines is definitely the decisive factor for the outcome of the war. The significance of greatly intensified submarine warfare is emphasised anew. **The Naval Staff is firmly convinced that German submarines, as in the [First] World War, are the decisive weapons against Britain. They possess even greater potentialities now, however, owing to the support they receive from the Air Force** [author's emphasis]. The great significance of submarine construction is not yet recognised in the general plan of armament production. Efforts to raise submarine construction capacity are ineffective because the necessary skilled workers are not available. The number of submarines newly constructed or nearing completion is totally inadequate.'

Once again, it is clear that this was very good advice, even without the benefit of hindsight. During an interrogation in May 1945, Goering stated that he advised Hitler to take Gibraltar:[57]

'Germany had saved Spain from Bolsheviks. Spain was in the German camp. I insisted on going to Spain, but to no avail. We could have bottled the British fleet in the Mediterranean, but no, the Fuhrer wanted to go to Russia. My idea was to close both ends of the Mediterranean. ... I am positive we could have taken Gibraltar. The Luftwaffe was ready and we had two divisions of parachutists ready and trained.'

So the Luftwaffe and Kriegsmarine both advised Hitler to undertake the same strategy, but he did not accept the advice from either.

It is obvious that the decision the Fuhrer made with respect to the strategy to follow would determine the outcome of the war. There were at the time three alternatives available to Nazi Germany.

(1) Attack the USSR

The whole of Germany's strategic situation revolved around the question of whether Germany had the capacity to continue the war against Britain and at the same time attack the USSR. Hitler's view that Germany did have the short-term capacity to do so was based on his estimate that the Wehrmacht could defeat the USSR in a brief campaign which he believed should be no longer than six months. Britain would be defeated thereafter. He told his generals that Stalin was only waiting for the chance to attack Germany when it was most embroiled in the war with the Western powers, but as is shown in Volume 2 of this work, his statement in this regard cannot be sustained by contemporary evidence. At the time, there was overwhelming evidence that the USSR did not contemplate an attack on Germany and that its diplomatic attitude was coldly detached from Britain, whose government was viewed with suspicion, if not outright hostility. This is obvious from the diary of Ivan Maisky,[58] the Soviet ambassador to Great Britain. This lack of intention to attack Germany was also confirmed by the troop dispositions and military infrastructure of the Soviet armed forces revealed after the launch of Operation *Barbarossa* in June 1941, with respect to which Field Marshals von Rundstedt and Manstein both opined that there were no indications of any short-term intention to attack Germany. Further compelling evidence that this was the case was the complete surprise which the Germans achieved when they invaded the USSR. It must also be remembered that Churchill had promoted intervention in Russia by the Western powers after the end of the First World War to help the Tsarist White Russian armies achieve victory over the communist Red Army. It is thus hardly surprising that Stalin did not view the Western powers – and particularly a Great Britain led by Churchill – with any warmth or trust. The recent non-aggression pact between Germany and the USSR, on the other hand, was viewed very positively by Stalin, which was stressed to Hitler by the German ambassador in Moscow, von Schulenburg, in every report he made. The main justification Hitler gave for his decision to attack the USSR in 1941 cannot therefore be accepted as being the real reason behind doing so.

The only other plausible explanation is that he wanted to attack the USSR as a consequence of his ideological racial dogma and belief in his mission to be the destroyer of communism, which he saw as being inextricably intertwined, and which he stated on numerous occasions had been the basis of his views since he started his political activities shortly after the end of the First World War.

(2) Defeat Great Britain

If Hitler had deferred the invasion of the USSR and concentrated on destroying the Mediterranean position of the British Empire, he could have done so at virtually no risk and with a mere fraction of the forces required to defeat the USSR, as pointed out by Grand Admiral Raeder and Reichsmarschall Goering. The destruction of Britain's Mediterranean position would also have significantly enhanced the power of Italy and reinforced Germany's economy through gaining access to the resources of (at the very least) the Middle East. Germany would then have been in a better position to attack the USSR by acquiring more oil and access to the other economic resources of the Middle East. Such a course would also have enabled Hitler to significantly augment the Wehrmacht before the invasion of either Britain or the USSR. It would also have meant that it would be less likely that the USA would be an enemy if Britain had either been defeated or compelled to make peace. From every point of view, therefore, defeating Great Britain was a much less risky venture than attacking the USSR.

(3) Consolidate the German position in Europe before expanding the war

The lowest-risk position Germany could have adopted was to consolidate its economy with the rest of Europe it had conquered and develop its economy through the very advantageous arrangement it had made with the USSR. This would have allowed the augmentation of its forces in line with a semi-defensive strategy while adding to the power of the Wehrmacht. Such a strategy would have allowed Germany to rebuild the Luftwaffe after the losses in the Battle of Britain and develop the sea war against Great Britain to the greatest extent possible. There was great productive capacity in France and technical (especially electrical) resources and expertise in Holland, which could have contributed significantly to the German war effort. However, these were not used to any significant degree at this stage of the war because of Hitler's preoccupation with defeating the USSR.

The position of the Kriegsmarine and the strategy advocated to Hitler by Raeder, which also happened to be that preferred by Goering, was therefore a much sounder proposal than the alternative which the Fuhrer adopted of attacking the USSR.

The Battle of the Atlantic and the defeat of the U-boats

The Battle of the Atlantic was possibly the most important maritime battle in history, lasting for the entire length of the Second World War. Its result tends to overshadow the extreme danger that was represented by the U-boat threat and how close the Allies came to disaster as a result. Doenitz states in his memoirs:[59]

> 'In June 1939 I reported to the Commander-in-Chief [Raeder] the anxiety [with] which I and my fellow officers regarded the possibility of an early war with Britain. Although, I said, I was only a captain and a subordinate combatant officer, I asked him to place my views before Hitler. I pointed out that if war with Britain came, the main burden of operations at sea would devolve upon the U-boat arm and that in its present numerically weak state this could achieve little more than a few pin pricks. On July 22, 1939, at Swinemuende, Raeder communicated Hitler's reply to the assembled officers of the U-boat arm on board the *Grille* [the Fuhrer's state yacht]: He would ensure that in no circumstances would war with Britain come about. For that would mean *Finis Germaniae* [the end of Germany]. The officers of the U-boat arm had no cause to worry.
>
> 'It will be appreciated that the effect of this unequivocal statement, made by the supreme head of state and the man responsible for directing German policy and denying categorically all possibility of war with Britain, was very great.'

On the outbreak of war, Doenitz addressed a memorandum to Raeder concerning the state of the U-boat arm and the necessity for its immediate expansion:[60]

'MEMORANDUM BY ADMIRAL DOENITZ, F.O. U-BOATS. DATE 1.9.39
'THE BUILDING-UP OF THE U-BOAT ARM

'The state of the U-boat arm at the present time of tension, and the impossibility of producing the desired results with the numbers of U-boats now available, make it my duty to express my views on the relevant questions, and draw the necessary inferences. I. The task of the U-boat arm – The Navy's principal task in the war, is the struggle with England. The focal point of warfare against England, and the one and only possibility of bringing England to her knees with the forces of our Navy, lies in attacking her sea communications, in the Atlantic. So long as we do not have sufficient numbers of surface forces which are suitable for this task it will fall chiefly to the U-boat arm.

'Even if our surface forces are equal to the task, the U-boat has the decisive advantage that it can reach and remain in operational areas in the Atlantic without support, and does not have to undergo the same dangers as surface forces. I therefore believe that the U-boat will always be the backbone of warfare against England, and of the political pressure on her.

'II. Forces required – The main weapon in the U-boat war against merchant shipping is the torpedo-carrying U-boat. About 90 are required simultaneously in the most important operational area, i.e. in the Atlantic, north of the Equator. In all, about 300 operational U-boats are necessary. (There follows a technical description of the different types of U-boats required.) How do these requirements compare with:

'III. The present situation. Of the 57 U-boats now in commission:

'18 U-boats are in the Atlantic.

'21 are in the North Sea or are intended for use in the North Sea.

'10 are in the Baltic.

'3 are not ready for active duties.

'4' are still undergoing trials.

'1 U-boat is set aside for A/S experiments.

'From a total of 26 U-boats suitable for operational duties in the Atlantic, 18 are in the Atlantic, 3 in the Baltic, 3 still not ready for active duties, and 2 still undergoing trials. ... At this time all available U-boats were sent out immediately and no reserves were held back as replacements. In the event of a war, it would therefore very soon become obligatory to reduce greatly the numbers of U-boats on operation, and later increase that number gradually to about one third of the available U-boats. The number of U-boats for the Atlantic would thus be reduced to about 8 or 9. We cannot expect the number of U-boats on operation to be more than a petty annoyance to British commerce, and we can expect still less from those numbers that will continue to be available. This means that: at the present moment we are not in the position to play anything like an important part in the war against Britain's commerce. ...

'IV. The development of the situation in the next few years – I have been informed that in the coming years we shall have the following numbers of U-boats available for Atlantic operations:

		Type VII b and c IX	*Type XI, XII*
'Beginning	1940	31	–
	'1941	49	–
	'1942	65	3
	'1943	81	7
	'1944	106	10

'1945	131	13
'End of 1946	160	18

'This means that if the required strength as shown in II is acknowledged, and if the present building programme is retained, it will be quite impossible for our U-boats to exercise anything approaching an effective pressure on Britain or her commerce within a reasonable space of time.

'V. Inferences – Measures must be taken even beyond the normal planning and existing Naval problems must be put aside, so that the U-boat arm can be brought as soon as possible to such a condition as will enable it to carry out its main task; that is, to defeat England in war. I nevertheless believe that such decisive measures can be carried out only under suitable conditions. I am therefore of the opinion that a central control office, with far-reaching powers and directly responsible to the C-in-C, must be created to deal with all questions relating to the building of the U-boat arm. I fully realise that the existing development of the U-boat arm after such a long break in U-boat building is an excellent performance, but incisive measures will be necessary in many departments if, in future conflicts with England, we want to stand forth with a really effective U-boat arm.'

I have quoted from this document at some length because it summarises the pre-eminent problem faced by Germany in the maritime war against Great Britain: it did not have the surface ships necessary to seriously challenge the Royal Navy and therefore the only way to inflict sufficient damage on British commerce was through the U-boat arm. However, neither were there enough U-boats to achieve this. Therefore, it was absolutely urgent that the number of U-boats be increased to the level needed to defeat Britain, as this would be the fastest and cheapest way to disrupt Britain's maritime trade, on which depended its entire capacity to carry on the war.

In order to achieve this increase in the U-boat fleet, it was necessary that Hitler order construction of submarines to be given the highest possible priority. As noted previously, although Hitler agreed to an increase in the number of U-boats to be constructed at the beginning of the war, he did not authorize the programme being given the highest priority. This was noted in the Fuhrer Conferences on Naval Affairs held on 1 September 1939:[61]

'3. The submarine construction programme has not yet been given priority by the Fuhrer, **as the replenishment of Army equipment and ammunition supplies is of prime concern at the moment** [author's emphasis]. The extensive construction programme is not possible with the present allocation of steel, metals, and labour. The question will be reconsidered in December. In order to carry out the large-scale submarine programme, continuous pressure will be necessary.'

It seems otiose to note that the need to replenish the German Army's stocks would not have arisen to the same degree if the invasion of the USSR had not been planned.

It is obvious that Hitler's decision to 'resolve' the Polish crisis which he had forced upon a reluctant Europe completely upset the rearmament plans of the entire Wehrmacht, no branch of which was ready for war at that time. This situation with respect to U-boat construction continued until an intervention by the Fuhrer in April 1943, as related by Albert Speer:[62]

'Without consulting me, after hearing a report from Doenitz, Hitler raised all naval armament to the highest priority. This happened in the middle of April, but only three months before, on January 22, 1943, he had already classified the expanded tank programme as the task of highest priority. ... This meant instead of the previous monthly production of twenty submarines of the smaller type totalling sixteen thousand tons displacement, producing forty U-boats per month with a displacement totalling more than fifty thousand tons.'

This order of Hitler's was too late to enable the U-boats to achieve the results intended because of the technical innovations the Allies had employed in the meantime to combat them. Hitler's tardiness in this regard must be regarded as one of the most crucial errors he made during the war. It can only be ascribed to Hitler's preoccupation with invading the Soviet Union and the consequent needs of the army, and his lack of understanding of the importance of defeating Great Britain in a prolonged war. In 1939, upon the outbreak of war, he believed that it would still be possible to negotiate a peace with Britain, despite the pronouncements of the British and French governments when war was declared. This was confirmed by Speer, who commented:[63]

'I do not think that in those early days of September, Hitler was fully aware that he had irrevocably unleashed a world war. He had merely meant to move one step further. To be sure, he was ready to accept the risk associated with that step, just as he had been a year before during the Czech crisis; **but he had prepared himself only for the risk, not [the] reality for the great war** [author's emphasis].'

That Hitler was reluctant to destroy the British Empire is confirmed by numerous entries in the diary of the Chief of the General Staff, Colonel General Franz Halder, a typical entry being:[64]

> 'The Fuhrer is greatly puzzled by Britain's persisting unwillingness to make peace. He sees the answer (as we do) in Britain's hopes on Russia, and therefore counts on having to compel her by main force to agree to peace. Actually this is much against his grain. The reason is that a military defeat of Britain will bring about the disintegration of the British Empire. This would not be of any benefit to Germany. German blood would be shed to accomplish something that would benefit only Japan, the United States and others.'

Hitler continued to publicly assert that peace would be possible even after the fall of France, stating in his speech to the Reichstag of 19 July 1940:

> 'In this hour I feel it to be my duty before my own conscience to appeal once more to reason and common sense in Great Britain as much as elsewhere. I consider myself in a position to make this appeal, since I am not the vanquished, begging favors, but the victor speaking in the name of reason. I can see no reason why this war must go on.'

The continuance of this belief, if truly held, further illustrates Hitler's limited understanding of other countries, and particularly the government of Great Britain, which had repeatedly and emphatically declared that it was prepared to continue the war indefinitely, even if it had to do so alone. It was the Fuhrer's inability to determine that Nazi Germany had to defeat Britain first, instead of seeking victory on land through attacking the USSR and then turning to defeat Britain, that led to the crucial delay in placing the highest priority on the construction of U-boats. This was certainly one of the most critical strategic errors of all of Hitler's miscalculations during the entire war.

That this was the case is reinforced by reflecting on the severity with which the Allies rated the threat posed by the U-boat war, which Churchill summarized as:[65]

> 'the dominating factor all through this war. Never for one moment could we forget that everything happening elsewhere, on land, at sea, or in the air, depended ultimately on its outcome.'

Doenitz's view of why the U-boat war was lost is contained in part of his evidence at Nuremberg:[66]

> 'The airplane, the surprise by airplane, and **the equipment of the planes with radar – which in my opinion is, next to the atomic bomb, the decisive war-winning invention of the Anglo-Americans – brought about the collapse of U-boat warfare** [author's emphasis]. The U-boats were forced under water, for they could not maintain their position on the surface at all. Not only were they located when the airplane spotted them, but this radar instrument actually located them up to 60 nautical miles away, beyond the range of sight, during the day and at night. Of course, this necessity of staying under water was impossible for the old U-boats, for they had to surface at least in order to recharge their batteries. This development forced me, therefore, to have the old U-boats equipped with the so-called "*Schnorchel*," and to build up an entirely new U-boat force which could stay under water and which could travel from Germany to Japan, for example, without surfacing at all. It is evident, therefore that I was in an increasingly dangerous situation.'

Doentiz wrote a paper after the war entitled 'The Conduct of the War at Sea', in which he stated:[67]

> 'The problem of location urgently required better reconnaissance. The U-boat itself, with its extremely limited range of vision, was the worst possible medium of reconnaissance. The most vital and necessary complement to the U-boat, which was our main instrument of battle, was the aircraft. Here the flaw in the conduct of the war at sea was revealed with painful clarity. *Fundamentally, it was the fault of the direction of the armed forces who in peace time had created a sea-air arm which in wartime was to be incorporated into the Luftwaffe; but the construction of the Luftwaffe to be employed in a purely land battle did not meet the demands of the navy* [emphasis in original].'

Ultimately, it was beyond Germany's power to re-equip the U-boat fleet amid the crises created by the war against the USSR, the disruption created by the strategic bombing campaign and the crisis presented by the destruction of the Luftwaffe and the loss of France. Hitler's decisions to commence the war ahead of the time advised to Grand Admiral Raeder by attacking Poland and then to attack the USSR before dealing with Great Britain as advocated by the Kriegsmarine were of fundamental importance to NAZI Germany losing the war.

Hitler Orders the Scrapping of the Surface Fleet

During 1942, the lend-lease supply convoys to the USSR from Great Britain and the USA became a regular feature of the Allied war effort. The Germans realized that if these were not disrupted, they would significantly enhance the capacity of the Soviet economy and armed forces to continue the war. The convoys that were sent to Murmansk were only part of the lend-lease supplies, the other main entry point bring from Iraq by rail, which the Germans could not do anything about. So it was crucial for the Germans that the convoys to Murmansk be disrupted. A typical convoy would carry hundreds of tanks, trucks or aircraft, together with strategic raw materials such as aluminium, copper, food and oil refining products. During the war, the USSR received approximately $11 billion (1944 dollar value) in supplies from the USA alone, so these convoys were of inestimable value and significantly contributed to the Soviet war effort. In 1938 the GDP of the USSR was equivalent to approximately US $23 billion, so the impact of the aid was very significant.

In an attempt to stop the convoys, a squadron of Kriegsmarine vessels, which included the heavy cruisers *Hipper* and *Lutzow* together with six destroyers, attempted to attack a convoy escorted by an inferior, although not inconsiderable, Royal Navy force on 31 December 1942. During the engagement, which became known as the Battle of the Barents Sea, the German commander mistook the escort for a larger force and retired, which meant that the convoy reached Murmansk with no losses.

When he heard of the result of the battle, Hitler was enraged. His anger was increased by Goering, who happened to be at Fuhrer headquarters at the time and said that he had to 'waste' squadrons of aircraft to protect the large surface units of the Kriegsmarine although they achieved nothing.[68] Upon hearing this, Hitler immediatey decided to have the large ships of the Kriegsmarine decommissioned and to use their armament and high-grade steel for other purposes. The impact of this decision would have been to release capital ships from the Allied navies which were being used to guard against the German surface fleet and enable them to prosecute the war even more aggressively.

The Fuhrer conference of 11 January 1943 records that Hitler addressed the following requirements to Raeder:[69]

'The Navy shall consider the following:

'1. Should the three aircraft carriers which were planned, be retained? Should other ships be converted into aircraft carriers (especially in case the *De Grasse* cannot be used)? Are the *Hipper* and the *Prinz*

Eugen, because of their great speed, more suited than the *Luetzow* and the *Scheer*, which have a more extensive operating radius? If the latter were lengthened, could they develop greater speed and could they be given a larger landing deck?

'2. Where would the heavy guns of these ships best be mounted on land?

'3. In which order should the ships be decommissioned? Probably the *Gneisenau* would be the first, since she will not be ready for active duty until the end of 1944. Next would probably be the ships which are now due for overhauling and repairs. Personnel of these ships will remain with the Navy.

'4. Can the submarine programme be extended and speeded up if the large ships are eliminated? The C-in-C, Navy, shall prepare a memorandum giving his views on the above. These comments will be of historical value. The Fuhrer will carefully examine the document.

'**The C-in-C, Navy, rarely had an opportunity to comment** [author's emphasis], but his final impression was that the Fuhrer, even though he described his decision as final, would reconsider some of his views if sound arguments were presented. Concerning the question of the C-in-C, Navy, whether the *Scharnhorst* and *Prinz Eugen* are to be sent to Norway, the Fuhrer replied in the affirmative and said that for the present, Norway is to be defended as strongly as possible. During a private conversation between the C-in-C, Navy, and the Fuhrer the C-in-C, Navy, tried to explain the reason for the delay in communications on December 31/January 1. It was explained that the Admiral Commanding Cruisers had expected to obtain reliable information from the radiogram with the date/time group December 31 at 1234, which would report success or failure of the operation and the presence of enemy cruisers. The C-in-C, Navy, further pointed out the difficulty in compiling a composite report from the two cruisers and six destroyers after they had anchored. Finally he mentioned that the teletype station Alta greatly delayed the transmission of the final report. The course of the operation itself was only briefly mentioned at the beginning of the discussion with the Fuhrer. At that time the C-in-C, Navy, explained that the Admiral Commanding Cruisers and the individual commanders had obeyed orders to the letter. **The orders of the Naval Staff strictly limited the extent of the operation** [author's emphasis].'

The orders referred to above forbad naval commanders from risking their ships against a superior force. In his evidence at the Nuremberg trials, Raeder recalled the meeting with Hitler relating to the Battle of the Barents Sea and stated:[70]

> 'Through Admiral Krancke he had all sorts of insults transmitted to me and demanded that I report to him immediately; and I could see that very strong friction would result. I arranged it so that I did not need to report to him until 6 days later on 6 January so that the atmosphere could first cool off a little. On 6 January I could go to him with a complete report; and in the evening, at a discussion at which Field Marshal Keitel was also present, **he made a speech of about an hour's duration in which he made derogatory remarks about everything that the Navy had done so far, in direct contrast to every judgment passed on the Navy up until this time** [author's emphasis]. From this I saw that he was anxious to bring about a break. I personally was firmly prepared to seize this opportunity to resign, **especially as it became ever clearer that the war was becoming a pure U-boat war** [author's emphasis], and I could therefore feel that I could leave at this moment with a clear conscience. After the Fuhrer had concluded his speech I asked to be permitted to speak with him alone. Field Marshal Keitel and the stenographers left and I told him that I was asking for my resignation as I could see from his words that he was entirely dissatisfied with me and therefore this was the proper moment for me to leave. As always, he tried at first to dissuade me but I remained adamant and told him that a new Commander-in-Chief of the Navy who would have complete responsibility would definitely have to be appointed. He said that it would be a great burden for him if I were to leave now since for one thing the situation was very critical – Stalingrad was impending – and secondly, since he had already been accused of dismissing so many generals. In the eyes of the outside world it would incriminate him if I were to leave at this point. I told him that I would do everything I could to prevent that happening. If he wanted to give the appearance as far as the outside world was concerned that I had not resigned because of a clash, then he could make me a general inspector with some sort of nominal title, which would create the impression that I was still with the Navy and that my name was still connected with the Navy. This appealed to him at once and I told him on 6 January that I wanted to be dismissed on 30 January. At this point I had concluded 10 years of service as Commander-in-Chief of the Navy under him. He agreed to this proposal and asked me to suggest two successors so that he could make a choice. On 30 January he then personally dismissed me by appointing me Admiral Inspector of the Navy.'

Raeder's move to the ceremonial position of Admiral Inspector of the Navy was in effect a resignation, without being termed as such. He carried out no duties in his new office; Doenitz was promoted to Grand Admiral and made commander-in-chief of the Navy on 30 January 1943.

While the emphasis of the German naval war thereafter changed to concentrating almost exclusively on U-boat operations, Doenitz managed to largely circumvent the consequences of Hitler's decision to decommission the larger ships. However, the German surface ships did not take any significant part in the war following the sinking of the *Scharnhorst* (December 1943) and the destruction of the *Tirpitz* (November 1944).

The Kriegsmarine and D-Day, 6 June 1944

During the invasion of France, the Kriegsmarine was in no position to affect the Allies' operations to any significant degree. In an interview conducted shortly after the end of the war, Admirals Doenitz and Wagner (who was in command of Naval OB West) answered a series of questions about the German naval capability around D-Day:[71]

> 'Q: What naval force could you actually move to the invasion area when it struck?
> 'A: Twenty to thirty E-boats,* six torpedo boats, twenty mine sweepers, three or four destroyers, and four to five submarines in the Channel east of Cherbourg.
> 'Q: How effective do you estimate these craft were in checking the invasion?
> 'A: They could inflict only fleabites.'

For the Germans, this was only too true. It was one of the long-term consequences of Hitler's mistimed attack on Poland, which severely disrupted the preparations of the Kriegsmarine for war with Great Britain, which were themselves quite misconceived.

Conclusions

1. It is abundantly clear that Hitler's decision to invade Poland in 1939, which precipitated the Second World War, completely disrupted the

---

* Author's note: German E-boats were considerably larger than allied Motor Torpedo Boats but performed much the same role.

Kriegsmarine's preparations for war, which had been based on his previous indications that there was not likely to be any conflict with Great Britain before 1944–45. Because of this situation, the Kriegsmarine had no real prospect of carrying out the strategy which it had intended to perform during the war.

2. The construction of the ships which were envisaged for the achievement of Plan Z – a German surface fleet 35 per cent of the size of the British Royal Navy, together with 229 U-boats – was a doubtful proposition because of limited construction facilities, limitations imposed by the cost of the existing rearmament programme and the small amount of steel available for the rearmament programme. If the ships had actually been built, there would have been significant problems supplying them with the necessary oil for operations in wartime. Once the war against the USSR commenced, this problem occurred even with the limited surface ships the Kriegsmarine possessed.

3. The strategy which the Kriegsmarine intended to carry out in wartime was based around commerce raiding by surface ships, which was outdated by the time of the Second World War. To have any chance of success, the strategy required more ships than Plan Z envisaged, as the British were expanding the Royal Navy to counter any expansion of the Kriegsmarine. In order that the strategy succeed as the situation existed in 1939, it was crucial for the Germans to develop close co-operation between surface ships, U-boats and reconnaissance aircraft. In practice this did not occur because the Luftwaffe was preoccupied with other problems of its own; it simply could not devote the resources necessary to effectively carry out the role intended for it with respect to maritime warfare.

4. Hitler's decision to invade Norway was shown from the German point of view to have been valid, and his involvement in its planning was a positive influence for the concept of the operation. However, the losses suffered by the Kriegsmarine were such that afterwards it was completely incapable of making any major contribution to the war effort with its surface ships. The failed sortie by the *Bismarck* (1941) and the sinking of the *Scharnhorst* (1943) were symbolic of the impossible position created by the inferiority of the German surface fleet to the Royal Navy. The result of the Battle of the Barents Sea, after which Hitler ordered the scrapping of German surface ships, illustrated the Fuhrer's lack of understanding of operational naval affairs and strategy. It also highlighted the inability of the Kriegsmarine to effectively counter the existential threat posed by the lend-lease convoys to the USSR.

5. After the conquest of France and the Battle of Britain, the Kriegsmarine recognized that it was very dangerous to attack the Soviet Union before Great Britain had been defeated. It advanced a strategy to Hitler to destroy the British position in the Mediterranean which, if properly co-ordinated with the Italians, would have caused great difficulties for the survival of the British Empire. Even if the British position had not been totally destroyed, access to significant resources which Germany lacked could have been gained by adopting this strategy. Additionally, the strategy would have required far smaller forces than the invasion of the USSR for its accomplishment. Proof that this strategy had a real chance of success can be seen in the problems caused to the British by the extremely modest forces commanded by Field Marshal Rommel in the Afrika Korps, which were only overcome with the utmost effort and difficulty. Hitler's decision to ignore this strategy and to unnecessarily attack the Soviet Union, thereby creating another enemy while Britain remained undefeated, is logically inexplicable when viewed in this context.
6. Hitler's delay in deciding that U-boat construction be given the highest priority in the arms programme resulted in the failure of the campaign which had the greatest potential to cause the defeat of Britain. His order that the construction of U-boats receive top priority in April 1943 was too late, as the Allies had by then overcome their initial technical problems in dealing with the U-boats and were effectively able to counter them from mid-1943 onwards. Ultimately, the technical innovations of the Allies effectively rendered the U-boat campaign almost completely ineffective.

Chapter 2

Hitler and the Luftwaffe

The terms of the Treaty of Versailles completely forbad Germany from having an air force. Although the German governments during the era of the Weimar Republic connived at some infractions of this requirement, no significant steps to create an air force were undertaken until Hitler came to power. As soon as he was made Chancellor on 30 January 1933, Hitler installed Hermann Goering as Minister for Aviation, an appointment which continued until 23 April 1945 when Goering was dismissed from all his offices by the Fuhrer as a result of a plot by Martin Bormann, Hitler's power-obsessed Party Secretary. Goering's original task was to co-ordinate all aspects of civilian air transport as the precursor to reconstituting the German air force.

The Luftwaffe was formally created on 21 May 1935 by the passing of the 'Law for the Reconstruction of the National Defence Forces'. This law also reconstituted the German Army with a peacetime strength of thirty-six divisions and created the Kriegsmarine, which had also been severely restricted by the terms of the Treaty of Versailles. The three services were together called the Wehrmacht (Defence Force), which was the term used for them throughout the Second World War. At the same time, Hermann Goering became a colonel general and was made the commander-in-chief of the Luftwaffe, a position he held until he was relieved of it by Hitler on 23 April 1945.

Intended Role of the Luftwaffe

Since the war, it has been widely believed that the Luftwaffe was conceived from the beginning almost as an auxiliary arm of the German Army and that its main role was to provide tactical support for army formations in their operations. This view seemed to be confirmed by the aircraft which were produced and the limited operational role which the Luftwaffe fulfilled by necessity during the war. However, this was not the role which the Luftwaffe was conceived to perform. The task which the Luftwaffe was actually intended to fulfil was stated by its first Chief of Staff, General Walther Wever:[1]

- To destroy the enemy air force by bombing its bases and aircraft factories, and by defeating the enemy air force attacking German targets;
- To prevent movement of large enemy ground forces to the decisive areas by destroying railways and roads, particularly bridges and tunnels, which are indispensable for the movement and supply of such forces;
- To support the operations of army formations, independent of railways i.e. armoured forces and motorised forces, by impeding the enemy's advance and participating directly in ground operations;
- To support naval operations by attacking enemy naval bases, protecting Germany's naval bases and participating directly in naval battles;
- To paralyse the enemy's armed forces by stopping production in the armaments factories.

'… We hope and believe that a modern army, co-operating with the air force, will find a means of preventing the positional warfare of massed armies. In the air force, we have a weapon which knows no boundaries; its operations cannot be impeded by national frontiers or by concrete fortifications.'

The Luftwaffe was thus intended to have a wider role, including that of strategic bombing, which required the production of four-engine bomber aircraft to have any chance of success. The role of heavy bomber was to be filled by the Heinkel 177, of which 2,000 were to be produced by 1943. However, when Wever died in a plane crash in 1936, Goering decided that the He 177 would not be produced and that it would be replaced by more medium bombers as a stopgap until a new heavy bomber was decided upon. The makeshift Luftwaffe production plan was for between 5,000 and 7,000 medium bombers to be available by 1942.[2] The timing by which Goering expected these would be needed reflects the assurances he had been given by Hitler as to when a war with the Western powers might occur, which he had stated to the three commanders-in-chief of the arms of the Wehrmacht to be most likely by 1944–45. Had either the He 177 or the increased number of medium bombers been produced in the numbers intended, the probability of the Germans succeeding in the Battle of Britain would have been significantly higher. Because war broke out in 1939, however, the Luftwaffe's plan was far from being completed and the Germans had to fight the war with the aircraft available.

Field Marshal Erhard Milch, who was Goering's State Secretary and effectively second-in-command of the Luftwaffe, wrote after the war:[3]

'Germany had no really adequate aircraft model for use in strategic operations: without any doubt, this is one of the reasons for the failure of the air offensive against Britain and for the Luftwaffe's inability to provide air protection for Germany's submarines at sea.'

The intended composition of the Luftwaffe

Because it has been assumed that the Luftwaffe was intended primarily as an adjunct to the ground forces, acting as 'airborne artillery' and combining with the new panzer formations to fulfil its role in blitzkrieg offensives, its intended composition has been presumed to have conformed to this role. This perception resulted from the fact that the Luftwaffe did not have strategic bombers during the war, and it is therefore assumed that this was always intended to be the case. However, this is not correct.

During the November 1937 conference detailed in the Hossbach Memorandum, at which Hitler outlined his foreign policy plans, the Fuhrer told the commanders-in-chief of the Wehrmacht that Germany's problem of *lebensraum* ('living space') could 'only be solved by force'.[4] At that meeting and afterwards, he repeatedly indicated at various times that he wanted the armed forces to be ready for a possible confrontation with the Western democracies by 1943 or 1944. The plan for the expansion of the Luftwaffe was based on this timetable, and originally included heavy as well as medium bombers:[5]

'Goering's object was to build up by 1944 a force of 2,000 heavy bombers, suitable for war against Russia, Britain and even the United States, to be supplemented by a medium-bomber force of 5,000 aircraft. This fitted in with the general pace of air force preparations, which were due to be completed in 1942 for a large war to be fought some years later.'

During a meeting in Rome on 16 April 1939, Goering mentioned this timeframe to Count Ciano, the Italian Foreign Minister.[6] There is therefore no doubt that Hitler and Goering intended to create an air force which had the capacity for waging a strategic bombing campaign. It seems unnecessary to state that if this level of armament had been achieved and the conflict with the Western democracies had occurred in accordance with Hitler's stated schedule, the chances of German victory in the Battle of Britain and the bombing campaign against British towns and cities would have been substantially increased. That this level was not achieved was due more to Hitler embarking on war before he told his service chiefs to be ready than any other factor.

Field Marshal Milch had calculated that these additional bombers would cost 500 million marks,[7] which was more than Germany had spent on the entire Luftwaffe programme in 1937–38, but Goering was unconcerned with this extra expense. When it was decided not to produce the He 177 as the heavy bomber for the Luftwaffe because it had developed problems with its engines and was not reliable, Goering ordered that between 5,000 and 7,000 medium bombers be produced by 1942[8] as a stopgap until the next heavy bomber was ready. Once again, had these bombers been available for use against Britain, the result could well have been different to that achieved in 1940.

On the basis of these facts, there is no doubt that Hitler intended the Luftwaffe to be capable of strategic bombing. Indeed, plans existed for the creation of a bomber force which would have enabled the Germans to attack Britain and France with every prospect of success by 1943–44.

However, upon the outbreak of war in September 1939, the Luftwaffe had only 1,182 bomb-carrying aircraft of all types, whether bombers or dive bombers.[9] This unpreparedness was one of the main consequences of Hitler provoking the outbreak of war when he did, and the subsequent inability of the Luftwaffe to fulfil its role was largely because of his precipitate action.

The Luftwaffe in Spain

The Spanish Civil War erupted in July 1936 and continued until 1 April 1939. It resulted from irreconcilable hostility between the political forces of the extreme right and left of the Spanish political spectrum, represented by the traditional centre of power in the Spanish state and forces ranging from anarchists to communists. The Nationalist 'Falangist' movement engineered a partially successful military coup, with most of the army, navy and air force remaining loyal to the Republic. The Falangists needed the support of the colonial army in Spanish Morocco and the Sahara to overcome the loyalist forces in Spain. The Nationalists' problem was that they did not have enough aircraft to transport the troops from Africa to Spain: when the coup occurred, there were only six Spanish transport aircraft available to transport the soldiers from Morocco.[10]

Both Hitler and Mussolini viewed the Spanish Civil War as a means of disrupting the status quo in Europe and eroding the position of the League of Nations, whose most important supporters were the Western democracies. By supporting the Falangist movement, they would also reinforce the anti-democratic forces in Europe, especially if they were successful and took over the government of Spain. The Falangists were ultimately headed by General Francisco Franco, who was the youngest general in the Spanish Army and commander of the Spanish African Colonial Army. An interesting detail of the German commitment in Spain was that a representative of the Minister of War, Field Marshal von Blomberg, was attached to Franco's staff in Spain and all German forces in Spain were made subordinate to him. This role was filled by Colonel (later General) Walter Warlimont, who subsequently became Deputy Chief of Operations at the OKW and wrote one of the most important books relating to the operations of Hitler's Fuhrer Headquarters to come out of the Second World War and which is quoted on many subjects in this and other works.

The early contribution of the Luftwaffe in transporting the Falangist troops to Spain from Africa was critical and allowed them to build their land forces to challenge and finally defeat the Republicans. At this early stage of the war, the Republicans made a crucial error in not interdicting the Falangist flights transporting troops from Morocco to Spain, which they could easily have done and which the Falangists were expecting.

Goering referred to the involvement of the Luftwaffe in the Spanish Civil War during his testimony at the Nuremberg trials:[11]

> 'When the Civil War broke out in Spain, Franco sent a call for help to Germany and asked for support, particularly in the air. One should not forget that Franco with his troops was stationed in Africa and that he could not get the troops across, as the fleet was in the hands of the Communists, or, as they called themselves at the time, the competent Revolutionary Government in Spain. The decisive factor was, first of all, to get his troops over to Spain.
>
> 'The Fuhrer thought the matter over. I urged him to give support under all circumstances, firstly, in order to prevent the further spread of communism in that theater and, secondly, to test my young Luftwaffe at this opportunity in this or that technical respect.
>
> 'With the permission of the Fuhrer, I sent a large part of my transport fleet and a number of experimental fighter units, bombers, and antiaircraft guns; and in that way I had an opportunity to ascertain, under combat conditions, whether the material was equal to the task. In order that the personnel, too, might gather a certain amount of experience, I saw to it that there was a continuous flow, that is, that new people were constantly being sent and others recalled.'

As soon as possible after the war commenced, the Condor Legion was formed from so-called 'volunteers' from the Luftwaffe, and planes for them to fly were procured through sham arrangements which enabled the Germans to maintain that they were not infringing rules set by the League of Nations relating to non-intervention in the war. These forces included bomber, dive bomber and fighter squadrons which fought the Republican forces who were supplied mainly by the USSR. While the communist USSR was supplying the Republic, and the Germans and Italians were supplying the Falangists, the Western democracies were standing on the sidelines supporting a failed policy of non-intervention which was being made a mockery of by the Germans and Italians.

During the war in Spain, the first mass bombing of a civilian target took place on 26 April 1937 at the town of Guernica, which was heavily damaged and suffered a high level of casualties, presaging later events in the aerial attacks on London and German cities. The aftermath was described by German pilot Lieutenant Harro Harder:[12]

> 'Today we flew to Guernica. It has been totally destroyed, and not by the Reds, as all the local newspapers report, but by German and Italian bombers. It is the opinion of all of us that it was a rotten trick to destroy such a militarily unimportant city as Guernica.'

Franco acknowledged in writing to the German government that the support of the Condor Legion's aircraft was vital to the success of the Nationalist forces.

Field Marshal Albert Kesselring, Chief of Staff of the Luftwaffe during most of the Spanish Civil War period, remarked on the use of German aerial forces in Spain:[13]

> '[T]he intervention of the "Condor Legion" in Spain was an incubus imperilling the work of organization, though in the long run it proved valuable. As one squadron after another was recalled from its baptism by fire there was a welcome progress in formation training, and instrument flying from being regarded as a black art became a commonplace. Fighter, dive-bomber, bomber and distance reconnaissance squadrons were equipped with the prototypes of the Me 109, the Ju 87, the Do (Dornier) 17 and the He 111, although short distance reconnaissance and sea-plane units had at first to be content with their obsolete, but still serviceable, aircraft. The flak artillery was equipped with the pioneer 8.8-cm., 2- and 3.7-cm. gun and air intelligence training attempted to reach naval wireless telegraphy standards.'

Although the scale of the commitment to the Spanish Civil War was minor in comparison to later campaigns, it gave the opportunity for all the Luftwaffe's weapons and systems to be tested and refined. It also gave the pilots the chance to test the tactics they used in combat against pilots who were from the air forces of other major nations, such as the USSR, as part of the international forces fighting for the Republic. This experience was invaluable and formed the vital base which was the difference between the Luftwaffe and the other air forces it faced in the opening campaigns of the Second World War. It was also the campaign in which the Germans discovered the full value of the 88mm Flak gun in an anti-tank role.[14] It subsequently transpired that the 88mm gun was probably the most effective anti-tank weapon of its kind during the war. The experience gained by the commitment of German forces in Spain was therefore extremely important for the development of the Luftwaffe.

The Luftwaffe on the outbreak of war

There is a great difference between the perception of the strength of the Luftwaffe at the outbreak of the Second World War and the actual position. German propaganda had been very effective in causing the enemies of the Reich to overestimate its strength, which is of course what was intended:[15]

> 'What were the actual figures? The one reliable and relevant German document – the daily strength report of operational aircraft, produced by the Quartermaster-General for the C-in-C Luftwaffe – tells a very different story. During the Polish campaign the operative Luftwaffe comprised Luftflotte 1 "East" under Air Force General Albert Kesselring, and Luftflotte 4 "South-East" under Air Force General Alexander Löhr. On September 1, 1939 they together had at their disposal not more than 1,302 first-line aircraft. In addition there were in the east 133 machines which came under the direct command of the C-in-C (Goering). Apart from two bomber squadrons for special missions they comprised only reconnaissance, weather reconnaissance and transport machines. Thirty-one reconnaissance and communications squadrons totalling 288 aircraft had been handed over to the army. Finally one may count the fighters whose role was the air defense of eastern Germany, though only a few of these became involved in the air battle over Poland, and that on its periphery. In administrative areas I (Königsberg), III (Berlin), IV (Dresden) and VIII (Breslau) they comprised twenty-four squadrons with a total of 216 machines. Thus at a generous estimate the total number of aircraft that the Luftwaffe could call up against Poland was 1,929. Of these only 897 were "bomb-carriers" – i.e., bombers, dive bombers and ground-attack machines – adapted to the actual air

offensive. Goering had thrown two-thirds of his entire strength into the east. The remaining third, which held watch in the west, comprised 2,775 front-line machines of all types. Of them only 1,182, or about forty per cent, were "bomb-carriers". These humble figures imply three things: at the outset of the war the Luftwaffe was substantially weaker than generally supposed; it was by no means a purely offensive weapon; at this early stage of its build-up, when Hitler chose to go to war, it was fit only for a short blitz.'

The total number of operational aircraft in the Luftwaffe at the outbreak of war was thus 4,704, of which 1,182 were medium bombers or dive bombers. There were other strengths which the Luftwaffe enjoyed as well. For example, as mentioned earlier, the campaign in Spain had provided invaluable experience for the Luftwaffe pilots and had contributed greatly to their efficiency. It had also allowed the Luftwaffe supply and communications services to be perfected under combat conditions, which was a very great advantage to them against the French and British, who had no such experience. The combat experience of the Spanish Civil War also made it possible for any problems with the German aircraft to be identified so that they could be modified or corrected in future production.

The Luftwaffe, while not as numerous as was thought at the time, was therefore a very modern and well-tested arm of the Wehrmacht when war was declared and at least a match for the air forces of the other major powers.

The Early Campaigns – Poland

The role of the Luftwaffe in the speedy victory over Poland was explained by Field Marshal Kesselring, who was commander-in-chief of Luftflotte 1, in his book *A Soldier's Record*:[16]

> 'The results of the first day guaranteed our hopes. Aerial photographs revealed that the Polish air force had been hard hit and general mobilization disrupted. Observation of the targets already attacked was now carried out and nuisance raids made irregularly over the enemy's back areas. During the next few days it became increasingly evident that our immediate task was to support the army and to harass enemy strategic concentrations and troop movements.
>
> '… Crises on the German side, as on the Tucheler Heath, in the Polish break-through battle on the Bzura and in the area covering Warsaw, were overcome by exemplary co-operation with the ground forces, and

by throwing in every available close-support aircraft and bomber in a recklessly concentrated attack. The main brunt of the fighting was borne by the Stukas, fighters and pursuit fighters, numerous sorties a day being the regular thing.'

The Polish Air Force was outnumbered, and the German aircraft and support systems were more modern. This meant the Poles were hopelessly outclassed from the start, but they still fought gallantly throughout. The Polish pilots were well trained and subsequently acquitted themselves with honour serving with the RAF during the Battle of Britain.

The role played by the Luftwaffe was central to the rapid success of the invasion of Poland. Once the Polish aerial forces were destroyed, which occurred early in the invasion, their army was at the mercy of the bombers and dive bombers of the Luftwaffe, which were involved in army support in the most important battles of the campaign. Once again, the experience which had been gained by the pilots of the Luftwaffe was important in achieving the excellence of its operational performance.

The early campaigns – Norway

The main objective of the German invasion of Norway was to ensure that the supply of Swedish iron ore to Germany was not disrupted by the Allies. During the winter months, when the normal supply route was stopped by ice, this ore was sent by train from Sweden to Narvik in Norway, from where it was then transported to Germany by ship. The ore at risk to Germany from this trade was approximately a third of the yearly total received by Germany. Additionally, if the Allies controlled Norway, which abutted Sweden, the Germans believed they would be able to take the steps necessary to totally stop the ore traffic from Sweden, which would cripple their military supply industries.

When giving his evidence at the trial of the major war criminals at Nuremberg, Colonel General Jodl, Chief of the Operations Staff of the OKW, stated the German view at the time of the importance of the invasion of Norway:[17]

'DR EXNER: Now, Grossadmiral Raeder has explained the facts from which England's plans could be deduced. Have you anything to add to that, or is the question settled?

JODL: On the whole, Grossadmiral Raeder has already submitted all the information. There is one thing which remains in my memory and which is also written in my notebook.

	That is the special insistence, quite openly advocated in the French press, that under all circumstances Germany must be cut off from the Swedish ore supplies.
'DR EXNER:	What would have been the consequences for us if England had got there first?
'JODL:	As to that I can refer to Grossadmiral Raeder's testimony, and can only say that once Norway was in British hands the war would have been half lost for us. We would have been strategically encircled on the northern flank and because of the weakness of our fleet we would have been incapable of ever rectifying this again.'

It was therefore a matter of critical importance for the Germans that Norway remain neutral, or that the ore supply from Sweden be otherwise guaranteed.

The Luftwaffe commitment to the Norwegian campaign was approximately 1,200 aircraft[18] of all types, virtually all of which were sent to France immediately after their short-term use in Norway. The type of aircraft reflected the needs of the operation, with a particularly large proportion of transport aircraft – 533 Ju 52s – being used. These were all incorporated into Fliegerkorps X, commanded by Lieutenant General Hans Geisler.

The Luftwaffe's contribution to the success of the Norwegian campaign was crucial. There were three main elements to the role assigned to its aircraft:

1. Transporting troops to the most important objectives in the initial invasion. When the invasion occurred on 9 April 1940, the Luftwaffe landed troops at Oslo and Bergen, both of which were secured, together with the important airfields, on the opening day of the campaign. These two principal Norwegian cities did not have any means of resistance, and although the army and government moved north from them as quickly as possible to defend the country, the successful occupation of these key centres by the Germans meant that it would be very difficult to eject them.
2. Attaining air superiority over the battlefield. The Luftwaffe occupied several of the most important airfields in Norway as far north as possible and conducted operations which extended across most of the country from the start of the campaign. Once the airfield at Vaernes (near Trondheim) was modified for military use, the coverage of the

country was extended to include Narvik, which made German air superiority over the entire country complete. The Royal Air Force could not dispute control because of the range from its bases in Britain, and the number and type of aircraft available on Royal Navy aircraft carriers were inadequate to do so. Throughout the entire campaign, the Luftwaffe was in complete control of Norwegian airspace, with decisive implications for the Allied ground forces, which did not have any meaningful anti-aircraft capability.

3. Reinforcing and supplying the troops at vital points during the campaign. Wherever there were airfields, the Luftwaffe transports landed supplies of all kinds and reinforcements, which sustained and added to the power of the invasion. The transport squadrons of the Luftwaffe were mainly equipped with Ju 52 aircraft, which were not a new design but were rugged and reliable. The large number used – 533 – was virtually the total available of these aircraft at the time. The total operational aircraft in the Luftwaffe upon the outbreak of war was 4,704, of which 2,079 were medium bombers or dive bombers. The use of so many of the transport types is conclusive evidence of the importance assigned to the operation.

The Luftwaffe also attacked elements of the British Royal Navy and largely prevented its intervention in the campaign. The only important exception to this occurred at Narvik, where the Royal Navy destroyed all ten of the Kriegsmarine's destroyers in the area in two battles early in the campaign. Nevertheless, although Allied ground forces took Narvik, they had to abandon it shortly after the main German offensive began on the Western Front as the Allies needed all the troops they had to deal with that emergency. Before they left, the Allied troops caused considerable damage to the port installations in an (unsuccessful) attempt to prevent Narvik's further use to facilitate the transport of ore to Germany.

The victory in Norway had long-term repercussions on the conduct of the war as it enabled the vital supply of ore to Germany to continue uninterrupted during the winter months throughout the whole of the conflict, when it would otherwise have been stopped. It also meant that Sweden remained neutral during virtually the entire war, supplying Germany with the ore needed for its weapons programmes; if Norway had been occupied by the Allies, Sweden would probably have been forced to stop the supply of ore to Germany.

In addition, as a direct result of the defeat in Norway, the Chamberlain government in Britain was replaced with the wartime British coalition government headed by the implacable foe of Nazi Germany, Winston Churchill.

The Luftwaffe in France – 1940

The air forces of the French and British in the Battle of France during the 1940 campaign were approximately equal in number to the Luftwaffe. However, the French Air Force was distinctly inferior to their enemy in the quality of its aircraft. It had a total of 1,286 aircraft available on 10 May 1940,[19] of which 632 were fighters, but most of these were obsolescent types. The best of the new French fighters was the Dewoitine D520, which was inferior to the Me 109 but better than any of the other German fighters – regrettably, only eighty of them were available. The French also had 262 bombers, but they too were mostly obsolete types. The French government was in the process of making major purchases of aircraft from the USA, but these did not reach them in time to participate in the 1940 campaign.

The French Air Force was augmented by the Royal Air Force, which had 416 aircraft committed to operations in France. These varied in quality, ranging from the Spitfires and Hurricanes – which were a match for any of the German types – to out-of-date bombers such as the Fairey Battle. There were also some of the new Bristol Blenheim medium bombers, which were comparable to the German types in performance. The Allied air forces thus had a total of 1,702 aircraft available with which to counter the German attack. During the campaign, the Allies lost 1,274 aircraft destroyed from all causes. The French also lost 460 aircrew killed and 120 taken prisoner, which represented 40 per cent of their officers and 20 per cent of their NCOs. The RAF lost 915 aircrew killed or missing and 184 wounded. The RAF also left behind an estimated one million pounds worth of equipment lost or destroyed.[20]

Only once were the Allied air forces committed in concentrated attacks on the German armoured forces, tactics which could have disrupted the development of the German offensive which broke through the French defences at Sedan, mainly due to being concentrated to cover the Allied forces' advance into Belgium. The one time the Allied air forces did mass for an attack was against the bridgehead at Sedan on 14 May:[21]

> 'About 152 bombers and 250 fighters concentrated over Sedan, suffering 11 per cent losses. The small size of the target made their task difficult, and the effectiveness of the operation was reduced by sending the planes in small groups of 10 or 20. Of 71 British bombers only 41 returned. According to the official RAF history, "[N]o higher loss in an operation has ever been experienced by the Royal Air Force."'

These losses were due to the concentrated anti-aircraft fire of the Luftwaffe Flak units attached to the army. RAF crews were flying slow and outdated Fairey Battles, which were unable to perform the role assigned. This tragic incident exemplified the appalling consequences of the neglect of the RAF by pre-war British governments.

According to Cajus Bekker's *The Luftwaffe War Diaries*:[22]

'The total strength in first-line aircraft available, on May 10, 1940, to Generals Kesselring and Sperrle, commanding Luftflotten 2 and 3, was as follows:

'1,120 bombers (Do 17, He 111, Ju 88)
'324 dive-bombers (Ju 87)
'42 "battleplanes" (Hs 123)
'1,016 short-range fighters (Me 109)
'248 long-range fighters (Me 110)
'plus reconnaissance and transport planes.

'They were divided up amongst six Air Corps. Of these I and IV (under Generals Ulrich Grauert and Alfred Keller) had Belgium and Holland as their zone of operations. II and V (under Lieutenant-Generals Bruno Loerzer and Robert Ritter von Greim) operated in front of the southern flank of the front facing north-east France and deployed the lion's share of the fourteen bomber Geschwader. Further, there was the "special purpose" Air Corps 2, responsible for the air landings in Holland, and finally VIII Air Corps under Lieutenant- General Wolfram Freiherr von Richthofen.'

It can therefore be seen that in the air as well as on the ground, the Germans did not enjoy any significant numerical advantage over the Allies. However, all the types of aircraft the Germans fielded were equal to or better than any in service in the rest of the world. Ironically, the Ju 87 Stuka was regarded as being obsolescent, but performed one of the most critical roles of any German aircraft in the offensive, providing accurate dive bombing on Allied ground forces in support of the army, especially at the main points of attack by the panzer breakthrough forces.

The losses sustained by the Luftwaffe during the 1940 campaign numbered 1,428 aircraft destroyed either by enemy action or through damage from other causes.[23] This represents almost 30 per cent of the available force when the campaign began. The number of aircraft produced by the Germans during 1940 included 6,201 fighter and bomber types, which bore the burden of these losses. The Luftwaffe therefore suffered losses in the 1940 campaign which were considered to be at the limit of tolerable levels.

The impact of the Battle of Britain

The Battle of Britain was an integral part of Operation *Sea Lion* and the first time that the Luftwaffe encountered determined opposition from an air force which was technically its equal. In addition, the RAF had several tactical advantages which meant that the contest between the two sides would be closer than anything that had occurred thus far in the war.

The main tactical advantage the RAF had was that it was operating from home bases over its own territory, meaning that it was not subject to any range or endurance issues and that any German pilots lost over the battlefield would become prisoners. These were substantial advantages.

The RAF also had an extensive radar network which had been completed in time to be completely operational during the battle. The Germans were aware that the RAF had a defensive radar network, but did not know the level to which it had been developed or that the RAF's pilots were connected by high-frequency radio to controllers who guided them to intercept targets. Adolf Galland, one of the most successful German aces, who later took command of the German fighter forces, remarked on the advantage brought by this radar network:[24]

> 'From the very beginning the English had an extraordinary advantage which we could never overcome throughout the entire war: radar and fighter control. For us and for our Command this was a surprise and a very bitter one. England possessed a closely knit radar network conforming to the highest technical standards of the day, which provided Fighter Command with the most detailed data imaginable. Thus the British fighter was guided all the way from take-off to his correct position for attack on the German formations.'

Air Chief Marshal Hugh Dowding, in charge of RAF Fighter Command, had championed the development and deployment of this crucial resource. The radar coverage of Britain is shown in the accompanying map (Map 1).

Galland pointed out another handicap faced by the Luftwaffe during the Battle of Britain:[25]

> 'Of further outstanding advantage to the English was the fact that our attacks, especially those of the bombers, were of sheer necessity directed against the central concentration of the British defense. We were not in a position to seek out soft spots in this defense or to change our approaches and to attack now from this direction, now from that, as the Allies did

later in their air offensive against the Reich. For us there was only a frontal attack against the superbly organized defense of the British Isles, conducted with great determination.'

The whole success of Operation *Sea Lion* would be determined by the Luftwaffe's ability to destroy the RAF, yet it did not possess the means to achieve this imperative necessity. The bombers which it did have were not adequate either in bomb load or in numbers to cause the destruction of the airfields upon which the RAF depended. Galland commented on this situation:[26]

'The bombing attacks on the British fighter bases did not achieve the expected success. Apart from the fact that it was purely coincidental if the respective fighter squadrons were grounded at the time of the attack, the quantity of bombs dropped on each target was by no means sufficient. Runways and buildings were usually only slightly damaged and could generally be repaired overnight. At Luftwaffe HQ, however, somebody took the reports of the bomber or Stuka squadrons in one hand and a thick blue pencil in the other and crossed the squadron or base in question off the tactical map. It did not exist any more – in any case not on paper. Reports of fighter and other pilots regarding numbers of shot-down enemy planes were also exaggerated as happens on both sides during large-scale air battles. Thus it came about that one day according to the calculations in Berlin there were no more British fighters, while we were supposed to have achieved a certain superiority; but we were far from achieving air supremacy. One of the main reasons for this was the short range of the ME-109, allowing only little penetration and in consequence reducing the range of the bombers.'

Galland continued:[27]

'The Luftwaffe, alas, had no heavy strategic bombers. General Wever, their champion, had demanded them energetically.
   '... On the death of Wever the development of a long-range strategic bomber force was stopped. It was considered sufficient to have Stukas and a large fleet of twin-engined medium-range bombers. Jeschonnek, the fourth Luftwaffe Chief of Staff after Kesselring and Stumpf, gave his specifications for a long-range twin-engined fast bomber as follows: 2,500-pound bomb load, 600-mile range, and a speed of 435 mph. His demands held fire because of the impressive initial successes at the beginning of the war and because Hitler's dislike of a war with England

made any new developments appear as of secondary importance. We therefore had to get used to the fact that our offensive could only be directed against a small and extraordinarily well-defended sector of the British Isles. But this sector included the capital, the heart of the British Empire, London. The seven-million-people city on the Thames was of exceptional military importance as the brain and nerve center of the British High Command, as a port, and as a center for armament and distribution. The fact that London was within the range of day bombing attacks with fighter cover, however inefficient and disadvantageous the German offensive was, must be regarded as one of the positive sides of our offensive.'

This halt in production was followed a short time later by the outbreak of the war, which meant that the development of other heavy bombers was not pursued vigorously enough, with the result that the Germans never had any heavy bomber forces comparable to those of the Allies. Goering had attempted to overcome this deficiency with some desperate measures:[28]

'In February 1940 Goering, worried by the raw-material shortage, ordained a policy of maximum economy. All long-term projects and developments were to be cancelled, and the available materials devoted to supplying the front with proven aircraft types "in the greatest possible number at the greatest possible speed". Thousands of engineers and technicians found themselves redundant and were conscripted to the forces. Any aircraft not ready for operations in 1940 need not be built, for by the following year at the latest the war would be won.'

The Luftwaffe's lack of a heavy bomber force also meant that it could not cause enough destruction to London to cause the panic reaction – the terror – which Hitler and Goering envisaged would ensue from concentrated attacks directed against large centres of population. This expectation was referred to in the Fuehrer Naval Conferences on 14 August 1940:[29]

'In addition on D-1 day, the Luftwaffe is to make a strong attack on London, which would cause the population to flee from the city and block the roads.

On 7 September, the Germans changed the focus of their attack to London, which gave RAF Fighter Command time to recuperate from the serious damage which had been done to some of the most important air stations in 11 Group (south-east England), which was bearing the brunt of the German attack, and the debilitating effects which constant combat had on the RAF aircrews and supporting services. Changing the focus of attack was an error which prevented the German strategy from having any chance of succeeding. The causes of the change are set out in Bekker's *The Luftwaffe War Diaries*:[30]

> 'The reasons for the new policy were two: one of them purely military, the other political. On September 3rd Goering met his two Luftflotten chiefs, Field Marshals Kesselring and Sperrle, at The Hague. He pressed the view that current tactical policy should now be abandoned in favour of a large-scale assault on the most important target – the English capital. The only question was: could such an attack be launched without undue risk to the bomber force? Had the British fighters become sufficiently weakened? Kesselring said Yes, Sperrle said No.
>
> 'Sperrle wanted the offensive against the fighter bases to continue. Kesselring put the view that they were expendable: if too badly damaged the fighter squadrons could withdraw to other bases behind London, and these, being beyond German fighter range, would thus be safe from bombers. He was indeed astonished that the British had not long since made this move to save them further losses. Their reasons must have been psychological, such as "holding the front line" and "setting an example to the people". But it was quite on the cards that they would withdraw to these more safely placed airfields now.
>
> '**"We have no chance," he said, "of destroying the English fighters on the ground** [author's emphasis]. We must force their last reserves of Spitfires and Hurricanes into combat in the air." This would only be accomplished by changing the target.
>
> 'Even before "Adlertag" ["Eagle Day", 13 August, the commencement of mass German raids against RAF airfields] the importance of London had been judged by II Air Corps to be so paramount that the English would hazard the last of their squadrons in its defence. **During the whole of August, however, Hitler for political reasons had forbidden any attack on the capital. Unfortunately, owing to a regrettable lapse in navigation on the part of a few bomber crews, it had happened. On the night of August 24th/25th some isolated bombs, destined for the aircraft works at Rochester and oil tanks on the Thames, had descended over the London area, and this had sparked off a whole chain reaction** [author's emphasis].
>
> '... Churchill demanded from a reluctant Bomber Command, who saw no military advantage to be gained by it, an immediate reprisal raid on Berlin. The following night, accordingly, eighty-one British

twin-engined bombers made the 600-mile each-way flight to the German capital.

'... It was the first of four British raids within ten days.

'For Hitler it was too much.'

Indeed, the Fuhrer now ordered that the Luftwaffe switch the focus of attack on London, which meant the start of the Blitz. In a speech on 4 September, Hitler stated:[31]

'And should the Royal Air Force drop two thousand, or three thousand, or four thousand kilograms of bombs, then we will now drop 150,000; 180,000; 230,000; 300,000; 400,000; yes, one million kilograms in a single night. And should they declare that they will greatly increase their attacks on our cities, then we will erase their cities!'

There is little doubt that this order of Hitler's stemmed from a desire to destroy London. Speer recalled that during a 'frenzy of destructiveness' Hitler had worked himself into during one of his nightly after-dinner sessions with his intimate circle, the Fuhrer said:[32]

'Have you ever looked at a map of London? It is so closely built up that one source of fire alone would suffice to destroy the whole city, as happened once before, two hundred years ago. Goering wants to use innumerable incendiary bombs of an altogether new type to create sources of fire in all parts of London. Fires everywhere. Thousands of them. They'll unite in one gigantic area conflagration. Goering has the right idea. Explosive bombs don't work, but it can be done with incendiary bombs – total destruction of London. What use will their fire department be once that really starts!'

That is indeed what the Germans attempted to do, but the Luftwaffe did not have the heavy bombers to carry enough bombs or sufficient fighters to protect daytime raids, as was proven by the severe losses suffered on the few occasions when the Luftwaffe tried to do so. Although the Germans raided London at night on many occasions from September 1940 until May 1941, the damage caused was not significant enough to achieve any of the aims of a strategic bombing campaign.

This diversion of effort which Hitler ordered resulted in the attacks on the British fighter stations ceasing and the Battle of Britain thus becoming a stalemate. In practice, the British had successfully prevented the invasion, the Luftwaffe's attempt to secure the conditions necessary for the launch of Operation Sea Lion having resulted in a strategic defeat for Germany. The primarily causes of this, as we have seen, were Hitler's insistence on the destruction of London and the Luftwaffe's lack of the heavy bomber force necessary for the task. If the RAF had lost daytime control of the airspace over southern England as a result of the Luftwaffe offensive from July–September 1940, the likelihood of a successful German invasion would have been much higher.

Johannes Steinhoff was a Staffelkapitan and fighter pilot on the front line of the fight in the Battle of Britain during August and September 1940, later being awarded the Knight's Cross of the Iron Cross with Oak Leaves. He recalled the difficulties of facing the RAF's skilled fighter pilots during the Battle of Britain:[33]

'The British were born fighters, very tough, well trained, and very enthusiastic. They were brave, and I never fought better pilots at any time during the war, including the Americans. We were almost evenly matched with the RAF in fighters against fighters, so true dogfights – even in the *Schwarm* ["swarm", a Luftwaffe tactical unit of four fighters] – were possible. They would take off and engage us, and with their radar, they knew where we were. They had a lot more fuel for the fight. The Battle of Britain, in my opinion, was the truest test of men and machines, and only the best survived. You learned quickly, or you did not survive.'

As far as can be accuratey determined, German aircraft losses during the Battle of Britain were as follows:[34]

Table 1: German Aircraft Losses: July–September 1940.

Single-engine fighters	–	518
Twin-engine fighters	–	235
Total fighters	–	753
Bombers	–	709
Total German losses	–	1,462

During the whole of 1940, the total German production of these types was 6,201 units,[35] so this level of loss was extremely damaging to the operational strength of the Luftwaffe.

But the losses were not confined only to aircraft; during August 1940 alone, Luftwaffe aircrew casualties, according to the Battle of Britain Historical Society, were as follows:[36]

Aircraft type	Pilots Killed	Injured	Captured
Me 109	57	41	3
Me 110	48	6	2
He 111	39	9	1
Do 17	22	14	2
Ju 88	33	5	4
Ju 87	20	5	1
Total	**219**	**80**	**13**

This level of loss of highly trained personnel was very significant to the Luftwaffe, even more important than the number of aircraft lost. Until 1942, when the training time for Luftwaffe pilots was changed due to the heavy losses sustained, a fighter or dive bomber pilot underwent about thirteen months of training with 150–200 flying hours, while a bomber or reconnaissance pilot received twenty months' training in addition to 220–270 hours flying. The personnel losses during the Battle of Britain were therefore a very important consideration for the long-term viability of the Luftwaffe.

The Battle of Britain was thus not only a strategic defeat for Germany, in that it ended in a stalemate, but also caused an important reduction in the fighting power of the Luftwaffe from which it never fully recovered. The defeat also meant that Operation *Sea Lion* could not be executed, which in turn led to Hitler's decision to attack the USSR, starting the chain of military events which concluded with his downfall.

The Luftwaffe and the invasion of the USSR

When Hitler made the decision to invade the USSR, he did so against the advice of Goering, who realized that the Luftwaffe needed time to refit following the French campaign and the Battle of Britain. Goering advised the Fuhrer that the Luftwaffe did not have the capacity to undertake a two-front war against both Britain and the Soviet Union, and that the Chief of Operations of the Luftwaffe, Major General van Waldau, had told him that to do so was 'impossible'.[37] Goering referred to this in his testimony at Nuremberg, which was confirmed by Field Marshal Milch:[38]

'DR STAHMER: Did you speak a second time to Field Marshal Goring about this war?
'MILCH: Yes.
'DR STAHMER: When was that?
'MILCH: On 22 May, on one of my tours, I again came into contact with the Commander-in-Chief for the first time after a long interval. It was in Veldenstein where Goring was at the time. There I discussed the question with him and I told him that, in my opinion, it would be a great historical task for him to prevent this war since it could only end with the annihilation of Germany. I reminded him that we should not voluntarily burden ourselves with a two-front war, et cetera. The Reich Marshal told me that he also had brought forward all these arguments, but that it was absolutely impossible to dissuade Hitler from this war. My offer to try to speak to Hitler once more was declared by the Reich Marshal to be absolutely hopeless. We had to resign ourselves; nothing could be done about it. From these words it was quite clear that he was against this war, and that under no circumstances did he want this war but that also for him, in his position, there was no possibility of dissuading Hitler from this project.
'DR STAHMER: Did it also appear from what he said that he had told Hitler of his misgivings?
'MILCH: Yes, it was quite clear to me, that he had also spoken about the question of a two-front war, and he told me that he had also laid before Hitler the arguments I had brought forward; but he told me that it was hopeless.'

So regarding the attack on the USSR at this time both the High Command of the Luftwaffe and the Supreme Command of the Army gave Hitler the same advice, which did not occur very frequently during the war. This is not to say that Goering was against war with the USSR at any time, just that he tried to dissuade Hitler from attacking at that time because he recognized that doing so while Britain remained undefeated was unnecessarily risky as it meant Germany having a war on two fronts.

Nevertheless, Hitler ordered the following as part of Directive 21 relating to Operation *Barbarossa*:[39]

> 'The air force will have to make available for this Eastern campaign supporting forces of such strength that the army will be able to bring land operations to a speedy conclusion and that eastern Germany will be as little damaged as possible by enemy air attack.'

The Luftwaffe was thus committed to a campaign which its commander-in-chief advised against and for which its chief of operations stated it was impossible for it to fulfil its intended role.

Adolf Galland also acknowledged the dangers of invading the USSR at this time:[40]

> 'Hitler's decision meant for Germany the renunciation of a safeguarded rear, while the struggle with the West was still undecided. … The fate of our battle in the west against the RAF was also decided at this moment.'

Despite the misgivings of its senior leadership, when the attack on the Soviet Union began, the Luftwaffe was initially extremely effective both in ground support and air superiority missions. One Soviet eyewitness to a ground support attack soon after the launch of *Barbarossa* stated:[41]

> 'The German bombing of our frontier forces was merciless. The weather was ideal for their planes – with long clear sunny days – and they rained bombs down on our troops as if they were conducting a military exercise. I came across the remnants of one of our units close to a forest. There were hundreds upon hundreds of dead. The German attack had been so rapid that most had not even had time to get out of their vehicles.'

This success was replicated in the air offensive against the Soviet air force. Johannes Steinhoff, who after fighting during the Batte of Britain also served with distinction on the Eastern Front, commented:[42]

> 'Our success was easy to explain. We fought as a team from the beginning. We had excellent training schools and great combat leaders from the Spanish Civil War, as well as the early campaigns in Poland and the West, who led by example. We were very successful from the beginning of the invasion from June 22, 1941. We did not have a lot of competition until the next year, as our greatest enemy was the weather.'

Indeed, the first winter of the war in the Soviet Union affected the operations of the Luftwaffe to a massive degree, as it did the entire Wehrmacht on the

Eastern Front. Erich Hartmann, who was the most successful of the German aces with an amazing 352 confirmed 'kills', described the situation faced by the Luftwaffe pilots in the Soviet winter:[43]

> '[W]e had a lot of problems with the motors. We used to have the crew chiefs start them every hour and run them for about 10 minutes around the clock to keep them operational. Then we got very lucky. We had a Russian prisoner, who was no fan of Stalin or the Communists, show us how to start our engines in the sub-zero cold by mixing gasoline into the oil crankcase ... Another guy showed us how to start a fire under the cowling, keeping the oil and coolant warm, and start the engine – another helpful hint. The same guy showed us how to keep the weapons firing.'

The commitment to and ultimate failure of Operation *Barbarossa* meant that the Luftwaffe had no opportunity to revitalize itself from the losses which had occurred during either the Battle of Britain or the early stages of the invasion of the USSR in 1941. The figures of aircraft lost and damaged during the period from the launch of the invasion until the spring of 1942 are shown below.

German Aircraft Losses on the Russian Front, 22 June 1941 to 8 April 1942[44]

	Lost	Damaged
22 June 1941–2 August 1941	1,023	657
3 August 1941–27 September 1941	580	371
28 September 1941–6 December 1941	489	333
7 December 1941–8 April 1942	859	636
Total	2,951	1,997

It can be seen that the losses during the winter months were almost equal to those suffered during the initial combat following the invasion, the highest rate of loss for the Luftwaffe to that time. During the winter, the number of sorties was markedly less than those flown during the initial invasion owing to the atrocious weather conditions, which made the attrition rate higher from causes other than combat.

During the same period, the production of aircraft for the Luftwaffe of all types[45] was 12,401 units, the proportion of which represented by losses on the Eastern Front alone being approximately 25 per cent.

Stalingrad

As mentioned earlier in this chapter and in Chapter 4 of Volume 2 of this work relating to Operation Barbarossa, Goering and others advised Hitler not to undertake the attack against the USSR in June 1941 because the Luftwaffe needed time to recover from its recent casualties and losses. Goering also warned that the Luftwaffe did not have the capacity to undertake a two-front war against both Britain and the USSR, and that the best strategy would be to finish off Britain before undertaking any campaign in the East. However, the Fuhrer believed that the Wehrmacht could defeat the Red Army in a short campaign which would leave Germany free to intensify its war against Britain or perhaps result in a negotiated peace when the Soviets were beaten. But Hitler's gamble did not succeed, the Germans suffering significant losses during the winter of 1941–42. Hitler believed that he had no choice but to strike again in the East in 1942, planning an offensive aimed at Stalingrad in a bid to finally shatter the power of the USSR.

The total number of aircraft of all types produced by German industry for the Luftwaffe in 1941 was 11,776, whereas British production was 20,094 and that of the USSR 15,735.[46] Germany was therefore being substantially out-produced without even taking into account the production of the USA, so unless the Wehrmacht could defeat the Soviets quickly, the writing was on the wall for Germany.

During 1942, due to Hitler's expansion of the war, the Luftwaffe continued to undertake the war against Britain and also became involved in campaigns in North Africa to support Germany's Italian allies with the Afrika Korps as well as in Crete, where it played the major part in the successful but costly airborne invasion of the island. The Luftwaffe's activities therefore increased exponentially, leading to greater losses than anticipated and a further dispersal of its forces.

When planning for the 1942 summer offensive, 'Case Blue', which ended in the Stalingrad disaster, the Luftwaffe assigned more than 60 per cent of its total available forces to support the operation. These were gathered together in Luftflotte 4, which had under its command Fliegerkorps IV and VIII. The combined total of aircraft in this grouping was 1,610 of all types,[47] which meant that the Germans had virtual parity in numbers with the Red Air Force in the air over the battlefield, and because of its qualitative edge was able to attain air superiority for the German ground forces to operate within. The main roles of these Luftwaffe formations were to support the ground forces and eliminate any Soviet aircraft that interfered.

The Luftwaffe's direct involvement in the Battle of Stalingrad commenced on 23 August, with bomber units dropping 1,000 tons of bombs on the city in forty-eight hours.[48] The intention of this bombardment was to create panic among the inhabitants, but it failed to do so and only made the defenders more determined to fight for the city to the last man and round. It also created a battlefield strewn with rubble, which acted as ready-made cover for the Soviet soldiers to maximize their defensive power.

During August, Luftflotte 4 was involved in non-stop operations supporting the army at Stalingrad and attacking the Soviet Air Force. This led to attrition and wear and tear on such a scale that the formation reported to Berlin its operational strength had been reduced to just 720 aircraft. The Luftwaffe command could not, however, withdraw aircraft from other fronts to assist, because it was stretched everywhere fulfilling its other roles.[49] The Luftwaffe was thus suffering serious losses even before the climax of the campaign was reached when the Red Army attacked north and south of Stalingrad to isolate the German Sixth Army on 19 November 1942.

When the Sixth Army was surrounded in Stalingrad, Goering assured Hitler that its troops could be supplied by the Luftwaffe. This assertion was strenuously questioned at the time by Colonel General Kurt Zeitzler, the Chief of the Army General Staff. The argument between him and Goering was witnessed by Albert Speer, who was at Fuhrer Headquarters at the time:[50]

> '[T]he fate of the encircled army was finally sealed. For Goering appeared in the situation room, brisk and beaming like an operetta tenor who is supposed to portray a victorious Reich Marshal. Depressed, with a beseeching tone in his voice, Hitler asked him: "What about supplying Stalingrad by air?" Goering snapped to attention and declared solemnly: "My leader! I personally guarantee the supplying of Stalingrad by air. You can rely on that." As I later heard from Milch, the Air Force General Staff had in fact calculated that supplying the pocket was impossible. Zeitzler, too, instantly voiced his doubts. But Goering retorted that it was exclusively the business of the air force to undertake the necessary calculations.
>
> 'Hitler ... revived at Goering's mere words, and had recovered all his old staunchness. Then Stalingrad can be held! It is foolish to go on talking any more about a breakout of the Sixth Army. It would lose all its heavy weapons and have no fighting strength left. The Sixth Army remains in Stalingrad.'

Hitler decided, without further investigation, to accept Goering's assurance that the Sixth Army could be supplied by the Luftwaffe. But the Luftwaffe had to attempt to undertake the task without the means of doing so, as its transport aircraft – mainly Ju 52s – were not capable of carrying large enough cargoes and were not available in the numbers to achieve the necessary tonnage required to keep the army supplied. Because it did not have the appropriate aircraft, the task was undertaken by medium bomber units, augmented by the comparatively few Focke-Wulf Condor and Heinkel 177 four-engine bombers available, which were not designed for the purpose and therefore of limited value in such a role. All the aircraft involved also had to fly in very bad weather conditions, further limiting their capabilities. The Red Army soon realized what was happening and set up numerous anti-aircraft emplacements under the flight paths into Stalingrad. These took a heavy toll of the German aircraft, which had to fly at low altitude because of the weather and were slowing to land at the few suitable airfields in the city. It soon became evident that Goering's claim was an empty boast, and the Sixth Army was never supplied with the minimum required for its proper maintenance:[51]

> '[O]n November 25th and 26th, the first two days of the airlift, Stalingrad received only sixty-five tons of fuel and ammunition in place of the required 300. And on the third day it received virtually nothing.
> "Weather atrocious," [General] Fiebig noted in his diary. "We are trying to fly, but it's impossible. Here at Tazi one snowstorm succeeds another. Situation desperate."'

Although the crews did everything possible with the available aircraft, the operation was a forlorn hope from the beginning. Disastrous damage was caused to the Luftwaffe by the flying conditions and the heavy anti-aircraft resources committed to the Stalingrad area by the Red Army. The result was the loss of over 500 of the aircraft involved in the airlift. This was over one-third of the Luftwaffe's total transport fleet. Worse still, over 1,000 aircrew perished in the operation, including instructors from the Luftwaffe's training establishments who had to be used for the flights. These were some of the most experienced flyers in the Luftwaffe and simply could not be replaced. The only positive which could be taken from the Luftwaffe's efforts was that 42,000 wounded, sick and specialist troops[52] were safely evacuated from the maelstrom of Stalingrad.

The net result of 'Case Blue' was not only a disaster for the German Army, but also for the Luftwaffe, which never recovered from the loss of experienced personnel and aircraft in the attempt to supply the surrounded Sixth Army. Hitler's gamble that the Wehrmacht could defeat the USSR had by this time become a nightmare, with enormous losses for Germany's ground and aerial forces. The Fuhrer had been warned about the dangers before the operation was launched, and he alone was responsible for its disastrous outcome.

On 19 January 1943, General Paulus, commander of the Sixth Army, exclaimed to one of the last Luftwaffe pilots to land at Stalingrad:[53]

> 'Why on earth did the Luftwaffe ever promise to keep us supplied? Who is the man responsible for declaring that it was possible? Had someone told me that it was not possible, I should not have held it against the Luftwaffe. I could have broken out. When I was strong enough to do so. Now it is too late.'

Hitler must bear the responsibility for the destruction of the Sixth Army. His acceptance of the assurance from Goering that the Luftwaffe could supply the surrounded troops was a perfect example of why his leadership was a calamity for the Nazi war effort.

The lost opportunity of the Me 262

The Me 262 was the first operational jet fighter to be produced by any country. It was far superior in terms of speed, climb rate and maximum altitude at which it could operate than any piston-driven aircraft. Its armament was also extremely powerful, with four 30mm cannon giving it the ability to disable or destroy the heavy bombers used in the Allies' strategic bombing campaign, while its speed of over 500mph and rate of climb of 3,937ft per minute made up for its comparative lack of manoeuvrability against the latest Allied fighters. These advantages meant that it could have been an extremely effective aircraft with which the Germans could counter the Allies' bombing campaign, if it had become operational early enough and in sufficient numbers. Its main operational limitations were the availability of fuel and that it needed a long runway from which to take off, meaning that the airfields it operated from were easy to identify.

German aces believed that this fighter, properly used, could give them a significant edge over anything the Allies had and seriously challenge the bombing offensive. General Adolf Galland, as commander-in-chief of the German fighter forces, reported his views on the Me 262 after his first flight in one on 22 May 1943:[54]

> 'This was no dream or fantasy, no daring project that would become reality in some distant future. The jet fighter ME-262, the fastest fighter aircraft on earth, was a fact. I had flown it. And I knew that with it we could beat any other fighter plane. Of course it still had to be nursed through its infancy. But all of us, who sat down for a round-table

conference were convinced that everything had to be done to make use of this unique opportunity. Risks had to be taken and unusual means had to be found. Thus a joint suggestion was worked out proposing an immediate start on the construction of a first series of 100 aircraft to serve simultaneously first technical and tactical tests. Such a procedure was contrary to the usual care applied in German aircraft construction. We wanted to prepare immediately for the final mass production, and we thought of using the time it would take until production really started to gather the necessary experiences with these first 100 aircraft. The changes we found necessary could then be applied to the first production series. This suggestion, together with the report of the flight, was worked out then and there and signed. A duplicate was sent to Milch, and I traveled on the same day with the original to Göring in Burg Veltenstein. Göring shared our enthusiasm. He would not have been a fighter pilot had he not shown full understanding for the train of thought resulting from my first trial flight with the ME-262. In my presence Göring telephoned to Milch, who also had the report and the suggestions in hand. He too was in complete agreement. All suggestions were accepted with amazing speed and enthusiastic resolutions. I thought that I had already won all along the line. The Reichsmarschall first had to get Hitler's sanction, which was necessary for such an important decision; but this would undoubtedly be granted, since we had such determined support from the experts. First thing next morning Göring wanted to see the Führer and inform him personally of all the details.'

However, there was no response from Hitler to the urgent representations of Goering or Galland and no authorization for production to go ahead. Galland commented:[55]

'Thereby the production of the ME-262 received a further delay of six months after it had already suffered a delay of about two years, due to the previous order given in autumn, 1940, to postpone all research developments. I believe that in this way about 18 months were lost in the development of the ME-262.

'When I was present at a demonstration of the latest Luftwaffe technical developments in December, 1943, at the aviation center at Insterburg in East Prussia, I did not know anything about the possible considerations not to use the ME-262 as a fighter. Hitler had come over from his nearby headquarters. The jet fighter ME-262 caused a special sensation. I was standing right beside him when he suddenly asked Göring, "Can this aircraft carry bombs?"

'Göring had already discussed the question with Messerschmitt, and replied, "Yes my Führer, theoretically yes. There is enough power to spare to carry 1,000 pounds, perhaps even 2,000 pounds."

'This was a carefully formulated answer which objectively could not be disputed. Among aviators this reply would have created no disturbance. Because any expert knew it was purely hypothetical. The ME-262 possessed no fixtures for releasing bombs and no bombsights. According to its flying properties and its safety conditions it was highly unsuited for an aimed-bomb release; diving or gliding were out of the question because of the unavoidable excess of the permissible top speed. At speeds of over 600mph the aircraft became uncontrollable. At low altitudes the fuel consumption was so high that the operative range became unprofitably small; therefore low-level attacks, too, were out of the question. There remained high-altitude bombing, yet here the given target had to be at least the size of a large town to be hit with certainty under the given conditions.

'But who could explain all this to Hitler at the moment? In any case, who would have had a chance of his argument being understood, to say nothing of being accepted? Of course it was the duty of the Reichsmarschall, with whom Hitler had spoken on these questions, to point all this out to him. I did not know if he had done so. Anyhow the Führer gave neither Messerschmitt nor ourselves an opportunity to explain.

'He said, "For years I have demanded from the Luftwaffe a 'speed bomber,' which can reach its target in spite of enemy fighter defense. In the aircraft you present to me as a fighter plane I see the 'Blitz bomber,' with which I will repel the invasion in its first and weakest phase. Regardless of the enemy's air umbrella it will strike the recently landed mass of material and troops creating panic, death, and destruction. At last this is the Blitz bomber! Of course none of you thought of that!"

'Hitler was right. Indeed no one had thought of that! And we were still not thinking of it. The existing programme for production and tests for the ME-262 continued unchanged. In collaboration with the Luftwaffe research unit and the Messerschmitt works, I formed a command of experienced fighter pilots, who started with tests in real action against English Mosquito daylight reconnaissance planes. At last we had a fighter which was superior to the fastest Allied aircraft. Soon the first kills were achieved.'

Hitler's interference in the adoption of this revolutionary aircraft because of his lack of technical understanding can only be looked at through a thankful prism. If he had listened to his experts, the air war over Germany would certainly have meant many more casualties among the Allied bomber fleets, although the ultimate result would have been the same – it was too late for the Me 262 to change the outcome of the war.

Hitler's role in the development and deployment of the Me 262 was commented upon by Albert Speer:[56]

> 'During the armaments congress at the air force test site in Rechlin (September 1943) Milch silently handed me a telegram which had just been brought to him. It contained an order from Hitler to halt preparations for large scale production of the Me262. We decided to circumvent the order. But still the work could not be continued on the priority level it should have had.
>
> 'Some three months later, on January 7, 1944, Milch and I were urgently summoned to headquarters. Hitler had changed his mind … on the basis of an excerpt from the British press on the success of British experiments with jet planes. He was now impatient to have as many aircraft of this type as we could make in the shortest possible time. Since in the meantime Hitler had let everything lapse, we could promise to deliver no more than sixty planes a month from July 1944. From January 1945 on, however, we would be able to produce two hundred and ten aircraft a month.
>
> 'In the course of this conference Hitler indicated that he planned to use the plane, which was built to be a fighter, as a fast bomber. The air force specialists were dismayed, but imagined that their sensible arguments would prevail. What happened was just the opposite. Hitler obstinately ordered all weapons on board removed so that the aircraft could carry a greater weight of bombs. Jet planes did not have to defend themselves, he maintained, since with their superior speed they could not be attacked by enemy fighters. Deeply distrustful of this new invention, he wanted it employed primarily for straight flight at great heights, to spare its wings and engines, and wanted the engineers to gear it to a somewhat reduced speed to lessen the strain on the still untried system.
>
> 'The effect of these tiny bombers, which could carry a load of little more than a thousand pounds of bombs and had only a primitive bombsight, was ridiculously insignificant. As fighter planes, on the other hand, each one of the jet aircraft would have been able, because of its superior performance, to shoot down several of the four-motored

American bombers which in raid after raid were dropping thousands of tons of explosives on German cities.

'At the end of June 1944, Goering and I once more tried to make Hitler see these points, but again in vain …

'… Hitler's order necessarily influenced long-range military planning, for the General Staff had been counting on this new type of fighter to bring about a decisive turning point in the air war. Desperate as we were over this aspect of the war, everyone who could claim any knowledge of the subject at all put in a word and tried to change Hitler's mind. Jodl, Guderian, Model, Sepp Dietrich, and of course the leading generals of the air force, persistently took issue with Hitler's layman's opinion. But they only brought his anger down on their heads, since he took all this as an attack on his military expertise and technical intelligence. In the autumn of 1944 he finally and characteristically brushed aside the whole controversy by flatly forbidding any further discussion of this subject.'

In order to ensure his orders were followed, Hitler took the step of promulgating a *Fuhrerprotokol* on 7 June 1944, which stated that[57] 'the Me-262s in production must be used exclusively as bombers'. Through taking this ridiculous stance, Hitler guaranteed that there was no possibility of the Luftwaffe effectively countering the Allied bombing offensive which was wreaking havoc throughout Germany, disrupting industry and greatly damaging infrastructure. Needless to say, the German fighter aces regarded this decision as a disaster. Galland, when interviewed soon after the end of the war, stated:[58]

'We have built a total of about 1,250 of this aircraft, but only fifty were allowed to be used as fighters – as interceptors. And out of this fifty, there were never more than 25 operational. So we had only a very, very few.

'When I was fired from my post of General of the Fighter Arm, I was to give proof that this jet was a superior fighter. And that's when we did it. I think we did it.'

According to Bekker's *The Luftwaffe War Diaries*:[59]

'On April 4th [1945] forty-nine Me 262s of JG 7 attacked a formation of 150 bombers over Nordhausen, claiming ten certainly, and probably fifteen, though on this day the Eighth AAF's attack was in the Hamburg region. Next day Galland's JV 44, taking off with only five Me 262s, accounted, without loss for two bombers out of a large, heavily escorted force.'

There seems no doubt that the Me 262 was markedly superior to the best Allied fighters available at the time. Galland certainly held high hopes for it if employed in the fighter role:[60]

> 'Today I still believe that it was not exaggerated optimism to expect from a mass action of ME-262 fighters a fundamental change in the German air defense even at that late hour. I was only afraid that the enemy might catch up to us in the development – or even surpass us. This worry remained one of the few that was unfounded.'

Galland was referring to the situation which would have applied if Hitler had authorized production to go ahead in mid-1943. While the Me 262 would not have changed the outcome of the Second World War, had Hitler agreed to the production of it as a fighter as soon as he was requested to do so, the air war over Germany would undoubtedly have been much more difficult for the Allies.

The Allied air commanders certainly took the potential of the Me 262 very seriously:[61]

> 'The correspondence between Spaatz and Arnold [General Carl Spaatz, commander of US Strategic Air Forces in Europe, and General 'Hap' Arnold, commander of the US Army Air Forces] on the threat of the German jet fighters reveals the extent to which the allies feared for the future of the bombing offensive. Spaatz wanted top priority for the development of the American jet fighter, the Lockheed P-80, and suggested that American bombers might have to change to night bombing or shallow penetration raids to keep losses to jet fighters within acceptable limits.
>
> 'By October [1944] he [General Doolittle, the commander of the US Eighth Air Force] warned that jet aircraft and enhanced weaponry, including the powerful 30mm cannon, might "overwhelm our defences" in attacks on Germany.'

Hitler's decision regarding the Me 262 can only be regarded as one of the very worst he made during the war, one that destroyed any remote possibility that the Luftwaffe may have been able to effectively dispute Allied air supremacy over Germany.

Defence of Germany against Allied strategic bombing offensive

The effects of the strategic bombing offensive carried out by the Western Allies against Germany were far greater than the mere physical devastation wrought. Germany had to take very serious steps to defend itself, which diverted enormous manpower and manufacturing resources from the Wehrmacht's defensive and offensive capabilities when they were most needed, and contributed significantly to Germany's defeat, despite the heavy losses caused to the Allied air forces.

The concept of a strategic bombing offensive and its effectiveness has been the subject of a great deal of debate since the end of the Second World War. As described by respected Italian air power theorist General Giulio Douhet,[62] strategic bombing involves the use of air forces in such a manner as to destroy the enemy's capacity to wage war, and thus to shorten its duration and the casualties caused. This strategy was seen by many proponents of air power at the time as a practical means of avoiding the enormous casualties which had occurred during the trench warfare of the First World War. Inherent in this approach was that the bombing of civilian targets would induce panic in the population and cause the morale of the workers to collapse, leading to a reduction in or elimination of the production of war materiel, the most important aim of any bombing campaign. If the intended results of Douhet's strategy are compared to the actual outcome of the campaigns on the Western Front in the First World War, the casualties involved would certainly be dramatically lower. The question was whether Douhet's hypotheses were not only correct, but feasible having regard to the available technology and means of implementation at the time. There were enthusiasts of Douhet's views in all the major air forces of the world during the 1920s, and these views were seriously taken into account by the RAF. Air Marshal Lord Trenchard, a fervent believer in Douhet's concepts, was Chief of the Air Staff from 1919–30, during which time he took steps to develop the RAF's bombing capabilities in an attempt to provide the means by which the Italian's strategy could be implemented. There was a prevailing view that 'the bomber will always get through',[63] despite developments with respect to fighter aircraft. After the defeat of France in 1940, and with there being no prospect of any short-term return to Europe by its land forces, the British government had little option to continue the war against Germany except by means of a bombing offensive, coupled with the traditional naval blockade, to cause food shortages – as had occurred in the First World War – degrade German industry and cause the morale of the workforce to collapse. However, the bombers available at the time were unable to undertake the scale of offensive necessary to achieve the strategic aims propounded by Douhet. The types could not carry the necessary bomb loads and there were far too few of them to attack German industry and military targets effectively.

When the campaign against German military targets was commenced, the poor results showed that the proponents of strategic bombing had dramatically underestimated the power of the defensive arrangements available through fighter aircraft and anti-aircraft artillery. For example, the raid on the German naval base at Wilhelmshaven on 18 December 1939 resulted in no appreciable damage to the ships of the Kriegsmarine but a 50 per cent loss of the attacking RAF force.[64] Similar loss rate was experienced in other raids carried out by the RAF at the same period of the war, leading to the realization that the only chance of waging a campaign with tolerable losses was to do so at night or to have fighter protection of the bombers for the duration of the operation, which was not possible because the fighters then available did not have the necessary range.

Night operations had their own complications for the simple reason that it was then difficult to navigate to the targets and to bomb accurately. However, there was no other choice available to the RAF if it was to carry out any major offensive action against Germany. The RAF strategic offensive grew from trivial beginnings into an enormous industrial and military undertaking to develop the aircraft and supporting technology in an attempt to implement the strategy Douhet envisaged, with the added complication of doing so at night. This meant that the offensive would be unable to primarily operate as a precision bombing campaign against individual targets due to the technology available at the time, but rather to target whole cities in pursuit of its aims, which was actually the way that Douhet envisaged the offensive would occur.

The United States Army Air Forces also believed in the strategy outlined by Douhet. However, the American view was that the best method of carrying out a strategic offensive was to target the most important parts of the enemy's industries and attack them through precision bombing. This approach held great attraction but entailed attacking in daylight, with its attendant risk of heavy casualties, and also required a high degree of accuracy in the bombing. The USAAF intended to obviate these problems by creating bombers which were so heavily defended that they would be able to defeat any attack by the enemy's fighter defences, and by the use of highly accurate precision bomb sights. When the USAAF commenced operations in Europe through the Eighth Air Force, the initial results confirmed the RAF's view that daylight bombing operations could not be carried out against the Luftwaffe's defences as the casualties involved would be too high until fighter escorts were available with long enough range to attend the bombers all the way to the target. It was not until January 1944, when long-range P-51 Mustangs and P47 Thunderbolts commenced flying with and ahead of the bomber fleets to attack the German fighters, that the US offensive was able to achieve its aim. The ensuing battles between the USAAF and the German fighters degraded the Luftwaffe to such a degree that the Allies were eventually able to enjoy air superiority over Germany.

Over time, the nature of US daylight and RAF night-time bombing offensives changed; the RAF became much more accurate while the USAAF also engaged in area bombing, mainly because of the difficulty of achieving the degree of accuracy expected due to the weather conditions over mainland Europe. The result was that Germany was bombed around the clock during 1944, leading to enormous destruction of infrastructure and industry. Despite all the efforts of the Germans to counter these offensives, the Luftwaffe's inability to defend the Reich led to great disruption in the production of all military and related materiel and was a significant contributor to the Allies' eventual victory. Although there has been much criticism of the Allied air offensives, any serious evaluation must acknowledge that this type of strategic campaign had never been attempted before and therefore it was to be expected that results would be imperfect.

Hitler was incensed by the bombing campaign by the Western Allies, characterizing their aircrews as 'terror flyers' and encouraging the shooting of captured crew from damaged aircraft. He also encouraged the German population to kill any Allied flyers captured after bailing out over German territory. This was a flagrant breach of existing agreements relating to the treatment of prisoners of war and was pursued at the Nuremberg trials. Such treatment of the Allied flyers was called '*Lynchjustiz*'[65] by the Germans, which literally meant 'lynching'. There were well documented cases of this occurring, as well as cases where Wehrmacht personnel intervened to prevent the populace from taking revenge in this way.

As will be seen, Hitler's decisions actually impaired the effectiveness of the Luftwaffe's attempts to defend the Reich against the strategic bombing campaign.

The actual tonnage of bombs dropped by Germany and the Western Allies during the war, including the V-1 and V-2 weapon strikes on Britain, were as follows:[66]

Year	Germany	Allies
1940	36,844	14,631
1941	21,858	35,509
1942	3,260	53,755
1943	2,298	226,513
1944	9,151	1,188,577
1945	761	477,051
Total	**74,172**	**1,996,036**

The disparity between these figures is enough to emphasize the essential point that Germany's Luftwaffe was woefully unprepared to prosecute a strategic war effectively, and this was above all the result of Hitler's insistence on invading Poland before the Wehrmacht's development was complete.

Luftwaffe defence against the RAF night strategic bombing campaign – The 'Kammhuber line'

Luftwaffe General Josef Kammhuber was appointed by Goering to create the means of defending Germany against the RAF's night bombing offensive in August 1941. The resultant 'Kammhuber line' consisted of radar installations across the main approaches to Germany taken by the British bombers and co-ordinated the night-fighter aircraft and other defences of the Reich. The main defences consisted of night-fighters and anti-aircraft artillery emplacements of varying calibres, together with searchlights, co-ordinated by radar operators.

Each of the radar emplacements managed a geographic box, within which night-fighter aircraft were directed by wireless operators using radar to plot the position of the German and Allied aircraft. By directing the fighters onto the Allied bombers, this defensive system could be very effective. Where the aircraft were otherwise engaged or missed the bombers, anti-aircraft artillery defences – which were also assisted by radar – took over.

The number of installations necessary was a significant drain on Germany's defence industries. Albert Speer, Hitler's Minister for Armaments, commented:[67]

> 'Had it not been for this new front, the air front over Germany, our defensive strength against tanks would have been about doubled, as far as equipment was concerned. Moreover, the anti-aircraft force tied down hundreds of thousands of young soldiers. A third of the optical industry was busy producing gun sights for the flak batteries. About half of the electronics industry was engaged in producing radar and communications networks for defense against bombing. Simply because of this, in spite of the high level of the German electronics and optical industries, the supply of our frontline troops with modern equipment remained far behind that of the Western Armies.
>
> 'Thus a serious shortage of army communications equipment developed – for instance, walkie-talkies for the infantry and sound-ranging apparatus for the artillery. In addition, further development of such devices had to be neglected in favor of anti-aircraft weaponry.'

Coming from the man who was in charge of the German war economy, this evidence is extremely important in revealing the significant resources necessary to fight the British strategic bombing campaign.

As part of the German defences and resources, 571,000 personnel were assigned to the Luftwaffe's Flak force in 1940. This was then significantly expanded, and by 1944 an additional 200,000 young men aged 15 and 16 were enrolled in the Flak force, along with as many young women as were available from the Bund Deutscher Madel (League of German Girls). These were augmented by over-age men or those who were otherwise unfit for normal military service, 100,000 Soviet POWs (who were given better rations) and as many ethnic Germans from the conquered territories as could be obtained.[68] This drag on the male German population, in addition to those who were fit for war service, was very significant.

Speer commented further on the mass production of anti-aircraft artillery having seriously deprived the army of anti-tank weaponry:[69]

'From February 1941 to 1943, we produced 11,957 heavy anti-aircraft guns (8.8 to 12.8 centimeter), but most of them had to be deployed for anti-aircraft purposes within Germany or in rear positions. During the same period 12,006 of the heavy caliber weapons (7.5 centimeters and up) were delivered, but only 1,115 were 8.8s. Fourteen million rounds of 8.8 or higher caliber flak ammunition were used for purposes other than anti-tank ammunition, for which only 12,900,000 were provided.'

Obviously, this drag on Germany's ability to provide artillery and ammunition to the army was very significant and restricted its power of defence, especially with respect to the 88mm, widely acknowledged as the best anti-tank gun on either side during the war.

Although their anti-aircraft artillery was of very high quality, the Germans did not develop the 'proximity' fuse as the Western Allies had, which was detonated by being close to a target. The lack of this capability significantly lowered the effectiveness of German defences. Ammunition consumption was much higher than would have been the case had the fuse been employed. The Germans calculated that it took an average of 16,000 rounds of ammunition for each Allied aircraft which was shot down.[70] Nevertheless, the intensity of the defensive barrage was such that the damage to aircraft and resulting casualties throughout the period of the night-bombing offensive were significant.

The first British attacks of any scale against German targets occurred in March 1942, when RAF Bomber Command sent 300 bombers to attack Lubeck and Rostov. The British Bomber Command did not remain idle. Harris prepared the first big blow against a German city. Lübeck was attacked on the night of March 28-29, 1942, by 200 to 300 bombers with a total load of 500 tons of high-explosive bombs and incendiaries. The damage was considerable. The casualties among the civil population for the first time reached four figures, with 300 killed. A month later Rostock was raided during the nights of April 24 and 27 by a similar force with a similar result. The losses of the attackers in these raids were insignificant. The formation flew in a wide arc and came in from the sea. The first two large-scale raids were a great shock to the German public, although it never learned the full extent of the losses, the strength of the attackers, nor the extent of the damage.[71]

> 'Within 90 minutes the center of the city lay in rubble and ruins, with 460 dead, 45,000 homeless, 3,300 houses and 36 industrial buildings totally destroyed, and 20 per cent of all buildings in the town damaged.'

On 30 May 1942, the heaviest British raid of the war so far was made on Cologne, using 1,000 heavy bombers. According to Bekker's *The Luftwaffe War Diaries*:[72]

> 'This massive onslaught showed up sharply the limitations of the German night-fighters. The time was gone when the British bombers passed singly through the ground-control interception zones, manned by one fighter apiece: they now came through in hordes. Though the fighters shot down thirty-six of the Cologne raiders, thereby raising their score for the war to date to 600 victories, it was only 3.6 per cent of 1,000. Harris had reckoned with the loss of fifty aircraft, Churchill with even a hundred. From all causes the armada lost forty and another 116 suffered various degrees of damage, mostly through flak. The calculation that the effectiveness would increase, and the quota of losses sink, according to the number of bombers engaged in a single raid, had been proved correct.'

In July 1943, the RAF and USAAF mounted a series of staggered attacks by night and day over a period of a week against Hamburg, using approximately 3,000 aircraft. These raids caused enormous damage and showed that the strategy the Germans had previously used with respect to the defence of the Reich had to change, with the Luftwaffe having to be deployed defensively in that role. Bekker continued:[73]

> 'For once the shock of the Hamburg raids acted as a unifying influence on its commanders. The men around Goering, such as Jeschonnek and

Milch, all began to clamour for the same thing. The whole directive must now be changed. All forces must be engaged to defend the homeland against the mass raids of the Allied bombers, by day and night. Only Hitler remained unteachable. At a situation conference on July 25th he turned furiously on his Luftwaffe adjutant, Major Christian (who had dared to utter a different opinion) with the words: "Terror can only be broken by terror! Everything else is nonsense. The British will only be halted when their own cities are destroyed. I can only win the war by dealing out more destruction to the enemy than he does to us … In all epochs that has been the case, and it is just the same in the air. Otherwise our people will turn mad, and in the course of time lose all confidence in the Luftwaffe. Even now it is not fully doing its job … "

'Top priority must be given to raids of revenge, he said, however inadequate the force available to the man appointed for this purpose – the "Angriffsführer England", Colonel Dieter Peltz – might be. But no one else concurred with this policy.'

The raids on Hamburg were a frightening portent of what was to come for the Germans, but the Fuhrer could not be made to see that the defeat of the bombers was possible through the use of the entire Luftwaffe fighter force. Had the Luftwaffe been redeployed in early 1943, the resulting losses for the Allied bombers could have been significantly higher, and if significant enough, could have led to changes in the Allied strategy.

When the strategic offensive began, the accuracy of the bombing was very poor and the number of aircraft used was comparatively insignificant. In 1941, the British government commissioned an examination of the results by Lord Cherwell, Churchill's scientific adviser, who analysed information derived from Bomber Command's own records. He concluded:[74]

'[O]nly one aircraft in three got within 5 miles of its target, and in the Ruhr, whose smog-bound industries formed the Command's main target, the figure was a mere one in ten.'

The bombing resulting from this low level of inaccuracy was obviously unacceptable. This was a major shock to the British and a damning verdict on the offensive's effectiveness to date.

Thereafter, the British introduced several technical improvements, including ground-defining radar which allowed the bomber crews to identify geographic and other features, thus enabling them to more accurately identify targets and the routes to them. The RAF also improved its operational practices, with specialist crews known as 'Pathfinders' used to mark the targets for the bomber fleet with flares and other indicators. By these and other measures, the accuracy of the bombing was significantly improved, resulting in increased damage to the targets.

The Germans also improved their response to the bomber offensive. During 1944, they developed a surface-to-air anti-aircraft missile called 'Waterfall'. Speer commented:[75]

> 'Approximately twenty-five feet long, the Waterfall rocket was capable of carrying approximately six hundred and sixty pounds of explosives along a directional beam up to an altitude of fifty thousand feet and hit the enemy bombers with great accuracy. **It was not affected by day or night, by clouds, or fog** [author's emphasis]. Since we were later able to turn out nine hundred of the big rockets [V-1s and V-2s] monthly we could surely have produced several thousand of these smaller and less expensive rockets per month. To this day I think that this rocket, in conjunction with the jet fighters, would have beaten back the Western Allies' air offensive against our industry in the spring of 1944.'

Instead of pursuing this advanced defensive rocket, Hitler decreed that the so-called 'vengeance weapons', the V-1 and V-2, were to be given absolute priority of manufacture. Although both were considerable technical achievements, they could not cause anything more than a mere fraction of the damage inflicted by the Allied bombing offensive and were ultimately a total waste of time, resources and effort as offensive weapons.

Speer called supporting the idea of the vengeance weapons 'one of my most serious mistakes'.[76] There is no doubt that the Waterfall missile had the potential to cause dramatic losses to the British strategic bombing campaign, as its operation was not affected at night. However, it did not fit with Hitler's offensive-centred approach to warfare and therefore was not used.

The Germans did, however, introduce radar on their night-fighters, which significantly increased their defensive potential. The fighters were adaptations of the Me 110, which was unable to compete with the latest single-engine day fighters, but was more than adequate for the role at night. They were also powerfully armed with a 20mm cannon, which ensured that if they were able to identify a target they could shoot it down. The Germans also developed a number of specialized night-fighters with steadily improved radar, performance and armament. The night-fighters were not available in large numbers but still posed a real threat to the bombers.

In addition to these steps, the Germans adopted other means of deceiving the night-bombers by means of dummy towns which were used as decoys to entice them to attack. Air Vice-Marshal Donald Bennett, in charge of the Pathfinder squadrons of Bomber Command, commented on this tactic:[77]

'Both before and after the advent of the Path Finder force, one of the most common customs was to create a target area adequately surrounded by defences and searchlights, and to let off dummy incendiaries, like our own, on the ground, so as to look as if there was a town being bombed and being defended. Many a crew would then drop their bombs in the middle of it all, fondly believing they were giving the real target a real pounding. Unfortunately, all too frequently this was simply a dummy town – in the open fields. The realistic nature of these dummies was quite staggering.'

The complexity and guile of the defences was improved as the bombing offensive became more destructive. However, the time involved in creating these dummies was not negligible, meaning that the defensive measures needed more men and materiel in the attempt to deceive the bombers.

RAF Bomber Command losses

During the Second World War, RAF Bomber Command air crew fatalities numbered 57,205, a 46 per cent loss rate from a total air crew of 125,000. This figure included those from the British Empire and other countries fighting Germany. Air crew personnel comprised the top level of recruits who received time-consuming specialized training, so this level of loss was particularly significant. In addition to these grievous losses, a total of 8,325 aircraft were lost in action.[78]

These losses emphasize the importance which was attached to the bombing campaign by the British and Allied governments. However high the loss ratio though, the actual number of personnel killed in the campaign was quite small in comparison to the losses incurred during trench warfare in the First World War. The rationale behind Douhet's theorems may thus have some validity, even though his proposals were never fully implemented.

Luftwaffe Fighter Command and the US bombing offensive

Adolf Galland was appointed by Goering to command the fighter forces of the Luftwaffe after the death of Colonel Werner Molders on 22 November

1941. Galland was one of the best fighter pilots in the Luftwaffe, with ninety-four kills to his credit, all of them in Western Europe, and had been a squadron commander. He did not wish to become a 'brass hat', but had no choice as he was ordered to take the position by Goering. He soon became a thorn in Goering's side, as he would not sugar-coat his views regarding the management of the Luftwaffe's fighter arm for anyone, including the Reichsmarschall or, on occasion, Hitler himself.

Fighter aircraft of the Luftwaffe were engaged on all fronts, but once the Allied bombing offensive began in earnest, its main role had to be the defence of the Reich to preserve German industry and civil infrastructure as well as preventing casualties to the civilian population. Galland remarked:[79]

> 'When the Battle of Britain petered out and the march to the east began, the time had come to prepare with the fullest energy the defense of the Reich. Denuding the air front in the west of fighter aircraft was almost like begging the enemy to stage an air offensive. Because of her central geographical position, Germany was exposed to air raids and was on several other scores particularly vulnerable from the air. Dense populations, concentration of industry, overloaded power supplies, a centralized network of transport, and many other factors presented excellent conditions for an attack from the air and therefore demanded timely and elaborate countermeasures. The leaders of the Luftwaffe certainly had enough hints, suggestions, and warnings in this direction. The hour for the defense of the Reich had struck. But no one wanted to admit that, at least in the west, we had lost the initiative, that we had been driven out of the role of attacker and into that of defender.'

Hitler was not disposed to using the fighters to defend the Reich, preferring to use anti-aircraft artillery and attacks on British targets as retaliation for raids on German cities. These retaliatory raids were completely ineffectual as the Germans had no heavy bombers to carry them out and resulted in very little damage. The Fuhrer's 'strategy' verges on the unbelievable, but is illuminated by the following extract from *The Luftwaffe War Diaries*:[80]

> '[D]efence – in Hitler's eyes – was always a matter of low priority. If Speer and Saur [Karl Saur, State Secretary in the Reich Ministry for Armaments and War Production], in 1944, raised fighter production to an all-time high, this took place against the express intent and wish of the Führer. As disaster followed disaster on every front, so did the choleric wrath of the German dictator increasingly descend on anyone

who dared gainsay him. Where the Luftwaffe was concerned, he listened only to talk of offensive action; to the need for air defence he was deaf. When, as late as August 1944, Speer and Galland personally expressed to him the crying need for German fighter strength to be concentrated in the defence of the Reich, Hitler merely threw them out, shouting that they should obey his orders. Next day he proclaimed that the whole fighter arm was disbanded, and instructed Speer to switch from fighter production to flak guns. As a practical proposition it of course made nonsense, and Speer was obliged to assemble figures and tables to prove it.

'Hitler's attitude coloured that of Goering, who never rose to the defence of his Luftwaffe, but simply passed downward the ruinous orders from above. Once in autumn, 1943, when the defence against an Allied raid had miscarried, he summoned his fighter commanders to Schleissheim near Munich, and heaped them with reproaches. Ever since the Battle of Britain, the Reichsmarschall declared, far too many fighter pilots had won decorations they did not deserve.

'At that General Galland wrenched his own Knight's Cross from his neck, and flung it down resoundingly on Goering's table. An icy silence ensued, but Goering took no action. He merely resumed the discussion, but with much greater sobriety and logic.

'Again and again Galland sought to ward off the annihilation of his weapon by building up a strategic fighter reserve. In the face of continuous enemy raids, he strove to hold back part of the output of fighter planes for the training of new pilots. The sudden appearance of a concentrated force, 1,000 or 2,000 strong, could still, after all, result in a resounding blow being struck against the Allies.

'Yet time and again Galland found himself robbed of his carefully fostered nucleus, and saw it thrown prematurely into battle. It happened, on Hitler's orders, at the end of July 1944, when a reserve of over 800 machines was squandered on the invasion front. Caught up in the turmoil of retreat, it was virtually wiped out. It happened again, though on a far greater scale, during the Ardennes offensive, after a new reserve of over 3,000 had been built up. Though its pilots had never been trained in ground attack, it was sacrificed in a brief and futile attempt to support the Army.

'"At this moment," Galland confesses, "I lost all spirit for further conduct of hostilities." Just as his fighter arm had again acquired astonishing strength, to the point when it could once more challenge Allied air control over Germany, it was given its final death blow by the crazy orders of its own high command.'

Hitler's fixation on the offensive was present in his attitude with respect to every branch of the Wehrmacht, to the detriment of the operations undertaken by them. When he did conduct defensive operations, his tactics were to attempt to hold every square metre of ground which the Germans had ever taken, regardless of its strategic importance, which invariably led to unnecessarily heavy losses. The effect of his attitude was apparent through the particularly egregious example of the Me 262 referenced in detail earlier in this chapter, which condemned the Luftwaffe to certain destruction alongside the cities and industries of Germany.

However, the crisis caused by the Allied bombing offensive was such that even Hitler could not ignore it, and by the spring of 1943 approximately 70 per cent[81] of the Luftwaffe's fighter aircraft were engaged in defending the Reich. The bomber offensive was thus easing the situation for the Red Army and Air Force even before the invasion of France by diluting the power of the Luftwaffe the Soviets had to face.

By early 1944, the US Eighth Air Force was a massive force, with approximately 2,000 heavy bombers and 1,000 fighter aircraft under its command. The development of the long-range P-51and P-47 fighters proved the death knell of the Luftwaffe. These aircraft were very powerfully armed and more than the equal of all German fighters except the Me 262, which as we have seen was primarily used as a bomber on the Fuhrer's orders. The Allied pilots were also a match for the best of the German flyers, whose level of expertise was declining because of the changes to training forced on the Luftwaffe by the reduction in available fuel. In January 1944, new tactics were adopted by the Eighth Air Force which allowed the fighters to roam ahead of the bomber formations and engage the defending Luftwaffe fighters before the bombers were attacked,[82] instead of closely escorting the bombers as had been done until then. This new tactic wore down the Luftwaffe and revealed the lower level of skill of its new pilots, resulting in the Allied air forces achieving air superiority over Germany. Ironically, this was the very tactic which the German fighter pilots had tried to convince Goering they should employ during the Battle of Britain, but which he would not allow.

While German aircraft production actually increased substantially during 1944 to a peak of over 40,000, including more than 25,000 fighters,[83] their use was hampered by lack of fuel. To further complicate the situation for the Germans, the fuel shortage also meant the Luftwaffe could not train its pilots to the same standard it previously had, additional unintended collateral damage caused by the strategic bombing campaign.

The damage to the oil supplies of Germany developed into another crisis during the second half of 1944, when both the US and British strategic air forces attacked the Reich's oil industry installations with devastating effect. In September that year, the production of all German oil products was only 5.5 per cent of its level at the beginning of the campaign in July.[84] Speer obtained Hitler's authority to use whatever number of workers were needed to repair the damaged plants, and by October 1944 some 350,000 of them were attempting to stem the disaster.[85]

The total weight of bombs dropped on German targets during the war by the USAAF was 393,548 tons.[86] This included targets in occupied Europe, but was more than five times the total dropped by Germany throughout the conflict.

US losses from the strategic bombing campaign

The US lost 6,363 heavy and medium bombers during the strategic bombing campaign.[87] Personnel losses were 31,155, which included 10,223 killed in action, which represented a 54.4 per cent loss of all those engaged.[88] As in the case of the British crews, their US counterparts were highly trained specialists, and once again these losses were a very high price to pay, indicating the importance the US attached to the bombing campaign.

German lost production

The effect on Germany of the Allied strategic bomber offensive in 1943 was summarized by Speer:[89]

> '[I]n 1943 I estimated that the air war was costing us – in terms of production for the Eastern Front – the equivalent of more than 10,000 heavy guns of more than 7.5cms caliber, and approximately 6,000 medium-heavy and heavy tanks.'

It is worth noting that this figure of lost tank production is considerably higher than the number of tanks the Germans were able to operationally deploy at any time during the war. It was thus critical to the defeat of the Wehrmacht, especially in the East, and exemplifies the vital contribution that the strategic bombing offensive played in the victory of the Red Army. Even if only 50 per cent of the 'lost' tanks were available, the number would still be more than the Germans were ever able to deploy on any front, even for Operation *Citadel* around Kursk on the Eastern Front in July 1943, the largest tank battle in history. It is important to note that the effect of the bombing offensive became proportionately greater in 1944 when command of the air space over Germany was irrevocably lost to the Allied air forces.

Speer commented further:[90]

> 'The unpredictability of the attacks made this front gigantic; every square meter of the territory we controlled was a kind of front line. Defense against air attacks required the production of thousands of antiaircraft guns, the stockpiling of tremendous quantities of ammunition all over the country, and holding in readiness hundreds of thousands of soldiers, who in addition had to stay in position by their guns, often totally inactive, for months at a time.'

These consequences were quite separate from the physical dislocation which the bombing campaign caused to Germany's cities. That these resources were a major detraction from the potential armed forces of Germany is obvious. Richard Overy, in his invaluable book *Why the Allies Won*, comments on the effects of the strategic bombing campaign in this regard:[91]

> 'In the air over Germany, or in the fronts in Russia and France, German forces lacked the weapons to finish the job. The combined effects of direct destruction and the diversion of resources denied German forces approximately half their battle-front weapons and equipment in 1944. **It is difficult not to regard this margin as decisive** [author's emphasis].'

The situation in which Germany found itself was the direct result of three of Hitler's most fateful decisions. The first was to go to war in 1939 when the development of the Wehrmacht, especially the Luftwaffe, was incomplete. The second decision was to attack the USSR before defeating Great Britain. He was universally advised against this step, including on this occasion by Goering, who was best-placed to know the capabilities of the Luftwaffe. Hitler attacked anyway. The third decision, for which there can be no logical explanation, was Hitler's declaration of war against the United States while still at war with Britain and the Soviet Union. He did so gratuitously at a time when it would have been very difficult for President Roosevelt to obtain a declaration of war on Germany from the US Congress, notwithstanding the attack on Pearl Harbor by Germany's ally, Japan. The Fuhrer compounded this egregious error by failing to secure the participation of the Japanese in the war against the USSR, although had he approached them at the time that *Barbarossa* was being planned, it is likely that they would have been only too happy to join in an attack on the Soviet Union. These key decisions, when viewed as a whole, defy logical explanation, unless one accepts the twisted logic of Hitler's preposterous dogma relating to the inferiority of the Slavic *'untermensch'* ('sub-humans') and the United States soldiery.

The Allied strategic bombing offensive has been criticized on a number of different levels since the war. The first and most contentious aspect relates to the morality of bombing innocent civilians, which also raises the wider question of the morality of war itself. The fact is that all combatants used strategic bombing to the extent that they were able, the only difference being the scale attained by each. One is reminded of Sherman's saying that 'war is hell', and also an appropriate quote from Churchill:[92]

> 'Never, never, never believe that any war will be smooth or easy, or that anyone who embarks on the strange voyage can measure the tides and hurricanes he will encounter. The statesman who yields to war fever must realize that once the signal is given, he is no longer the master of policy but the slave of unforeseeable and uncontrollable events.'

The lesson being, of course, that it is impossible to foresee what course a war will take once it is started, or whether it will be fought humanely because each side believes it must use all means to win. Despite the ferocity of the conflict in all theatres, there were types of warfare which were not used during the Second World War by any of the combatants, the most notable being gas warfare.

The second avenue of criticism is that the strategic bombing of Germany was not effective. This argument is comprehensively rebutted by the information previously provided from Albert Speer and quoted by Richard Overy. The reasoning behind the view that the campaign was not successful seems to be that it did not achieve the objective of winning the war by itself, which was the position of the partisans of a bombing campaign during the interwar period. Of course, it did not win the war by itself, but without its effects the Germans would have had many more weapons, the war would have taken longer and there would have been more avoidable deaths.

In further confirmation of the effect of the campaign on tank production, Richard Overy writes:[93]

> 'Speer's deputy responsible for tank production explained to his post war interrogators that bombing forced measures that contradicted mass production: "the breaking down and dispersal of plants, starting up factories on account of their geographical position instead of their technical capacity ... As German factories moved into smaller, camouflaged premises, into woods or even underground, it became

progressively more difficult to expand production." There was enough momentum in the Speer reforms to carry German industry to a peak in September 1944, but bombing made it impossible for managers and workers alike to achieve the maximum.'

The effect of the campaign was exhaustively analysed by both the major Western allies during and after the war, with the most comprehensive investigation being that known as the *United States Strategic Bombing Survey*, which is quoted (and misquoted) on many subjects and in many publications.

The United States Strategic Bombing Survey (USSBS)

The USSBS, a project commissioned by President Roosevelt, comprised three parts: The Combined Bomber Offensive Survey, The Strategic Bombing Effects Survey and The US Bombing Research Mission. It commenced operations before the end of the war and was tasked with analysing the effects of the Allies' strategic bombing campaign against Germany and the (largely US) bombing campaign against Japan. It was carried out by a team of 2,300 researchers, headed by civilians, with the intention that the military could not influence the findings of the survey to cover up any shortcomings which may have occurred. The resulting report comprised over 100 volumes and the summaries alone extended to some 200 pages. The report is therefore a gold mine of information regarding every aspect of strategic bombing carried out during the Second World War, although some of its conclusions are limited by the information which was then available.

There are several findings which are established that are crucial. Firstly:[94]

'No complete and accurate figures on German civilian air raid casualties, covering the entire period of the war, were available. Local reports of recorded deaths from aerial attacks were secured from a number of cities and proved to be comparatively accurate. The Report of the German Statistical Office, listing deaths by cities, was obtained and found to be generally correct for the years 1940 through 1943. Estimates of air raid deaths for 1944 and 1945 were prepared based upon the known tonnage of bombs dropped and the known locally recorded deaths per ton for sample cities graded by population size. The result yielded an estimated total of 422,000 deaths. It was further estimated that an additional number, approximating 25% of the known deaths in 1944 and 1945, were still unrecovered and unrecorded. With the addition of this estimate of 1944 and 1945 unrecorded deaths, the final estimation gave in round numbers a half a million German civilians killed by Allied aerial attacks from the beginning of heavy bombing to the end of the European war.'

This figure was subsequently largely confirmed by unearthed German records, which provided a somewhat larger figure. This number of deaths needs to be read in context to understand its full magnitude. In comparison to this figure, the total war dead of civilians and combatants for the entire British Commonwealth from 1939–45 as recorded by the *Encyclopedia Britannica* was 466,000 (quoting official British and Commonwealth country records). So the total number of German civilians killed in air raids during the Second World War alone exceeds the combined civilian and combatant deaths for the whole British Commonwealth. Obviously, such a figure reflects a level of disruption to the civilian population which would have been felt by the entire community. The moral question relating to the inflicting of this level of death and suffering cannot be covered in this work, but undoubtedly the human consequences involved are comprehensible and appalling to contemplate.

Secondly, the bombing campaign meant absenteeism became a problem, and as one would expect was related to the intensity of the bombing experienced at each location:[95]

'At the Robert Bosch industries in Stuttgart, to take one example, during the very heavy air raids of 1943 and 1944, only 30% of the employees – both officials and laborers – were present for work in the first week after the raids. At the end of one week approximately 50% were present, and at after four weeks 70% to 80%. In these figures are included the sick who contributed 15% to the rate (5% for the male, and about 20% for the female employees). In most cases, transportation difficulties and preoccupation with personal affairs subsequent to bombings were given as reasons but the personnel director believed that very minor illnesses were used as excuses and may, therefore, render the statistics unreliable.'

Whether or not the employees were using excuses does not alter the fact that they were absent. Such a level of absenteeism could not fail to disrupt armaments production, where any delay or reduction in production at one site would cause delays in the production of finished products and components for large units such as tanks or aircraft.

Thirdly, disruption of the transport system caused by bombing throughout the Reich had other significant consequences which undermined the German government's efforts at self-sufficiency in food:[96]

'Every attempt was made to increase Germany's self-sufficiency through a highly organized system of food production, storage and distribution, and food rationing. The success of this delicately balanced, highly integrated organization was dependent upon the integrity of the German transportation and communications system. Since the productive capacity of all German land was strained to the utmost to attain even the degree of self-sufficiency which has been described in this report, any damage to the factors supporting this productivity obviously contributed to malnutrition in that country. The bombing in which the German transportation system was disrupted, and the air attacks in which sources of fertilizers, farm machinery, and fuel were destroyed, caused the ultimate breakdown of the German food supply system. Disruption of transport, in particular, made the *uniform* [emphasis in original] distribution of food to all areas impossible.'

The Nazi government made intensive efforts prior to and during the war to promote a policy of 'autarky' – which can also be described as 'self-sufficiency' – which was intended to reduce the level of imports of vital resources. These efforts were made across all industries and in agriculture, and was assisted for much of the war by simply taking food from the conquered territories. As the above finding illuminates, the effects of the bombing campaign made it very difficult to transport food and therefore led to large parts of the population suffering varying degrees of malnutrition during the latter stages of the war.

Fourthly, the survey also found that the bombing campaign was responsible for destroying 20 per cent of living accommodation in Germany, including houses and apartments. This was a major problem due to the displaced people who had to be accommodated somewhere else and also because the level was so great that no significant attempt at repair could be made while the war was being fought.

These findings alone are sufficient to show that the damage and disruption caused by the bombing campaign was very significant and a major problem for the German regime and people. Together with Speer's views quoted earlier, they show that the strategic bombing campaign was indeed the 'lost front' as he described it in *Spandau: The Secret Diaries*,[97] quoted previously, even if it may have been successful for reasons which were not wholly contemplated at the time it was initiated.

That the Germans were able to dramatically increase the production of armaments is no evidence that the campaign was not successful, as Speer himself indicates that German industry was being run on almost a peacetime basis until he became Minister for Armaments in February 1942. The evidence shows that the increases which the Germans could have achieved without the burden of the Allied bombing would have been much greater than those which actually occurred. That the German people's morale did not break entirely is also no evidence that the campaign was ineffective, because there is no doubt that the bombing did cause significant absenteeism from the vital war factories and affected many people's lives dramatically. This did not mean the Germans 'couldn't take it', just that they were exposed to a great deal more bombing that they had to take – there is no comparison to the level of bombing that the Germans were subjected to and that which was endured during the Blitz by the people of Britain, significant as it was.

Additionally, any comparison of the Allied bombing and Douhet's prewar postulations must take into account the basic fact that the campaign, formidable though it was, never approached the level of intensity necessary to achieve the result which Douhet proposed or which the chiefs of the Allied air forces wished. The reality was that there was no possibility of any of the governments involved in the war procuring the number of aircraft necessary to fulfil Douhet's vision, having regard to the expense involved and other priorities of wartime production. It will thus never be known if air power exercised as Douhet postulated could have won the war, as put forward by the supporters of strategic bombing, but it seems unlikely having regard to all the evidence.

The determination as to whether the Germans could have effectively resisted the Allied air offensive will also never be conclusively answered, and is a separate question in itself. However, it is certain that Hitler's decisions negatively impacted the defence of the Reich in at least three ways:

- Firstly, because he squandered the fighter reserve which had been built up by General Galland, the chief of fighter command, to inflict a defeat on the daylight bombing campaign on two separate occasions in vain attempts to assist the German Army. These occasions were both during 1944 and simply meant that the fighter reserve was destroyed piecemeal instead of being committed together in a massive attack on the bomber fleets, as Galland intended and for which the pilots had been trained.[98]
- Secondly, because he delayed the production of the Me 262 jet aircraft on two occasions, meaning it did not become available until too late to affect the air war; and when it did become available, the Fuhrer ordered its deployment as a bomber, not a fighter. Characteristically, this was against the advice of all the experts, on this occasion including Goering, who argued with Hitler several times in vain attempts to get him to change his mind.

- Thirdly, because he did not specify that the Waterfall surface-to-air anti-aircraft rocket should be produced as a priority and deployed as soon as possible against the British and US bomber fleets.

As Hitler had taken over exclusive control of these decisions and would not allow anyone else to make them, responsibility for them and the disastrous consequences which ensued for Germany is his alone.

Conclusions

1. The impact of Hitler precipitating the war in 1939 meant that the Luftwaffe did not have the capability to fulfil its intended role, especially with regard to strategic bombing, as the bomber fleet which was envisaged as being available by the time he previously specified when hostilities were likely to break out with the Western democracies (1944–45) was not available.
2. Hitler's decision to attack the USSR while still at war with Britain was taken against the advice of his air force commanders, including Goering. This aggravated the difficulties in keeping the Luftwaffe up to strength after the losses sustained in the French and Battle of Britain campaigns.
3. The Fuhrer's decision to attempt to supply the trapped German forces in Stalingrad using the Luftwaffe was taken only on the advice of Goering, who had previously been told by the Luftwaffe general staff that this was not possible. It resulted in the loss of significant numbers of transport aircraft, and also specialist instruction crews who were brought in to man every transport aircraft the Germans had access to. These losses were extremely damaging and were a significant factor in the mid- to long-term decline of the Luftwaffe's power and the quality of its air crews.
4. Hitler's decision to delay the production of the Me 262 and then to order its use as a bomber rather than a fighter, as intended, was against all the advice he received and meant that the opportunity to significantly reduce the impact of or defeat the Allied strategic bombing campaign was lost. There is no question that this was one of the most vital decisions of the war which Hitler made concerning the Luftwaffe, and its effect was entirely negative.
5. Hitler's deployment of the fighter reserve which had been brought together by Galland in support of the army in 1944 finally destroyed any chance the Luftwaffe had of attempting to defeat the Allied bomber fleets over Germany. This decision meant that the last slim chance of wresting back control of German airspace was gone.

Chapter 3

Hitler's Involvement in Weapons Development Programmes and Production Priorities

Throughout the entire period of the Third Reich, Hitler exercised ultimate control over the development of new weapons programmes and the manufacturing priority assigned to the production of all the requirements of the Wehrmacht. This included everything from the types of trucks used by the army to the massive research projects relating to the 'vengeance weapons', the V-1 and V-2 rockets. The weapons thus produced were therefore an accurate reflection of the Fuhrer's view regarding the best which could be provided and the relative importance they assumed for the German war effort.

One of the fundamental matters which Hitler had learned from Germany's experience in the First World War was that the whole economy of the country had to be mobilized to ensure that the war effort could be maintained. He ascribed to Hindenburg's view that the armed forces had not been beaten in battle in the autumn of 1918 but were 'stabbed in the back' by the home front, which had been subjected to the British naval blockade that caused food shortages among the civilians and workers, leading to the politicians giving in to demands for the war to end and the revolt which subsequently overthrew the Imperial government. The Fuhrer, determined that history would not repeat itself in that respect, undertook a process to transform the German economy:[1]

'By 1939 Germany devoted almost a quarter of its national product, and more than a quarter of its entire industrial workforce to military production. From the mid-1930s the state sponsored a colossal programme of capital investment – more than two thirds of all German industrial investment – to build a solid foundation of material resources on which to raise the later superstructure of military output. Across Germany sprang up the world's largest aluminium industry; a new iron and steel complex, planned on a scale to eclipse Magnitogorsk (this was a new city created by the Soviets east of the Urals where large production facilities for tank production were centred and which was crucial to the USSR's high level of production), was built from scratch on the large ore fields of Brunswick in central Germany; the chemical industry began to construct whole new plants for the synthetic production of oil and rubber, resources vital for mechanised warfare, but controlled on world markets in their natural form by Germany's potential adversaries. By 1939 Germany possessed the kind of military-industrial complex that would be developed by the two super-powers after 1945. Its productive potential was enormous, all the more so when, bit by bit, Germany assimilated the valuable resources of central Europe – iron ore and machine-building in Austria, brown coal (for oil production) and armaments from Czechoslovakia, coal iron and steel from the areas of conquered Poland.'

Together with this investment in industry, there was also heavy expenditure in fertilizer production for farmers to increase food supply and state-sponsored schemes for opening up new farmland and revitalizing unused agricultural land. However, the transformation of the German economy was not complete when the country went to war. Furthermore, the military bureaucratic structure of the Nazi state stultified efforts at increasing production in all respects, as Richard Overy writes:[2]

'No organisation was more guilty of limiting Germany's war potential than the military. Answerable only to Hitler, the armed forces treated the German industrial economy as an annex to the front line. Military priorities dominated arms production, from the design and development of a weapon through to the final factory inspection. Military officials were posted to factories to monitor production. Changes to design and specification were made endlessly in response to every cry for improvement from the battlefield. Production schedules were set by military agencies; consultation with the industrialists and engineers who had to produce the goods was rare and one-sided.'

Overy also states that the high quality and wide range of weapons manufactured in Germany was actually a weakness in wartime:[3]

'[Germany produced weapons] of very high quality, with a level of finish and attention to detail that astonished the Allies when they inspected crashed aircraft or captured guns. By the end of the war German designers had developed many of the weapons that armed NATO a decade later. But the pursuit of advanced weaponry came at a price. Instead of a core of proven designs produced on standard lines, the German forces developed a bewildering array of projects. At one point in the war there were no fewer than 425 different aircraft models and variants in production. By the middle of the war the German army was equipped with 151 different makes of lorry, and 150 different motor-cycles.'

The consequence of this approach by the army and the tradition of craftsmanship of German manufacturers indicates that the hierarchy did not properly understand the fundamental concepts of wartime mass production and illustrates the difficulties which Speer had when he took over as Minister for Armaments in 1942. Speer also found that Hitler was not really interested in the organizational changes which were fundamental to significant increases in production:[4]

> 'Whenever I explained my organizational plans to Hitler, he showed a striking lack of interest. I had the impression that he did not like to deal with these questions; indeed, in certain realms he was altogether incapable of distinguishing the important from the unimportant. He also did not like establishing lines of jurisdiction. Sometimes he deliberately assigned bureaus or individuals the same or similar tasks. "That way," he used to say, "the stronger one does the job."'

Such an approach was hardly conducive to the structures, attitudes and policies which are the bedrock for efficient mass production.

The degree of detailed control which the Fuhrer exercised over each of the armed forces' development and procurement programmes differed according to his interest in the type of weapon and the branch of the Wehrmacht. His interest in the three arms of the Wehrmacht and knowledge with respect to their weapons systems and requirements largely reflected his own experiences, but this did not inhibit his proclivity to interfere whenever he felt inclined. Because he involved himself so deeply across the three services, Hitler had to make decisions which involved highly technical and specialized matters with respect to which he had no specific knowledge. Speer commented:[5]

> 'Hitler's technical horizon, however, just like his general ideas, his views on art, and his style of life, was limited by the First World War. His technical interests were narrowly restricted to the traditional weapons of the army and the navy. In these areas he continued to learn and steadily increase his knowledge, so that he frequently proposed convincing and usable innovations. But he had little feeling for such developments

as, for example, radar, the construction of an atom bomb, jet fighters and rockets.'

After the invasion of Norway and the loss of so many German surface ships, the wartime involvement of the Kriegsmarine was increasingly centred on the U-boat campaign. However, U-boat weapons development programmes did not absorb a high proportion of Hitler's attention. Similarly, the Luftwaffe's development was largely regarded as Goering's sphere, Hitler only becoming significantly involved after Goering's influence began to wane in 1943. The Fuhrer was kept informed of developments in the arms programmes of all three services, but only became involved in those projects which interested him or he felt were of significance, such as the Me 262. However, he did not initiate discussion with respect to the Luftwaffe and Kriegsmarine's requirements to the same degree he did with those of the German Army.

Speer commented on Hitler's intellectual attitude toward making decisions about any matter:[6]

'Amateurishness was one of Hitler's dominant traits. He had never learned a profession and had remained an outsider to all fields of endeavour. Like many self-taught people, he had no idea what real specialized knowledge meant. Without any sense of the complexities of any great task, he boldly assumed one function after another.

Speer added that Hitler made decisions in a completely isolated environment, without any input from other parties unless he requested it:[7]

'Without much fuss, and without any rebellion on the part of those concerned, Hitler continued to make all decisions himself, in total disregard of any technical basis. He dispensed with analyses of the situation and logistical calculations. He did not rely on any study group which would examine all aspects of offensive plans in terms of their effectiveness and possible countermeasures by the enemy. The headquarters staff were more than competent to carry out these functions of modern warfare; it would only have been necessary to activate them. To be sure, Hitler would accept information about partial aspects of situations; but the grand synthesis was supposed to be born solely in his head. His field marshals as well as his closest associates had, therefore, merely advisory functions, for his decision had usually been forged long beforehand and only minor aspects of it were subject to change. Moreover, whatever he had learned from the eastern campaign

This picture shows the whole of Hitler's '*maison militaire*', the usual military personnel who were in his entourage. Keitel is on Hitler's right, Jodl on his left. On Jodl's left is Martin Bormann who was the Chief of the Nazi Party Chancellery, tried in absentia at the Nuremberg trials and sentenced to death.

This picture shows Hitler with his chosen successor, Hermann Goering on the balcony of the Reich Chancellery in March 1938. Goering accumulated a vast array of offices in addition to being Commander-in-Chief of the Luftwaffe, but almost entirely neglected the duties which went with them. He was found guilty of war crimes and committed suicide prior to being hanged at Nuremberg.

This picture shows Hitler with his only Minister of War, Field Marshal von Blomberg. On his left are Goering, Commander-in-Chief of the Luftwaffe, Colonel-General von Fritsch, C-in-C of the Army and Admiral Raeder, C-in-C of the Kriegsmarine. In 1938 Hitler retired both Blomberg and Fritsch, primarily because they had reservations about this expansionist policies, created Oberkommando der Wehrmacht (the High Command of the Armed Forces) through which he took over the office of the Minister of War and exercised direct command of the Wehrmacht.

Hitler speaking before the Reichstag in 1939. It was located at the Kroll Opera House after the fire during the election of February 1933. It was heavily damaged in an RAF attack during 1943.

This photo shows Hitler with his architect Albert Speer at the Berghof in 1938 reviewing construction plans. Speer was appointed Reich Minister for Armaments after the death of Dr. Todt on 8th February 1942. Speer was able to increase production in all classes of war material and became one of the most powerful figures in Nazi Germany.

Hitler with Field Marshal Keitel on the left, Commander in Chief of the Army Field Marshal von Brauchitsch and Chief of the General Staff Colonel-General Halder. Hitler got rid of Brauchitsch in December 1941 blaming him for the failure of Operation Barbarossa, the invasion of the USSR. Halder was sacked in September 1942 after many disagreements with Hitler over strategy and tactics and particularly Hitler's tactics after the failure of Barbarossa and during the Stalingrad offensive.

Hitler situation conference with Field Marshal von Manstein (extreme left) and Colonel-General Zeitzler on Hitler's left.

Hitler showing Mussolini the wrecked conference room following the attempted assassination on 20 July 1944. Hitler was only slightly wounded and continued with his schedule for the rest of the day. The effect of the attempted coup was to strengthen Hitler's paranoid suspicion of all generals and made any real co-operation between him and the Supreme Command of the Army virtually impossible.

The Messerschmidt Me-262 was the first operational jet aircraft in the world. It outclassed any allied fighter at the time in terms of speed, rate of climb and operational ceiling. Its armament of 4 x 30 mm cannon was formidable and could have inflicted significant losses on the allied bombers causing such great damage and disruption to Germany. Hitler's insistence that it be used as a bomber was nonsensical and squandered its potential as the means by which the allied bomber offensive could be defeated or limited.

The V-1 was the first operational cruise missile. Its main weaknesses were its relatively low speed which meant that it could be shot down or moved off course by defensive fighters and its launch ramp which could easily be identified by allied reconnaissance aircraft. Nonetheless if it had been produced in the numbers Hitler intended it could have inflicted significant damage on London.

The V-2 was the progenitor of all modern intercontinental ballistic missiles. There were no defensive measures available against it at the time of its production. It took much longer to perfect than originally expected and was not deployed until September 1944. By the time of its deployment, the war was already lost and the number available could do nothing to alter its course.

Werner Heisenberg was Hitler's go-to expert on nuclear physics and had won the Nobel prize for physics in 1925. Based on his views the Germans decided not to pursue the creation of the Atomic bomb because it would take too long to develop to affect the result of the war. This decision was correct because as Speer stated they did not have the resources to commit to such a project.

Werner von Braun in 1941. He was in charge of the program to develop the V-2 rocket. This photograph shows him with General Olbricht (2nd from the left in the front row) who was Chief of the Army Reserve and one of the plotters involved in Operation Valkyrie. Von Braun was employed by NASA after the war heading the development program for rockets to carry the lunar landing craft and other projects.

The Tiger PzkfwVI. These were very powerfully armed but were expensive, time consuming, complex to service, had limited operational range and there were never enough of them. They were also very heavy and required special flatcars to be transported, which meant that they were also time consuming to transport and unload.

The 'King Tiger' was the final development of German tank design and was once again a very powerful tank. It was even more expensive than the Tiger 1 and still had the other flaws noted for it.

The Panther was a very powerful tank which the Germans classified as medium despite weighing 45 tons. Had the Germans concentrated on the production of this tank instead of producing the Tigers, they would have had many more of them and they were sufficiently powerful and armoured to be a real problem for the allies. This picture illustrates the long calibre 75mm main gun which was a very effective weapon against all the allies' tanks.

The Heinkel 177 was the 4 engined bomber designed before the war which was intended to provide the Luftwaffe with the ability to carry out a strategic bombing campaign. The aircraft had two paired engines in the two wing nacelles and was mechanically unreliable and tended to catch fire. Its projected bombload was 13,000 pounds, which was significant improvement on other German bombers. Although its operational record was far from satisfactory approximately 1,200 were produced.

Hitler's Involvement in Weapons Development Programmes 113

in the years 1942–43 was rigorously repressed. Decisions were made in a total vacuum.'

The Fuhrer thus made all the important decisions for the German armed forces with respect to the type of equipment they were provided with completely on his own, lacking any technical knowledge and having regard only to the experience he had as a soldier during the First World War. Plainly, this was an inadequate basis for such important and involved decisions.

Speer described his involvement with Hitler's regular 'weapons conferences':[8]

'Every two or three weeks I travelled from Berlin to spend a few days at Hitler's East Prussian, and later in his Ukrainian, headquarters in order to have him decide the many technical questions of detail in which he was interested in his capacity as Commander in Chief of the army. Hitler knew all the types of ordnance and ammunition, including the calibres, the lengths of barrels, and the range of fire. He had the stocks of the most important items in his head – as well as the monthly production figures.

'... I could never predict what the result of our conferences would be. Sometimes he instantly approved a proposal whose prospects seemed exceedingly slight. Sometimes he obstinately refused to permit certain trivial measures which he himself had demanded only a short time before.'

Speer also gave an interesting description of the way in which Hitler inspected new weapons and how they were demonstrated to him:[9]

'Our technical conferences were usually combined with a demonstration of new weapons which took place in a nearby field. A few minutes before we would have been sitting intimately with Hitler, but now everybody had to line up in rank and file, Field Marshal Keitel, chief of the OKW (High Command of the Armed Forces) on the right. Obviously, Hitler laid stress on the ceremonial aspect of the occasion, adding a further note of formality by entering his official limousine to cover the few hundred yards to the field. I took my place in the back seat. Hitler would then step out, and Keitel would report the presence of the waiting line of generals and technicians.

'This ritual concluded, the group promptly broke up. Hitler looked into details, clambered over the vehicles on portable steps held in readiness for him, and continued his discussions with the specialists. Often Hitler and I would make appreciative remarks about the weapons, such as: "What an elegant barrel," or, "What a fine shape this tank has!"

– a ludicrous relapse into the terminology of our joint inspections of architectural models.'

These conferences covered all aspects and types of weapons and manufacturing priorities. Sometimes, when the Fuhrer was at his retreat at Berchtesgaden in the Bavarian Alps, these conferences would consist of presentations by the senior officers of the arm of the Wehrmacht involved, such as Admiral Doenitz. On other occasions, for example with matters relating to the V-1 and V-2, Hitler would view films while a presentation was being made regarding the weapons. Usually, Hitler made decisions on the spot at the conclusion of the meeting, which would then be actioned through what were known as Fuhrer Protocols or other formal orders to industry and government departments.

Hitler and the development of the panzers

There is no doubt that the creation of Germany's panzer and mechanized forces prior to the war was due to Hitler's enthusiastic support. He recognized that they provided the potential to overcome the defensive power of the weapons and strategies which had dictated the character of the First World War, giving Germany the opportunity to achieve quick, decisive victories against its potential enemies. He read the works of several of the interwar proponents of armoured warfare, including De Gaulle and Guderian, referring to them on numerous occasions in his private and military circles.[10] Without Hitler's support, it is very unlikely that the panzer forces would have been created, the Weimar Republic governments prior to the Nazis being very focussed on avoiding any overt actions which could have caused friction with the victors of the Great War. Hitler's claim that he was the father of these forces is therefore quite valid.

It is obvious that the mere number of tanks produced does not guarantee victory on the battlefield. Hitler's approach was to have the best tanks available to overpower those of the enemy, rather than to try to win through preponderance of numbers alone. This meant integrating the latest available technology into the design and manufacture of the tanks and to emphasize the quality of the product rather than merely their number. This was generally in accord with the tradition of German craftsmanship, but not necessarily conducive to large-scale manufacture. During the interwar years, there had been covert co-operation between the Soviet and German high commands relating to the development of the types of tanks and tactics for armoured formations, but this had never been on a large scale.

Hitler's Involvement in Weapons Development Programmes 115

There are several critical elements in tank performance, and every type of tank represents compromises in these elements – speed, endurance, armour, hitting power, communications and serviceability. Ultimately, these aspects of design and performance determine the tanks' effectiveness on the battlefield and the number of operational tanks available for use. Nevertheless, if the disparity in numbers becomes too great, numbers can also be a vital factor in victory.

The types of tank with which the German panzer divisions commenced the war were not the most powerful or best-protected of the time. The Mark III and IV panzers were the most powerful German designs, but were outclassed by the French Char B, which was by far the most powerful tank at that time. The French had more than enough of these to cause a real problem for the panzer divisions if they were deployed and co-ordinated in large-enough formations with appropriate air force support and correctly used tactically. Unfortunately for the French, their tanks were not optimally deployed, and the training of the crews and the formations as a whole were far from complete, as pointed out in Volume 1 of this work. The German tanks, meanwhile, were faster, and each was radio-equipped, whereas approximately 80 per cent of the French tanks were not, which made a significant difference to the co-ordination and tactical flexibility of the formations in combat. When the Germans attacked through the Ardennes in May 1940, the French and British forces, including their armoured formations, were moving to their pre-arranged positions in accordance with the plan to defeat an attack through northern Belgium, instead of the actual route taken by the Germans. Consequently, the Allied armoured formations were never deployed in a large-enough mass to make a difference to the course of the main German attack.

The Panzer Mk III and IV models were still the best tanks the Germans had at the commencement of Operation *Barbarossa* in June 1941. The percentages and types of tanks and assault guns involved in the invasion of the Soviet Union were as follows:[11]

PzKpfw I	8 per cent
PzKpfw III	49 per cent
PzKpfw IV	13 per cent
Stug III	7 per cent
PzKpfw 35(t)	4 per cent
PzKpfw 38(t)	19 per cent

The PzKpfw I was by this time little more than obsolescent, being armed with only two 7.92mm machine guns in a lightly armoured turret, and was mainly used for reconnaissance work. The Stug III was an assault gun intended as an infantry support weapon, based on the chassis of the Panzer Mk III. While very useful, it did not have a rotating turret, the main gun being placed in its hull and thus having limited ability to engage targets. However, it was cheap to manufacture and had the hitting power of a tank. The 35(t) and 38(t) were Czechoslovakian types, further complicating the German problems in maintaining the spare parts of their panzer forces.

The PzKpfw IV was upgraded on several occasions and improved with respect to its armament and armour. However, its basic armour configuration was inferior to the Soviet T-34, which was sloped, and it had comparatively narrow tracks that were not able to cope adequately with the mud and snow encountered in the autumn and winter on the Eastern Front. General Gunther Blumentritt, who took part in *Barbarossa*, commented on the strengths of the T-34 in *The Fatal Decisions*:[12]

> 'We were confronted by another and equally unpleasant surprise at this time. The first Russian T34 tanks appeared during the Battle of Vyazma. In 1941 this was a most spectacular A.F.V. [armoured fighting vehicle] which could only be dealt with by other tanks or by the artillery: it was impervious to the infantry's anti-tank weapons, for at that time our infantry was equipped only with 37mm and 50mm anti-tank guns. These had been capable of knocking out the Russian tanks we had hitherto encountered but they had no effect on the T34. Thus a very serious state of affairs arose for the infantry divisions, which felt themselves naked and defenceless against this new tank. A gun of at least 75mm calibre was needed, and such a gun had first to be built. At Veraya the Russian tanks simply drove straight through the 7th Infantry Division to the artillery positions and literally ran over the guns. The effect on the infantryman's morale was comprehensible. This marked the beginning of what came to be called "the tank terror".'

The advent of the T-34 tank was a profound shock to the Germans, outperforming their tanks in every respect. It was more powerfully armed, with a 76mm gun, than any German tank at that time. It also had sloping armour, which made it almost impervious to any anti-tank guns the Germans had except the 88mm Flak gun when used in the anti-tank role. Furthermore, it had wider tracks, was more manoeuvrable and could go where the German tanks could not, especially in the autumn and winter months. The T-34 was therefore a technological triumph which comprehensively made all German tanks virtually obsolete and showed the absurdity of the Nazi racial doctrine which asserted that all Slavic peoples were inferior '*untermensch*'. It also outclassed all of the tanks the Western Allies then produced. The T-34 made all the German assumptions relating to the technical superiority of their equipment outdated, and it was only the superior experience and tactics of the panzer divisions and the relatively small number of T-34s then available to the Red Army which allowed the Germans to avoid a complete disaster on the Eastern Front in 1941.

The development of the German tank-building programme between 1942 and 1943 was succinctly outlined by Guderian in his book *Panzer Leader*. Guderian, who became the Inspector General of Panzer Troops in March 1943, wrote that on 23 January 1942 the design of the new Panther tank was submitted to Hitler, who approved it in May and ordered that production be set at 600 units per month.[13] He added:[14]

> 'Hitler expressed an opinion which was to be a continual source of confusion to him in his understanding both of the technical development and of the tactical and operational employment of tanks. He believed that the hollow-charge shell, which was about to be issued to the artillery, and which showed increased power of armour penetration, would lead to a considerable decrease in the future effectiveness of tanks. He believed that if this new development should, in fact, fulfil its promise, the answer was to have much more self-propelled artillery and he therefore wished to divert tank chassis to the artillery for this purpose.'

This diversion of tank production capacity made it more difficult to achieve the rate of production required, which indeed was never met. Guderian also noted that in March 1942, Hitler instructed that the Krupp company prepare designs for a tank that was to weigh 100 tons;[15] then in June 1942, the engineers Grote and Hacker were told to design a monster tank weighing 1,000 tons, which Guderian characterized as a 'fantasy'. These diversions of effort were entirely without any useful result. Such monster tanks would have been impossible to use in operations for many practical reasons, including transporting them and manoeuvring them on the battlefield. The heavy Mouse tank destroyers, which weighed in at 90 tons, were a complete failure when committed in Operation *Citadel*, and thus a total waste of resources.

Hitler changed the tank production programme again in September 1942, demanding that 800 tanks be produced per month, including a new Leopard light tank. In January 1943, production of the Leopard was ordered to cease, with resources to be directed to other tank types. Guderian stated that the General Staff later asked Hitler to discontinue production of all tank types other than the Panther and Tiger, with all efforts allocated to producing as many as possible of these types. This chopping and changing of programmes and requirements was plainly detrimental to achieving optimum results. Guderian continued:[16]

> 'This new plan contained only one major weakness; with the abandonment of the Panzer IV Germany would, until further notice, be limited to the production of 25 Tigers per month. This would certainly have led to the defeat of the German Army in the very near future.'

The programme was therefore changed again to ensure that the army had tanks in the interim between the cessation of the production of the Panzer Mk IV and the new tanks becoming available.

It was obvious that the Mk IV had to be replaced if the Germans were to regain a qualitative edge after the advent of the Soviet T-34. The result was that Hitler ordered that creation of the PzKpfw V, known as the *'Panther'*, be brought forward as soon as possible. This medium tank had been in development since 1937 and was re-specified following developments in 1941 to be superior to the T-34. As was typical of all tank types, the Panther had teething problems, which meant that it was not ready for combat when Hitler ordered that it be committed to the Kursk offensive in summer 1943. Because it had not finished testing and the crews had not been fully trained in its operation, the results were very disappointing. However, once these initial problems were dealt with, the Panther became a very successful tank, regarded by many as the best tank design of the Second World War.

Hitler also ordered the development of a new heavy tank, known as the Tiger, the designation of which was PzKpfw VI. This tank was very heavily armed, using a version of the Krupp 88mm anti-tank weapon which had proved so effective against all types of Allied tanks. The Tiger Mk I also had extremely strong armour, with a maximum 8in frontal thickness, which made it very difficult to destroy. However, because of its 57-ton weight, the Tiger could not use many bridges in Europe, and even fewer in the Soviet Union. It therefore had to cross on pontoons or at river fords that it could negotiate, causing significant problems if it became stuck on the banks of any waterway it could not ford because its weight made it extremely difficult to move. It also had to be transported on specially built railway flat cars, which meant there were frequently delays in its commitment to battle.

There were several characteristics of the new German designs which were significantly different from previous examples. The new suspension systems consisted of torsion bars with large, interleaved running bogeys which were very heavy, difficult to service and also became clogged with mud during the autumn and winter on the Eastern Front. The mud frequently froze overnight in winter, with the result that the tank was immobilized. The new suspension arrangement did, however, provide very stable cross-country performance and made the tank a very good gun platform in operation. The new Panther and Tiger tanks also had excellent Zeiss optical systems, which meant that coupled with their powerful main armament they could destroy targets at longer ranges than Allied tanks could effectively fire on them.

The Panther 'Ausf A' variant had the following characteristics:[17]

Weight	-	45 tons
Speed	-	46kmph
Endurance	-	177km
Main armament	-	75mm KwK 42 L/70
Machine guns	-	2 x 7.92mm MG 34

Total of 4,800 units produced between September 1942 and April 1945

Each Panther cost 117,100 Reichsmarks (RM) and took approximately 150,000 man hours to build and assemble, more than any of the Allied tanks by a significant margin.

The Panthers and Tigers were also complex to service, which made their battlefield durability a problem. When captured and examined by the Allies, the new German tanks were regarded as being unnecessarily complex and over-engineered.

The characteristics of the Tiger Mk I, which was the more numerous of the Tigers, were as follows:[18]

Weight	-	57 tons
Speed	-	38kmph
Endurance	-	100km
Main armament	-	88mm KwK 36 L/56
Machine guns	-	2 x 7.92mm MG 34

Total of 1,347 units produced between August 1942 and August 1944

Tigers were also much more time-consuming to construct and cost significantly more than any Allied types. The total time to produce a Tiger I and all its components is estimated to have been 300,000 man hours, while the cost was approximately 400,000 RM, which was equal to $160,000 at the time. In comparison, the cost of each US Pershing M26 medium tank, which had a 90mm main armament and was more than capable of dealing with the Tiger or Panther, was $84,000. While the US Sherman tank had a lower-powered 76mm gun, it was stabilized, which made it more accurate when fired on the move. The armament was upgraded several times and included a variant with the British 17-pdr gun known as the Firefly, which could also knock out a Tiger. Furthermore, over 40,000 Shermans were constructed until production ceased in 1942, and the design was found to be reliable and rugged. It cost $44,000 for the early variants, but that figure increased later as its capabilities were upgraded. However, it was still significantly cheaper than the new German tanks.

The Mk II version of the Tiger, known as the King Tiger, was even more powerful, heavier and incorporated refinements following experience with the Mk I. Its vital statistics were:[19]

Weight	-	68 tons
Speed	-	38kmph
Endurance	-	110km
Main armament	-	88mm KwK 43
Machine guns	-	2 x 7.92mm MG 34

Total of 485 units produced between January 1944 and March 1945

King Tiger tanks were used in Normandy in June 1944 and the Ardennes offensive in December that year, and although very powerful were once again resource-intensive and expensive to produce, taking an estimated 300,000 man hours to assemble and build and costing 800,000 RM. The number of tanks produced was severely restricted by the Allied bombing campaign, with the main Henschel factory producing them being heavily bombed twice in 1944.

The Germans were also handicapped by their tank-manufacturing programme not being optimized to achieve the highest number of operational tanks on the battlefield. Speer provides evidence of how Hitler had a negative impact on this issue:[20]

> 'One of his worst failings was that he did not understand the necessity for supplying the armies with sufficient spare parts. General Guderian, the Inspector of Tank Ordnance, frequently pointed out to me that if we could repair our tanks quickly, thanks to sufficient spare parts, we could have more available for battle, at a fraction of the cost, than by producing new ones. But Hitler insisted on the priority of new production.'

Guderian confirmed Speer's claims when recording a meeting with the Fuhrer on 4 August 1941 to discuss the future course of Operation *Barbarossa*, which included the needs of the panzer divisions and the maintenance of their tanks:[21]

> 'I stressed the fact that our tank engines had become very worn as a result of the appalling dust; in consequence they must be replaced with all urgency if any more large scale tank operations were to be carried out during the current year. It was also essential that replacements be provided for our tank casualties from current production. After a certain amount of humming and hawing **Hitler promised to supply 300 new tank engines for the whole Eastern front, a figure which I described as totally inadequate. As for new tanks, we were not to get any, since Hitler intended to retain them all at home for the equipping of newly set-up formations** [author's emphasis]. In the ensuing argument I stated that we could only cope with the Russians' great numerical superiority in tanks if our tank losses were rapidly made good again. Hitler then said: "If I had known that the figures for Russian tank strength which you gave in your book were in fact the true ones, I would not – I believe – ever have started this war." [The figure for Soviet tank strength which Guderian had given in his book *Achtung – Panzer* was 10,000 in 1938.]'

The necessity for an adequate supply of spare parts was surely self-evident to anyone of even average intelligence, which makes this decision by Hitler inexplicable on any rational basis. However, it is apparent that such problems existed for the panzer forces throughout the war due to the Fuhrer's lack of understanding of this elementary matter.

Hitler's decisions had a particularly damaging effect with respect to servicing of the over-engineered Tiger tanks:[22]

> 'The Tiger tank required a small army of mechanics to keep it in the field, while the ratio of spare parts produced was derisory. For every ten Tiger tanks only one spare engine and one transmission were produced. The new heavy tanks were supposed to be repaired at the front line, but the absence of heavy repair equipment or adequate stocks of spare parts meant a long trail of tank transporters carrying damaged vehicles back to repair depots in Germany.'

While it is always desirable to have the most powerful and technologically advanced types of military equipment available, ultimately their numbers are restricted by the time involved in manufacture and cost of the items. Achieving the correct balance in such matters is the key to successfully supplying any armed forces. Furthermore, while types may be superior when they are produced, this edge in quality is frequently eroded by the actions of the enemy, who is likely to improve the performance of its types in response. This is precisely what happened with the different types of tanks produced by the Allies during the war, particularly the US and Great Britain, who lagged behind the Germans and the Soviets in this matter when the invasion of France was launched in June 1944. While the German tanks were superior in some respects, notably the range at which they could destroy Allied tanks because of their advanced Zeiss optical systems, they were complicated, difficult to service, costly to produce and there were never enough of them.

Ultimately, the effectiveness of the German tank-production programme was affected by a combination of the factors mentioned above, but especially because the Allies caught up far enough in terms of design quality with those of the Germans and significantly out-produced them in terms of numbers. In particular, Soviet industry produced the T-34 for the Red Army in 1941, the type being continually upgraded and remaining a competitive design until the end of the war. Meanwhile, Hitler's impact on the design of German tanks and his apparent inability to understand the basic necessity of manufacturing enough spare parts for the panzers was a major factor in restricting the number of operational tanks the Germans could field on all fronts and at all stages of the war. His influence can therefore be seen to have reduced the effective power of the panzer forces of Nazi Germany.

The Waterfall anti-aircraft missile

The Waterfall ground-to-air defensive rocket was a surprisingly advanced weapon developed to the stage where production could have started in 1942. Speer, a supporter of the project, commented:[23]

> '
> Approximately 25 feet long, the Waterfall rocket was capable of carrying approximately six hundred and sixty pounds of explosives along a directional beam up to an altitude of fifty thousand feet and hit enemy bombers with great accuracy. It was not affected by day or night, by clouds or fog. Since we were later able to turn out nine hundred of the offensive big rockets monthly, we could surely have produced several thousand of these smaller and less expensive rockets per month.'

Professor Carl Krauch, the commissioner for chemical production in the Reich, sent a paper to Speer on 29 June 1943 in which he argued:[24]

> 'Those who advocate accelerated development of aerial weapons are proceeding on the principle that that terror is best answered by terror and that the rocket attacks against England will necessarily lead to a decrease

in the missions flown against the Reich. Even assuming that the large long-distance rockets were available in unlimited quantities, which at the moment they are not, previous experience suggests that this reasoning is unjustified. On the contrary those elements in England who formerly opposed the use of terror-bombing against [the] civilian population … have been moved, since our rocket attacks, to urge their government to launch massive raids against our densely populated areas. We are still helplessly vulnerable to raids of this sort … Such considerations point to the necessity of concentrating heavily on antiaircraft weaponry, on the C-2 device of Waterfall.'

This logic was extremely strong, but the problem was that Hitler was not disposed to undertake defensive measures, relying always on attack. The project was thus not made a priority and the Waterfall rockets were never used operationally. Speer concluded:[25]

'To this day I think that this rocket, in conjunction with the jet fighters, would have beaten back the Western Allies' air offensive against our industry from the spring of 1944 on. Instead, gigantic effort and expense went into developing and manufacturing long-range rockets which proved to be, when they were at last ready for use in the Autumn of 1944, an almost total failure.'

Speer's enthusiastic support for the Waterfall project continued, and he wrote that he considered its demise to be one of the worst mistakes the Fuhrer made during the war.

The 'Vengeance' weapons

Hitler intended to use the V-1 and V-2 'Vengeance' weapon programmes to take revenge on the Western Allies for the strategic bombing campaign and the destruction it caused to Germany. The creation and production of the V-1 and V-2 were the most expensive weapons programmes the Germans undertook during the war, costing over 5 billion RM, according to Albert Speer.

The Vengeance weapons had their beginnings in the 1920s when the German Army undertook research to determine whether rockets could be effectively used as artillery. By 1935, sufficient progress had been made for a research facility to be established at Peenemunde on the Baltic coast. The first employee working on the programme was Wernher Freiherr von Braun, who subsequently headed the entire research projects at Peenemunde and went on after the war to do the same for the NASA space programmes in the United States. Peenemunde was the location for secret development programmes for the army and Luftwaffe and became the largest research facility developed by the Reich. However, it was vulnerable to attack as its location made it accessible to the Allied bomber fleets and it was relatively easy to identify because it was on the coast.

The V-1 programme was run under the auspices of the Luftwaffe, and is now regarded as the world's first cruise missile. It was primitive by modern standards, but was revolutionary for its time. The V-2, meanwhile, was managed through the army; known as the A4 programme, it was a much more complex weapon system.

The V-1 flying bomb

The V-1 was a relatively simple weapon and therefore cheap to produce in significant numbers. However, its launch relied on a ramp being installed. These ramps were large enough to be identified by reconnaissance aircraft and thus gave away their positions, so the sites were repeatedly bombed. The Germans changed the type of launch site so that they were more difficult to detect, but the Allies were still able to spot them. Thereafter, mobile ramps were used, which offered greater concealment. Hitler had intended that the deployment of the V-1 would result in hundreds of flying bombs being sent against London daily, but the early results were not encouraging:[26]

> 'The first ten bombs were launched on the night of 12th/13th June [1944]. Five crashed shortly after launching, and a sixth went missing; of the remaining four, one fell in Sussex, and the others near Gravesend, near Sevenoaks and at Bethnal Green.'

Speer described the first mass deployment and operational use of the flying bombs:[27]

> 'Fifty-five positions had been prepared along it [the Pas-de-Calais coast], from which several hundred "flying bombs" were to be launched against London daily.
>
> '... Hitler and all of us hoped that this new weapon, the V-1, would sow horror, confusion and paralysis in the enemy camp. We overestimated its effects.
>
> '... In response to Hitler's premature command, the first V-1 pilotless jets were catapulted off their launch ramps in great haste. Only ten of

them could be dispatched, and only five reached London. Hitler forgot that he himself had insisted on rushing matters and vented his fury at the bungled project upon the builders. ... Hitler was on the point of deciding to halt the production of flying bombs on the grounds that it was a wasteful blunder. Then the press chief handed him some exaggerated, sensationalized reports from the London press on the effects of the V-1. Hitler's mood promptly changed. Now he demanded increased production.'

Following waves of bombardment were more successful, but never approached the consistent level which had been expected:[28]

'In the 24 hours beginning at 22.30 on 15th June, Wachtel [Colonel Max Wachtel of Flak Regiment 155, in charge of the deployment of the V-1s] launched more than 200 flying bombs, of which 144 crossed our coast and 73 reached Greater London. 33 were brought down by the defences but 11 of these came down in the built up area of Greater London.'

Subsequently, Britain's anti-aircraft defences became much more proficient, being established in a belt along the flight path to London of the V-1s. By using the proximity fuse, the number brought down steadily increased. The British also used their fast fighters, including the Typhoon and the new Meteor jet when they came into service, to tilt the wings of the V-1s, which nudged them off course.

The British had been tracking the V-1 experiments at Peenemunde by radar and knew their flight characteristics.[29] They were also able to feed misleading information to the Germans when the V-1 bombardment of London started, but it was tricky to get the level of deception just right:[30]

'The dilemma facing M.I.5 was that the Germans were now telling their supposed London agents to report the times and places of flying bomb incidents in London. If, to preserve the security of possible future deceptions, we were to supply truthful information to the Germans, this would be aiding the enemy. If, on the other hand, we supplied false information, then this could be checked by German photographic reconnaissance, in which case the agents would be "blown" and future deception plans ruined.'

The solution was to provide accurate information regarding where the bombs fell, but with misleading times, which were adapted to reflect the known flight characteristics which the British had been able to obtain through their radar tracking of the Peenemunde tests. The result was that the accuracy of the bombs was significantly affected. It also turned out that because of the RAF's dominance of the skies over London, photographic reconnaissance, which would have been crucial to the Germans in tracking the accuracy of the V-1s, simply had not been possible. Scientific military intelligence expert R.V. Jones has called this 'one of the biggest surprises of the war', intelligence staff not realizing until after the war the weakness of the Luftwaffe's reconnaissance capability.[31]

The V-1 bombardment of London depended on the launching sites being within range of London, but as the Allies broke out of Normandy in the summer of 1944 and forced the Germans closer to their borders, the sites were overrun and the ability to attack London thus diminished. The last V-1 struck Britain on 29 March 1945.

Of the approximately 10,500 V-1s launched again London, only some 2,400 landed within Greater London, causing 6,000 fatalities and 18,000 serious injuries.[32] The V-1 was therefore a comparatively cost-effective weapon when compared to the cost of inflicting casualties with conventional bombing.

The V-2 rocket

The V-2 was the prototype of all intercontinental ballistic missiles which have subsequently been developed. Speer noted that Hitler was first shown a film of a V-2 rocket taking off on 7 July 1943 in one of the conference halls at the Fuhrer HQ, and commented on his reaction:[33]

> 'After a brief introduction the room was darkened and a color film shown. For the first time Hitler saw the majestic spectacle of a great rocket rising from its pad and disappearing into the stratosphere. Without a trace of timidity and with a boyish sounding enthusiasm, von Braun explained his theory. There could be no question about it: From that moment on, Hitler had been finally won over.'

After the meeting, Hitler immediately ordered:[34]

> 'The A-4 [Aggregat-4, better known as the V-2, one of a series of ballistic missile designs developed in Nazi Germany] is a measure that can decide the war. And what encouragement to the home front when we attack the English with it! This is the decisive weapon of the war, and what is more it can be produced with relatively small resources. Speer, you must

push the A-4 as hard as you can! Whatever labor and materials they need must be supplied instantly.'

Delays relating mainly to the missile's guidance system meant that the V-2 could not be deployed until September 1944. Hitler had intended that 5,000 rockets be sent against London on the first day, but the Allies had discovered the existence of the programme and disrupted it with bombing attacks on Peenemunde. When the V-2 offensive eventually started at the beginning of September, just twenty-five rockets were sent against London over a ten-day period.[35]

The V-2 was much more difficult to counter than the V-1, as its trajectory reached stratospheric levels and it descended at such high speed that no anti-aircraft defence was usable against it. Therefore, the Allies had to concentrate on destroying it at its source. Ultimately, through a combination of information from the Polish resistance and Ultra decrypts, the British learned of the locations to which the V-2 programme had been moved after Peenemunde had been attacked in August 1943. From then onwards, the British were able to track the development of the V-2 and the location of the factories where it was being produced, which were then severely disrupted through air attack. In an effort to negate the Allies' bombing, the Nazis developed a bomb-proof underground factory in the Harz mountains of central Germany to produce the V weapons, operated by the SS. The V-2s were then produced there using a combination of concentration camp inmates and slave labour, who worked in barbaric conditions.[36]

More than twenty years after the end of the war, Speer commented on a study that was carried out to compare the effectiveness of the V-2 with a conventional bomber:[37]

'According to the US Air University Review, Vol. XVII, No. 5 (July–August 1966), a four engine B-17 (Flying Fortress) cost $204,370. A V-2, on the other hand, according to David Irving's precise documentation, cost only 144,000 Reichsmarks, or one sixth that of the bomber. Six rockets delivered four and a half metric tons of explosives (1,650 pounds per rocket). Each one was destroyed by use. A B-17 bomber, on the other hand, could be sent on any number of missions, had a range of 1,000 to 2,000 miles, and could deliver two tons of explosives on the target. On Berlin alone, 49,400 metric tons of explosives and bomb shrapnel were dropped, damaging or totally destroying 20.9 percent of the dwelling units (Webster and Frankland, *The Strategic Air Offensive against*

Germany [London 1961], Vol IV). To deliver the same load over London we would have to use 66,000 large rockets, or the production of six years.'

From this, it is obvious that the effectiveness of the V-2 as a war-winning weapon was greatly overrated, as Speer himself commented:[38]

'The whole notion was absurd. The fleets of enemy bombers in 1944 were dropping an average of three thousand tons of bombs a day over a span of several months. And Hitler wanted to retaliate with thirty rockets that would have carried twenty-four tons of explosives to England daily.

'I not only went along with this decision of Hitler's part but also supported it. That was probably one of my most serious mistakes.'

Combined with the difficulties in producing the rocket, the Allied countermeasures meant that the number of V-2s which were launched was far below the level Hitler had specified. Of the total of 5,200 rockets produced, approximately 1,300 were targeted at London and these inflicted around 9,000 casualties, of whom 2,700 were killed.

The V weapons projects were a spectacular failure. They cost over 5 billion RM[39] and diverted precious resources from projects which could potentially have made a real difference to Germany's defensive efforts against the Allied air offensives, such as the Waterfall surface-to-air anti-aircraft missile. The funds allocated to the V programmes would have generated an additional 24,000 German aircraft, according to the US Strategic Bombing Survey. Even half such a number would have made a significant difference to Germany's defensive position. This encapsulates the futility of Hitler's fixation with offensive measures to strike at the enemy rather than developing effective defensive weapon systems.

The German A-bomb

During the 1920s and early 1930s, Germany was ahead of the rest of the world in the study and research relating to nuclear physics. However, in 1935 the Nuremberg Laws relating to the employment of Jews in Germany came into force, imposing many discriminatory measures against the Jewish population of Germany. Because of this discrimination and Nazi persecution, Albert Einstein and many other Jewish scientists left Germany and resettled in either Great Britain or the United States, where they carried on their academic endeavours.

Britain had an advanced nuclear physics research capability centred on its universities well before the war began. After hostilities broke out, it commenced a programme under the code name 'Tube Alloys' to establish the practicability of developing an atomic bomb in association with Canada, before the USA began its own similar project. The British realized that the development of a nuclear weapon was very expensive and that their research facilities were within range of German bombers, so they decided to partner with the United States in developing an atomic bomb, and both agreed to share their resources during the war as part of the Quebec Agreement signed on 19 August 1943. The code name of the programme was the 'Manhattan Project'. The most expensive weapons development programme ever undertaken until that time, the Manhatten Project was centred in several large secret sites in the United States and employed tens of thousands of scientists and researchers. The cost of the programme was $1.89 billion, which although immense, represented only 0.61 per cent of the total war budget of the United States ($261 billion).[40]

There has been much speculation and myth-making with respect to Germany's nuclear programme and its capacity to produce an atomic bomb. For a programme of the scale required for the research and development of an atomic bomb to occur in Nazi Germany, it was essential that it have the enthusiastic support of Hitler. In turn, this depended on the Fuhrer's understanding of the potential presented by nuclear weapons and his acceptance that such a programme would take years to complete.

Albert Speer, the German Armaments Minister and in charge of weapons development for the entire Nazi war effort, made the following comments relating to Hitler's attitude to the production of an atomic bomb:[41]

'Hitler sometimes spoke to me about the possibility of an atom bomb, but the idea quite obviously strained his intellectual capacity. He was also unable to grasp the revolutionary nature of nuclear physics. In the twenty-two hundred recorded points of my conferences with Hitler, nuclear fission comes up only once, and then it is mentioned with extreme brevity. Hitler did sometimes comment on its prospects, but what I told him of my conference with the physicists confirmed his view that there was not much profit in the matter. Actually, Professor Heisenberg [Werner Heisenberg, a pioneer of quantum physics and leading scientist in the German wartime atomic bomb programme] had not given any final answer to my question whether a successful nuclear fission could be kept under control with absolute certainty or might continue as a chain reaction. Hitler was certainly not delighted with the possibility that the earth under his rule might be transformed into a glowing star.'

Apart from Hitler's attitude, Speer said the German scientists faced another significant practical problem:[42]

> 'Difficulties were compounded, Heisenberg explained, by the fact that Europe possessed only one cyclotron, and that of minimal capacity. Moreover, it was located in Paris and because of the need for secrecy could not be used to full advantage. I proposed that with the powers at my disposal as Minister of Armaments we build cyclotrons as big or bigger than those in the United States. But Heisenberg said that because we lacked experience we would have to begin by building a relatively small type.'

The Germans were therefore confronted with a lead time for the necessary equipment to be designed and built for the research programme before it would be possible to commence developing and building the bomb itself. This shows how much they had to do before they could even start the project for the creation of the bomb itself.

As in every project involving Hitler, there was an ideological element behind his attitude to the whole question of an atomic bomb project. Speer commented:[43]

> 'Our failure to pursue the possibilities of atomic warfare can partly be traced to ideological reasons. Hitler had great respect for Philipp Lenard, the physicist who had received the Nobel Prize in 1920 and was one of the few early adherents of Nazism in the ranks of the scientists. He had instilled the idea in Hitler that the Jews were exerting a seditious influence in their concern with nuclear physics and the relativity theory. To his table companions Hitler occasionally referred to nuclear physics as "Jewish physics" – citing Lenard as his authority for this. This view was taken up by Rosenberg. It thus becomes clearer why the Minister of Education was not inclined to support nuclear research.'

Speer dealt with the question of whether and how long it would have taken for the Germans to develop an atomic bomb:[44]

> '[E]ven if Hitler had not had this prejudice against nuclear research and even if the state of our fundamental research in June 1942 could have freed several billion instead of several million marks for the production of atom bombs, it would have been impossible – given the strain on our economic resources – to have provided the materials, priorities and

Hitler's Involvement in Weapons Development Programmes 131

technical workers corresponding to such an investment. For it was not only superior productive capacity that allowed the United States to undertake this gigantic project. The increasing air raids had long since created an armaments emergency in Germany which ruled out any such ambitious enterprise. At best, with extreme concentration of all our resources, we could have had a German atom bomb in 1947, but certainly we could not beat the Americans, whose bomb was ready by August 1945. And on the other hand the consumption of our reserves of chromium ore would have ended the war by January 1, 1946, at the very latest.'

Speer added that the German atomic bomb programme was eventually shut down in 1942 for the following reasons:[45]

'On the suggestion of the nuclear physicists we scuttled the programme to develop the atom bomb by the autumn of 1942, after I had again queried them about the deadlines and been told that we could not count on anything for three or four years. The war would certainly have been decided long before then. Instead I authorized the development of an energy-producing uranium motor for propelling machinery. The Navy was interested in that for its submarines.'

Richard Overy comments on the situation in his book *Why The Allies Won*:[46]

'Though German scientists knew of American research they remained reasonably confident that they were ahead in the atomic race throughout the war, despite its low priority. This arrogant assumption, shared, it should be added, by the anxious enemy, was the product of a science establishment heavily weighted towards pure theory. When the theoreticians turned to the practical development of the ideas they ran into difficulties.

'... As it was the sceptics were borne out by events; even the Americans, with vast resources, 150,000 workers, and top priority for the project, failed to produce a bomb until the war in Europe was over.'

Speer mentioned one of the main reasons why the German atomic bomb programme was never revived:[47]

'In the summer of 1943, wolframite [tungsten] imports from Portugal were cut off, which created a critical situation for the production of solid core ammunition. I therefore ordered the use of uranium cores for this type of ammunition. My release of our uranium stocks of about twelve hundred metric tons showed that we no longer had any thought of producing atom bombs.'

The cessation of these imports, which was a very real problem for the Germans, was brought about by British diplomacy. Portugal and Great Britain have a very long trading history going back to a treaty which was ratified on 9 May 1386, and the British leveraged this relationship to obtain a contract for all the tungsten which Portugal could supply. The Germans were simply left out in the cold by this coup.

It can therefore be stated with certainty that the Germans had not even commenced a programme with the aim of producing an atomic bomb during the war. Speer's evidence is also clear that even if the Germans had assigned all the resources they had to such a programme, it would not have been able to beat that of the Allies, which required tens of thousands of scientists and huge funds to succeed.

Nevertheless, Speer is also adamant that Hitler would not have shrunk from using the bomb if he had possessed it:[48]

'I am sure Hitler would not have hesitated for a moment to employ atom bombs against England. I remember his reaction to the final scene of a newsreel on the bombing of Warsaw in the autumn of 1939. We were sitting with him and Goebbels in his Berlin salon watching the film. Clouds of smoke darkened the sky; dive bombers tilted and hurtled toward their goal; we could watch the flight of the released bombs, the pull out of the planes and the cloud from the explosions expanding gigantically. The effect was enhanced by running the film in slow motion. Hitler was fascinated. The film ended with a montage showing a plane diving toward the outline of the British Isles. A burst of flame followed, and the island flew into the air in tatters. Hitler's enthusiasm was unbounded. "That is what will happen to them!" he cried out, carried away. "That is how we will annihilate them!"'

We have seen that there were four main reasons why a project to develop an atomic bomb by the Germans was not commenced. The first was that Hitler was not sufficiently supportive of commencing such a project because he believed it was based on 'Jewish physics'. Without Hitler's support, such a major project could never occur in the Nazi state. An example of this is shown by the fate of the Me 262 jet aircraft, as analysed earlier. The most significant project undertaken by the Germans during the war was the V-1 and V-2 programme, which was only able to proceed because the Fuhrer saw them as war-winning weapons that would turn the tide against the Western Allies.

Secondly, infrastructure needed to be built to support the research necessary as a prelude to the construction of the bomb. So even before the programme could start, equipment such as a cyclotron had to be constructed, together with other important research facilities. These preliminary requirements would have added further delays to the project, meaning that the time factor would be too long for the Germans to contemplate, which is in fact what was realized when the programme was terminated in 1942.

Thirdly, Germany did not have the spare resources necessary to commence such a programme during the emergency created by the war. Germany was experiencing a severe shortage of labour for its existing projects, and already had to use foreign workers and slaves to produce many materials. As noted earlier, the successful Allied Manhattan Project employed over 150,000 scientists and researchers, and even with this scale of commitment did not result in a useable bomb until after the war in Europe was over. The Germans simply did not have the resources available to undertake such a massive project.

Finally, Speer stated that the effect of the strategic bombing campaign had caused an armaments emergency in Germany, meaning everything had to be concentrated on providing existing arms for the Wehrmacht.

The result of all these considerations is that the Germans themselves realized there was no possibility of the atom bomb being produced by Germany during the war, so they cancelled any ongoing activities involving research into such a project in 1942.

Conclusions

There is no doubt that Hitler exercised a negative influence on the development of German weapons programmes in several important respects:

1. His influence in the design and manufacture of tanks acted to limit the number of operational panzers which the Germans could commit to battle at any time because the design and manufacturing process of the types of tank he required were extremely resource intensive, involved complex engineering and were expensive. The evidence shows that the Tiger tanks were not sufficiently superior to the Allied tanks they were committed against to justify the resources they consumed. Additionally, they were too heavy to be easily transported to and used on the battlefield, and too difficult to service. Had the resources used for the production of the Tiger been used for additional production of the Panther, or an improved version

of the Panzer Mk IV, the number of tanks produced could have been significantly raised.

2. Hitler's decision relating to the production of spare parts for the various tank types is completely unfathomable. Any intelligent person can understand the requirement for adequate maintenance and spare parts for mechanical vehicles, so the Fuhrer's ideas in this respect cannot be reconciled with reality. The impact of this on the army commanders who had to try to manage the multiple fronts that Hitler's strategy caused with the limited number of tanks available because of this ludicrous decision can easily be imagined.

3. The German Vengeance weapons programme was ultimately a waste of resources for the German war effort. The time and effort involved could have been used much more efficiently on the production of additional fighter aircraft or the Waterfall surface-to-air missile, either of which would certainly have made the Allies' strategic bombing campaign much more costly.

4. Hitler's involvement in the potential development of a German atom bomb was inimical to its prospects of success in a number of respects. Firstly, because of the 1935 Nuremberg Laws which institutionalized persecution of the Jewish population of Germany, many of the leading figures in nuclear research left the country, never to return. This constituted a drain of expertise which made it much more difficult for the Germans to create an atom bomb, but also meant that the Allies had access to knowledge that would otherwise have been utilized by their enemies had the anti-Jewish policies not existed. Secondly, as related by Speer, because the Reich's economy was stretched to the limit by the existing war programmes, Germany did not have the resources to commit to a project of the scale required to create the atom bomb; this would not have been the case had the V weapons programmes not been in place. Thirdly, due to the destruction of German industry and infrastructure caused by the Allied strategic bombing campaign, Nazi Germany's war economy was suffering an emergency which restricted the existing programmes and the capacity to undertake any other significant initiatives did not exist.

5. The Fuhrer's decision with respect to the Me 262 is incomprehensible considering the additional defensive power it would have added to the Luftwaffe if used in the fighter role it was designed to perform. His insistence that the 262 be used as a bomber was against all the advice received from all the responsible front-line commanders, including Galland, head of the German Fighter Command. The decision can only be ascribed to a complete inability to understand the issues involved.

Chapter 4

The Generals' View of Hitler as Commander-in-Chief

During the course of the Second World War, Hitler's standing within the Wehrmacht – and especially its higher-level commanders – fluctuated, mainly based on their perception of the military situation at any particular time. Within the most senior levels of the military hierarchy, however, many officers regarded Hitler as a dilletante part-time commander or a crass *parvenu* from the beginning of the Third Reich to its end. After the defeat of France in 1940, Hitler was at the peak of his power and of his standing within the military at all levels. Part of this was undoubtedly because it appeared that he had been proven to be correct in the majority of instances where he had disagreed with his senior commanders over the operations he wished to undertake. On almost every occasion, they had resisted the Fuhrer's wishes based on a rational evaluation of the situation, only for it to appear subsequently through the course of events that Hitler's view was correct.

While President Hindenburg was alive until August 1934, Hitler moved cautiously and did not make any major changes to the senior military hierarchy. However, upon Hindenburg's death and Hitler's combination of the office of President and Chancellor into the new one of Fuhrer and Reich Chancellor, he was freed from any restraining power. From then on, he increasingly interfered in the composition, size, role and senior personnel appointments of the Wehrmacht, especially the army.

Hitler's position as Fuhrer was accompanied by a level of deliberately promoted idolatry by the Nazi propaganda machine, which also contributed to the submission he received from the military and the German people. Speer commented on this matter:[1]

'Hitler's entourage certainly bore a measure of the blame for his growing belief in his superhuman abilities. Field Marshal Blomberg, Hitler's first and last Minister of War, had been overfond of praising Hitler's surpassing strategic genius. Even a more restrained and modest personality than Hitler ever was would have been in danger of losing all standards of self-criticism under such a constant torrent of applause.'

Blomberg was dismissed by Hitler in 1938, as outlined in Volume 1 of this work, and the torrent of praise only increased with his early victories, which gave a deceptive appearance of success to the overall strategic situation.

The Generals of the Oberkommando der Wehrmacht (OKW)

During March 1938, Hitler took over the office of Minister for War and assumed direct command of the administrative structure which went with it. He created a new staff called the High Command of the Armed Forces (Oberkommando der Wehrmacht, or OKW), which occupied a position above the supreme commanders of the three services to act as his personal military staff. He appointed Field Marshal Wilhelm Keitel at its apex, with the title of Chief of the Armed Forces High Command. Hitler's choice of Keitel was not based on any regard for his military abilities – he remarked at the time to Field Marshal Blomberg that he was looking for someone to be 'the person who runs his office'.[2] In reality, none of the members of the OKW staff, including Keitel, had any executive authority, except that specifically with reference to an order Hitler told them to carry out, although they were in a very influential position because of their constant contact with the Fuhrer.

During the war, the generals of the OKW did actually influence Hitler and became very powerful because of their proximity to him. This influence occurred in different ways with the two most senior of the OKW generals, Keitel and Alfred Jodl. Keitel's influence usually occurred as a result of agreeing with Hitler in a proposed course of action. By doing so, it meant that other courses were not likely to be undertaken, as Hitler would use Keitel's agreement against anyone arguing for a different decision. An instance of this type of negative influence was Keitel's expression of opinion to Hitler regarding the proposed retreat from Stalingrad. When Zeitzler, the Chief of the Army General Staff, implored Hitler to order a breakout from Stalingrad, the Fuhrer asked Keitel his view. Zeizler recalled Keitel's response:[3]

> 'Keitel, standing to attention and with his eyes flashing said "My Fuhrer! Do not leave the Volga."'

Colonel-General Jodl, the Chief of the Operations Staff of the OKW, routinely briefed and discussed military situations and operations with Hitler separately from the Chief of the General Staff of the Army, and thus had the opportunity to propose courses of action which were different from those which the Army Command would put forward. Hitler had also divided the responsibilities of the Supreme Command of the Army and the OKW, so that the Chief of the General Staff was only responsible for the Eastern Front. This also frequently led to Hitler deciding to undertake operations which were different from those advised by the army commander-in-chief of a particular front. Examples of this were the plans of operations for the defence of Normandy and the winter 1944 Ardennes offensive, neither of which were developed through the responsible army theatre commander. The creation of the OKW command staff was therefore a source of friction between the generals of the Supreme Command of the Army, the generals of the OKW and Hitler. This was intentional on the Fuhrer's part as the effect of these changes was to reduce the power of the army generals, whom he largely did not trust.

Field Marshal Keitel

Keitel was the object of the ill-concealed contempt of many of the generals of the Army High Command and those in command of armies in the field, due to what they saw as his supine acquiescence to Hitler's wishes. Directly after the war and before he was executed following the Nuremberg trials, Keitel wrote a draft of his memoirs and was interviewed by American psychiatrist Dr Leon Goldensohn. In those memoirs, Keitel stated:[4]

> 'For the execution of his [Hitler's] plans, which were unknown to us, he needed impotent tools unable to inhibit him, men who would be obedient and faithful to him in the real soldier's tradition. How easy it is for all those who are not exposed to the ball and shot and do not have to face up to a **demon like that man** [author's emphasis] day after day to criticise!'

During an interview with Goldensohn on 17 May 1946, Keitel said:[5]

> 'He was a **demonlike man, possessed of inordinate willpower, who whenever he had something in his mind, had to accomplish it** [author's emphasis]. Hitler had charm, loved children, charmed women. But in political respects he would stop at nothing.

During the war, Keitel became a man whom Hitler could manipulate at will, which accounts, at least in part, for his longevity as head of the OKW. Speer wrote of Keitel:[6]

> 'From an honourable, solidly respectable general he had developed in the course of years into a servile flatterer with all the wrong instincts.

Basically, Keitel hated his own weakness, but the hopelessness of any dispute with Hitler had ultimately brought him to the point of not even trying to form his own opinion. **If, however, he had offered resistance and stubbornly insisted on his own opinion, he would merely have been replaced by another Keitel** [author's emphasis].'

Ultimately, Hitler did not want a debating society, just people who carried his will into execution, regardless of their or anyone else's views, and he had the power to dismiss or appoint anyone he pleased.

Colonel General Alfred Jodl

In his role as Chief of the Operations Staff of the OKW, Jodl was in almost daily contact with Hitler for the entire war. He declared during his evidence at the Nuremberg trials:[7]

> 'Hitler was a leader to an exceptional degree. His knowledge and his intellect, his rhetoric, and his will power triumphed in the end in every spiritual conflict over everyone. He combined to an unusual extent logic and clarity of thought, skepticism and excess of imagination, which very frequently foresaw what would happen, but also very often went astray. I really marveled at him when in the winter of 1941–42, by his faith and his energy, he established the wavering Eastern Front; for at that time, as in 1812, a catastrophe was imminent. His life in the Fuhrer headquarters was nothing but duty and work. The modesty in his mode of life was impressive.'

For Jodl, who was reputedly an intelligent person, to make these remarks after the crimes of the Nazi regime were known shows that his absorption of Nazi propaganda and submission to Hitler's will were complete. It also shows that he was not capable of any objective assessment of Hitler's military 'strategies', for if he had been, he would certainly have seen that the position of the German Eastern Front in 1941 was significantly different from the circumstances surrounding Napoleon's retreat of 1812. Napoleon's army had become an undisciplined mob after being cooped up for months in Moscow, and as they had to deploy for a march in appalling weather were in a very poor position to defend themselves from the Imperial Russian Army, which could choose where and which parts of the French Army it attacked. The position of the Wehrmacht in 1941, although potentially dire, was different because it was still intact, cohesive and fully capable of defending itself despite Hitler's faulty generalship. The experience of its troops and excellence of its middle-level commanders meant it was still a force to be reckoned with, even when not deployed to maximize its defensive power. As pointed out in Volume 2 of this work, however, the main reason for the survival of the Germany armies in 1941 was because of Stalin's errors, which were of the same nature as those of Hitler – he did not concentrate his forces against Army Group Centre, as proposed by Zhukov, but attempted too many offensives and thereby dissipated the power of the Red Army. Meanwhile, Hitler's strategy in defence in 1941 was seriously flawed and did not take advantage of the German Army's greatest strengths, as was pointed out by numerous of its most senior operational commanders who were at the front, while Jodl – and Hitler – were not.

Jodl's record at the OKW is uneven at best. Two of his most egregious errors were his support of Hitler's determination to hold Stalingrad, a position which was militarily untenable and was contrary to the views emphatically and repeatedly expressed by the best German commanders, and his refusal to wake the Fuhrer to obtain the release of the panzer reserves when requested by Field Marshal Gerd von Rundstedt on 6 June 1944. These were both crises of the first order, in which Jodl's supposed military abilities should have told him that the action required of him was the opposite of that which he actually took. In both instances, his view was the opposite of the best operational commanders in the German Army, and he should have deferred to them as he had no operational command experience that was in any way comparable to theirs. The result of his support for Hitler's views and methods was on both occasions disaster on a Wagnerian scale for Germany. It may be that his opting to recommend the views of the operational commanders would not have changed the result or Hitler's actions, but the consequence of his not doing so is that he too must be regarded as a servile flatterer of Hitler, at least as culpable for the mismanagement of the German war effort as Keitel.

General Hasso von Mantueffel, who commanded a panzer army in the Ardennes offensive in December 1944, made the following observation regarding Jodl:[8]

> 'Jodl had also lost contact with the front. He never took the opportunity of talking to me when I came directly from the front line to report to Hitler. On the few occasions when I saw him in Hitler's presence **I could not help noticing his subservience toward Hitler and his arrogance toward his juniors, including myself, even though I was the commander in chief of an army** [author's emphasis].'

The basis of one of Jodl's defences at Nuremberg was that if he had opposed Hitler overtly there was no telling what would have happened to him, and he believed that by staying at his post he was lessening the effect of Hitler's worst orders. The other main contention was basically that he was only following orders. These excuses were dismissed by the tribunal, and he was sentenced to death. Jodl would have served his country and his own reputation much better if he had followed the course of the honourable soldier he attempted to present himself as being.

General Walter Warlimont

For others, however, the emperor's clothes were never in evidence. General Walter Warlimont was Jodl's Deputy Chief of the Operations Staff in the OKW and held this post for most of the war, only leaving it on 6 September 1944 on medical grounds resulting from an injury he sustained in the bomb explosion during the 20 July attempt to kill Hitler. Having attended most of Hitler's daily conferences through which the war was managed, he was appalled by the Fuhrer's lack of command ability:[9]

'[E]very day I would get back shaken to the core by what had occurred during the hours I was in Hitler's presence, shaken not only by the man himself but by his method of command [author's emphasis].'

Warlimont's view of Hitler as military commander is quite clear. He was dismissive of Hitler's command of the German Army after sacking Field Marshal Walther von Brauchitsch, and specifically during the 1942 Stalingrad offensive:[10]

'[T]his is not to say that Hitler purposely neglected his job of commanding the Army – the time and attention he gave to it are enough to show that. Nevertheless it was only too obvious what a difference there was between him and a *military* [emphasis in original] commander who throughout his career had prepared himself for this great responsibility and had no other object in life. A man like Hitler could not be expected to grasp the full import of the job which he had taken over; quite apart from the fact that in many respects he was ignorant of the basic principles of the exercise of command, he was overloaded with other responsibilities, and finally it was not in his nature. As regards enemy intelligence he only accepted what suited him and often refused even to listen to unpalatable information. **As before, time and space were for him only**

vague ideas [author's emphasis] which should not be allowed to affect the determination of a man who knew where he was going. As a soldier of the First World War, he felt himself better qualified than any of his advisers to judge the capacity of the troops, and **this was the subject of interminable and repetitive dissertations** [author's emphasis]. In the end, however, it was generally pushed into the background and forgotten. He had already shown that **strategically he did not understand the principle of concentrating forces at the decisive point; now he proved incapable of applying it tactically also, so nervous was he of exposing himself to attack anywhere** [author's emphasis].'

These comments could be applied to any of the military operations which Hitler commanded. Apart from any other consideration, the Fuhrer did not have the time to seriously undertake the role of commander-in-chief of the Army while also Head of State, Supreme Commander of the Wehrmacht, head of the Nazi Party and executive head of the entire government. No one could have adequately fulfilled all these roles simultaneously, and it should come as no surprise that Hitler failed to do so. It is a clear symptom of his all-consuming arrogance, ego and hubris that he thought he could.

Coming from a senior and very able military professional who was in Hitler's presence almost every day from the outbreak of the war until September 1944, Warlimont's comments must be given great weight. The fact that Warlimont was able to retain his independence from Hitler and from the supreme command structure and the people within it without becoming subservient, yet without being dismissed by Hitler or Jodl (although he had many disagreements with the latter), showed great strength of character.

The Supreme Command of the Army, the OKH and the Chiefs of the General Staff

Colonel General Franz Halder

Halder was Hitler's choice as Chief of the General Staff and fulfilled the role from August 1938 until September 1942. He therefore witnessed Hitler's reactions to all kinds of military events, including the most noteworthy victories and the prelude to the worst defeats. Halder's attitude to Hitler was clearly that he regarded his interference in higher-level military affairs – especially operationally – as wholly negative. His remarks in his diary[11] are mostly restrained, indicating an intellectually based analytical approach to all problems and issues which arise, but there are a significant number of entries which are very critical of Hitler, and these are not confined to *Barbarossa* or other unsuccessful operations. During the successful 1940 campaign, Halder's diary is replete with examples of the limitations of the German supreme command, of which two examples follow. On 18 June 1940, toward the very end of the campaign, Halder noted:[12]

> 'The Fuhrer has left for consultation with Mussolini. So for a day and a half we will be our own masters. We are going to make the most of this time and push our drives in the prearranged directions, so as to establish a basis for armistice negotiations.'

The following day he added:[13]

> 'Some days ago I tried desperately hard to get permission to commit the armor and motorized divisions of Kleist's right wing. At the time the plan was directly vetoed on at the top level. Now, after these forces have been racing off in a southeastern direction for several days and not meeting any organized resistance, they have to be reversed and ordered in a northwestern direction.
> **'It is indeed an effort to keep calm in the face of such dilettantish tinkering with the business of directing military operations** [author's emphasis].'

This chopping and changing became a frequent source of dispute between Hitler and Halder, as is noted with increasing exasperation in his diary entries during the opening phases of Operation *Barbarossa*, especially regarding the diversion of the panzer forces from Army Group Centre for the Kiev offensive.

Warlimont noted a particularly vociferous dispute between Hitler and Halder at which he was present during the Fuhrer's daily situation conference on 24 August 1942 concerning the defence of the Rzhev salient, which had resulted from the Soviet 1941 winter offensive and was a particularly difficult and costly position to hold:[14]

> 'Halder again urged that the Ninth Army, which was fighting at Rzhev, should be allowed the necessary freedom of manoeuvre and authorized to withdraw to a shorter line which could be held by its dwindling forces. This led to a collision which, only nine months after the departure of its Commander-in-Chief, was to deprive the German Army of its Chief of the General Staff who had been the real brain behind its victorious campaigns. The proposal ran counter to Hitler's cardinal principle of command and obviously annoyed him. "You always come here with the

The Generals' View of Hitler as Commander-in-Chief 143

same proposal" he threw back at Halder, "that of withdrawal", and then in the same breath proceeded to make a series of highly disparaging remarks which in this case even included the fighting troops. He ended his tirade with the words: "I expect my commanders to be as tough as the fighting troops." There was an atmosphere of extreme tension; Halder was now furious and he raised his voice as he replied: "I am tough enough, my Fuhrer. But out there brave men and young officers are falling in their thousands simply because their commanders are not allowed to make the only reasonable decision and have their hands tied behind their backs." Hitler recoiled, fixed Halder with a long malevolent stare and ground out hoarsely: "Colonel-General Halder, how dare you use language like that to me! Do you think you can teach me what the man at the front is thinking? What do you know about what goes on at the front? Where were you in the First World War? And you try to pretend that to me that I don't understand what it's like at the front. I won't stand that! It's outrageous!"

'… It was now clear that the final breach between these two men, who were as different as chalk from cheese, could not be far off.'

It is noteworthy that Hitler did not attempt in his reply to address the purely military question raised by Halder. Even a cursory examination of a map setting out the dispositions of the German forces at the time will lead to the conclusion that Halder was correct in his view. Hitler ultimately could not stand the criticism of his operations, both overt and implied, in the observations and recommendations which Halder made. He was therefore dismissed with every mark of opprobrium and without any recognition of the outstanding contributions he had made during the victorious Western campaigns and the planning of *Barbarossa*. Halder and his wife were imprisoned in concentration camps after the 20 July plot to assassinate Hitler without any evidence of his involvement, such was the hostility to him among the sycophantic upper echelons of the Nazi leadership because of his disagreements with the Fuhrer.

Halder gave a scathing review of Hitler's performance in the role of Supreme Commander:[15]

'In the last phases of the tragedy, Nazi Party Offices formed military formations out of children and old men. These were barely equipped with weapons, were without communications equipment, almost without supplies. But with high-sounding orders they were thrown against a well-equipped enemy and given tasks for which even elite formations in full battle order had proven inadequate. **Is this a military genius at**

work? Or is it rather a sign of insanity that a man should think himself capable of making up for military training and weapons by Party Fanaticism, and the requirements of organisation by the power of his will? [author's emphasis]'

After Halder was relieved of his position, Hitler said to him:[16]

> 'In view of the tasks now facing the Army, rather than relying on technical competence, it must be inspired by the fervour of belief in National Socialism.'

This statement came from someone who claimed that he knew what the men at the front wanted. However, what they actually wanted above all else was to go home, not be sacrificed on the altar of Hitler's overweening arrogance and ego, or due to the programme of a party to which most of them did not belong, whose aims most did not in any event support, particularly with respect to aggressive warfare.

Although he was conscious of his duty to the men of the German Army, Halder equally could not abide working any longer with Hitler and was no doubt relieved not to have to do so any longer.[17]

Colonel General Kurt Zeitzler

Zeitzler had the misfortune to be appointed as Chief of the Army General Staff in September 1942, just before the disaster at Stalingrad. Upon taking up his duties, he observed that 'Hitler trusted no-one'.[18] He also noted that 'in the atmosphere which thus prevailed at Supreme Headquarters, any frank and objective discussion of the situation was impossible'.[19]

Once he had analysed the position of the German forces on the Eastern Front, Zeitzler warned Hitler on numerous occasions of the danger associated with the use of Romanian, Hungarian and Italian armies to cover the extended flank north of Stalingrad, correctly predicting where the Red Army's attack would occur. Hitler ignored his warnings, as he had ignored those of Halder and everyone else.

After the Red Army attack on the allied armies to the north of Stalingrad occurred on 19 November, with the obvious aim of cutting off the German forces in and around the city on the Volga, Zeitzler tried repeatedly to obtain Hitler's consent to order the Sixth Army to break out from its encirclement, saying to him:[20]

'There is, therefore, only one possible solution. You must immediately order the Stalingrad army to turn about and attack westwards. This will save the Sixth Army from encirclement, will inflict great damage on the Russian armies that have broken through, and will enable us to use the Sixth Army in building a new front to the west.

'Hitler now lost all self-control. He crashed his fist down on the table shouting: "I won't leave the Volga! I won't go back from the Volga!"'

Apart from cutting off and destroying the German forces in Stalingrad, disastrous as that was, the Soviet offensive had wider strategic aims. Once they had established the cordon around Stalingrad and while the catastrophe was unfolding for the Sixth Army, the Red Army was also attacking towards the vital German position at Rostov, well in the rear of Stalingrad, placing in peril the whole of Army Group A in the Caucasus as well as the forces in Stalingrad and those attempting to reform a defensive line to the west. Hitler had sent Army Group A into the Caucasus to secure the oil resources of the Baku and Caspian Sea region as part of the 1942 offensive. The operation had begun promisingly, but due to problems with supplying the lengthening front line (which Hitler had been warned would occur prior to the offensive beginning) and the increasing resistance of the Red Army, it had stalled. When this occurred, Hitler had decided to send Jodl to Army Group A commander Field Marshal Wilhelm List's headquarters with imperative orders to get the offensive moving again. This precipitated a serious dispute between Jodl and the Fuhrer. When he returned from List's headquarters, Jodl told Hitler that he agreed with List's view of the situation and that he had only been following Hitler's orders which had led to the offensive stalling. Jodl described Hitler's reaction in his testimony at Nuremberg:[21]

'Never in my life did I experience such an outbreak of rage from any human being.'

This was one of the few times that Jodl disagreed with Hitler before an audience, and because of the vociferous reaction it provoked was probably the reason he never did so again. Nevertheless, Hitler sacked List and also intended to sack both Jodl and Keitel from their positions, but changed his mind as the Stalingrad crisis developed, which meant he had to keep them at their posts.

Zeitzler (and all of Hitler's responsible military advisers) realized that the position of Army Group A in the Caucasus was extremely perilous and urged the Fuhrer to order its withdrawal to avoid another disastrous encirclement on the same lines as Stalingrad. Zeitzler recalled:[22]

> 'I made a second attempt to secure Hitler's authorization for an evacuation of the Caucasus. He refused to listen then or on many other occasions … Finally, towards the end of December, he appeared to give way. I was alone with him. I described the situation in the south, and I ended with the words: "Unless you order a withdrawal from the Caucasus now, we shall soon have another Stalingrad on our hands."'

Hitler at last allowed Zeitzler to order the withdrawal. However, when Zeitzler returned to his headquarters there was a message to call the Fuhrer. In the meantime, Hitler had decided not to allow the withdrawal. Based on previous experience, Zeitzler had expected this would happen and had already issued the orders to move back, which Hitler then decided not to countermand. Thus, by the narrowest of margins, Army Group A was saved from the same fate as the Sixth Army in Stalingrad, and the whole German Army on the Eastern Front were saved from a complete and irreparable disaster.

Several months later, after a German recovery on the Eastern Front, Zeitzler was instrumental in planning and implementing Operation *Citadel*, the attempt to destroy the Red Army forces in the Kursk salient in July 1943. He was fully supportive of Field Marshal Erich von Manstein's view that an operation be launched before the Red Army had time to recover from their efforts during the preceding winter campaign and the reverses they had suffered at Belgorod and Kharkov, which had been retaken in a riposte by the forces of Army Group South commanded by Manstein. Manstein told Hitler in writing that he favoured waiting for the Soviets to attack, as he felt was inevitable, and then to use the concentrated power of the German panzers to deal a crushing blow 'on the backhand'. Hitler, however, decided to attack first and not to wait for the Soviets to move, a decision which Zeitzler supported. In an effort to build up German forces and add weight to the attack at Kursk, the Fuhrer delayed its commencement for three months longer than Manstein had stipulated was the latest date that the circumstances would be favourable for a German riposte. This additional time, however, also gave the Red Army longer to prepare its defences and reinforce its own armies. The eventual German attack was repulsed with heavy casualties and the Red Army then went over to the offensive both north and south of the Kursk positions. The Germans had suffered losses which they could not replace, allowing the Red Army to gain the initiative for the rest of the war. After the Kursk attack was defeated, Hitler was heard to say that 'this is the last time I will listen to the council [sic] of my general staff'.[23]

Zeitzler made the following general observation regarding Hitler:[24]

> 'Hitler never once admitted that he himself was to blame or that he might have made a faulty appreciation of the situation. To listen to him, he was always and invariably right. If his plans miscarried, it was always due either to unpredictable and incalculable factors beyond his control or to the inefficiency or worse of those charged with the execution of the orders he had signed.'

This observation applied to Hitler's attitude at all times during the war, and was the single most dominant factor in his character – he believed he was never wrong, and this belief formed the basis of all his commands. That the Fuhrer could still think himself infallible after all the instances during the war when his plans went awry or led to disastrous results illustrates the extent of his arrogance and hubris. Zeitzler did not formally retire from his position as Chief of the Army General Staff, but apparently suffered a nervous breakdown in July 1944, after which he went on medical leave for the rest of the war.

Colonel General Heinz Guderian
Guderian is probably the most famous of the German generals with respect to the development of the role and strategy for the tank forces. During the interwar period, he wrote several papers for German military publications and a book entitled *Achtung – Panzer* about the role and composition of armoured units, all of which were widely read and influential. He was the German commander whom Manstein stated was operationally most responsible for the successful implementation of his plan for the 1940 victory over France and Britain, and was at the forefront of the victories of Army Group Centre during the opening stages of Operation *Barbarossa* and the offensive Hitler ordered at Kiev in 1941. He also commanded the Second Panzer Army during Operation *Typhoon*, the last attempt to take Moscow before the Soviet counter-offensive which commenced on 6 December 1941. He was then relieved of his command despite his successes after a dispute with the commander of the Fourth Army, Field Marshal Gunther von Kluge.

Guderian was made Chief of the Army General Staff on 21 July 1944, Zeitzler having left the role as a result of stress brought on by working with Hitler and the insoluble problems which had to be dealt with after the Allied invasion of Normandy and the catastrophic situation on the Eastern Front after the destruction of Army Group Centre. Because of the separation of the theatres of war which Hitler imposed, Guderian was then only operationally responsible for the Eastern Front. He had many occasions during his tenure at the OKH – and also in previous commands and during his time as Inspector General of Panzer Troops – to observe Hitler and his technique of military command. His conclusions are noted in a discussion relating to Hitler in his book *Panzer Leader*:

> 'His most outstanding quality was his will power. By the exercise of his will he compelled men to follow him. This power of this worked by means of suggestion and, indeed, its effect on many men was almost hypnotic. I have frequently observed such cases. **At OKW almost nobody contradicted him; the men there were either in a state of permanent hypnosis, like Keitel, or of resigned acquiescence like Jodl** [author's emphasis].'[25]

Guderian makes many operational references in his book to decisions of Hitler's, but his summary of how the Fuhrer made his plans, compared to how he carried them out, is most interesting:

> 'The Western Campaign showed another facet of Hitler's character. Hitler made his plans with great boldness. Norway was a courageous undertaking, as was the armoured break-through at Sedan. In both these cases he gave his approval for the boldest proposals. But when, in the execution of those plans, he was confronted by the first difficulty – a contrast to his unshakeable pertinacity when faced by political trouble – he would give in, **perhaps because he was instinctively aware of his lack of talent in the field of military science** [author's emphasis].'[26]

He states with great clarity the situation which pertained once the defeat of the USSR had not been achieved in 1941, when Hitler also surprisingly declared war on the United States:

> 'The Russian war soon showed the limitations of Germany's strength. But Hitler did not conclude from this that he must either break off the undertaking or at least choose more modest objectives; on the contrary, he plunged in to the unlimited. He was determined, by means of reckless violence, to force defeat upon the Russians. With incomprehensible blindness he was simultaneously courting war with the United States. … **between that and actual, open warfare there might have lain a very long road had Hitler's overweening arrogance not closed it** [author's emphasis].'[27]

His comments on Hitler's strategy in the winter of 1941 are undoubtedly correct, as was shown by many examples in Volume 2 of this work, and could actually be applied with equal validity to any of his operations:

> '**Hitler's strategy, lacking in consistency, and subject to continual vacillation in its execution** [author's emphasis], had crashed. From now on ruthlessly harsh treatment of his own troops was to make up for a failure of capability on the part of the controlling mind. For a time this proved successful. But in the long run it was not enough simply to remind his soldiers of the sacrifices made by Frederick the Great's Grenadiers on the orders of that powerful king and commander.'[28]

Guderian's summary of the Fuhrer's fanaticism is reflected in Hitler's own words. This was his credo from long before he admitted defeat, until the end of his dictatorship in the ruins of the Reichstag in Berlin:

> 'With a fanatic's intensity he grasped at every straw which he imagined might save him and his work from destruction. His entire and very great will power was devoted to this one idea which was now all that preoccupied him – "never to give in, never to surrender."'[29]

It is clear that Guderian did not hold Hitler in high regard as a military commander, his analysis going straight to the substance of the problems which he exhibited.

The three wartime Chiefs of the Army General Staff who had to work with Hitler were quite different, but each was an extremely competent commander of the first rank. The fact that all three of them could not work with Hitler and had very low opinions of his military ability is enough to establish beyond doubt that he was unfit to fill the position which he aspired to above all others and so unsuccessfully carried out, that of the world-conquering warlord.

The field commanders

This section contains the views on Hitler's military competence of those who I believe were the most important field commanders in the German Army who left written accounts of the subject or gave interviews which were later published.

Field Marshal Gerd von Rundstedt

Von Rundstedt has the distinction of being the most sacked and reinstated of all Hitler's senior commanders. He was and still is acknowledged as being in the first rank of commanders of both sides during the war. He held important command positions in every one of the major campaigns of the war, from Poland to the Ardennes – although he completely disowned the latter offensive in 1944, which was undertaken against his advice and virtually without his involvement. He therefore had many instances of being in direct command relationships with Hitler and the senior personnel of the OKW. Rundstedt is on record as having disagreed with the following major decisions made by Hitler:

- The decision to halt General Ewald von Kleist's armour before it cut off the British Expeditionary Force from Dunkirk.
- The decision to attack the USSR.
- The strategy used in the attack on the USSR.
- The decision to attack at Rostov, which led to his first dismissal on 1 December 1941.
- The strategy for the defence of France in 1944.
- The conduct of the Normandy campaign.
- The Ardennes offensive in 1944.

Each of these differences is discussed in detail in Volumes 1 and 2 of this work. Such a catalogue of disagreements shows beyond doubt that Rundstedt had significant reservations concerning Hitler's conduct of the war, both on the strategic and operational levels. If any further proof is needed, it is provided by Rundstedt's reaction upon receiving Hitler's plan for the Ardennes offensive:[30]

> 'I was staggered. Hitler had not consulted me about its possibilities. It was obvious to me that **the available forces were far too small for such an extremely ambitious plan** [author's emphasis]. Model [Field Marshal Walter Model, commander of Army Group B] took the same view of it as I did. In fact, no soldier believed that the aim of reaching Antwerp was really practicable. **But I knew by now it was useless to protest to Hitler about the possibility of anything** [author's emphasis].'

The last sentence succinctly encapsulates Rundstedt's contempt for Hitler's military abilities. He knew that Hitler did not understand the operational possibilities of military undertakings and was completely unrealistic in his expectations and views, and realized that it was useless to try to change his mind in these respects.

Field Marshal Eric von Manstein

Von Manstein is acknowledged as being at the very apex of the commanders on both sides of the war. His strategy relating to the 1940 campaign in France and the Low Countries was the main reason for its success, as Guderian and others have acknowledged. His observations relating to the partial victory which it achieved are therefore extremely instructive:[31]

> 'The success in Northern Belgium was not as complete as it might have been. The enemy succeeded, according to Churchill's figures, in evacuating 338,226 men (26,176 of them French) from Dunkirk, though they lost all their heavy weapons and equipment in the process. **This successful evacuation must be attributed to the intervention of Hitler** [author's emphasis], who twice stopped the onward sweep of our armour – once during its advance to the coast and again outside Dunkirk.
>
> 'Three different reasons have been given for the latter order, **the true effect of which was to throw a golden bridge across the Channel for the British Army** [author's emphasis].
>
> '… **Whatever the answer may be, Dunkirk was one of Hitler's most decisive mistakes** [author's emphasis]. It hampered him in attempting the invasion of Britain and subsequently enabled the British to fight in Africa and Italy.'

There can be no doubt that this statement is correct. If anything, Manstein understates the importance of the mistake, for if Britain had been eliminated from the war in 1940, either by conquest or negotiation, the history of the world would have been significantly different.

During Operation *Barbarossa* and the remainder of the war in the USSR, Manstein commanded some of the most important operations carried out, both offensive and defensive. His feat in taking Sevastopol and the Crimea led to his promotion to field marshal, and Hitler selected him to command the relief force intended to save the Sixth Army at Stalingrad. He was then given command of Army Group South and the major formations involved in the *Citadel* offensive in the summer of 1943. He was therefore in contact with Hitler on an almost daily basis for more than two-and-a-half years until he was relieved, and thus fully able to form a considered view as to Hitler's military command abilities. He devoted a whole chapter to this in his book *Lost Victories*, which included the following:[32]

> 'While Hitler may have had an eye for tactical opportunity and could quickly seize a chance when it was offered to him, **he still lacked the**

ability to assess the prerequisites and practicability of a plan of operations. He failed to understand that the objectives and ultimate scope of an operation must be in direct proportion to the time and forces needed to carry it out – to say nothing of the possibilities of supply [author's emphasis]. He did not – or would not – realize that any long range offensive operation calls for a steady build-up of troops over and above those committed to the original assault. All this was brought out in striking clarity in the planning and execution of the 1942 summer offensive. Another example was the fantastic idea he disclosed to me in autumn of 1942 of driving through the Caucasus to the Near East and India with a motorized army group.'

These comments are undoubtedly valid. The shortcomings he mentions are present in every one of the operations which Hitler controlled after taking direct command of the German Army. Manstein does not include the Normandy campaign or the Ardennes offensive because he did not take part in them, but the same comments could certainly be made with respect to them.

Manstein also revealed his view of Hitler's command ability by trying to convince him to give up his operational command of the army and hand it over to someone with the requisite ability. Unsurprisingly, Hitler did not agree to his suggestions:[33]

'I made no less than three attempts, in the interest of a more rational conduct of the war, to persuade Hitler to accept some modification of the Supreme Command. **From no other quarter, as far as I know, was the inadequacy of his military leadership ever put to him quite so bluntly** [author's emphasis].'

Ultimately, Hitler decided that he did not need Manstein's ability at the time for the following reason:[34]

'[T]he time for grand-style operations in the east, for which I had been particularly qualified, was now past. **All that counted now, he said, was to cling stubbornly to what we held** [author's emphasis].'

Such was the rationale Hitler gave for dispensing with the services of his best operational commander. It was, of course, a smoke screen to mask the real reasons, which were that he had a personal aversion to Manstein, as is recorded in Volumes 1 and 2 of this work, and that Manstein was too independent for Goering and Himmler's liking.

The Generals' View of Hitler as Commander-in-Chief 153

At the trial of the major war criminals at Nuremberg, Manstein was called as a witness and was asked about the resistance by the military leadership to Hitler:[35]

> 'DR LATERNSER: Do you know, Field Marshal, whether other military leaders, too, had differences with Hitler?
>
> 'VON MANSTEIN: These differences were, no doubt, very numerous. That becomes apparent from the following facts alone:
>
> 'Of 17 Field Marshals who were members of the Army, 10 were sent home during the war and 3 lost their lives as a result of 20 July. Only one Field Marshal managed to get through the war and keep his position as Field Marshal. Of 36 Generalobersten, 18 were sent home and 5 died as a result of 20 July or were dishonourably discharged. Only 3 Generalobersten survived the war in their positions.'

These figures indicate the depth of the resistance to Hitler by the senior army commanders. They can only have resulted from a deep-seated aversion to both the substance and the methods behind Hitler's *modus operandi* of command. That Hitler could not appreciate that his own survival depended on having the willing co-operation of the commanders of the army in his undertakings, and that therefore he had to obtain their best contributions to his operations, further illustrates the depth of his arrogance, obstinacy and hubris.

Field Marshal Ewald von Kleist

Von Kleist was one of the most important and effective commanders during the 1940 campaign in France and the 1942 offensive in the Caucasus. He was promoted to field marshal after successfully evacuating the Caucasus following the disaster at Stalingrad, which prevented the Red Army from surrounding Army Group A. He was relieved by Hitler on the same day as Manstein and never used in command again. He related in an interview with US Army psychiatrist Leon Goldensohn on 25 June 1946, while waiting to give evidence as a witness at the Nuremberg trials, that it was because of Hitler's order to halt his panzer group before cutting the British off and preventing them from entering Dunkirk in May 1940 that they were able to escape across the Channel:[36]

> 'It was nonsense – those orders of Hitler's in those days. We could have wiped out the British Army completely or taken the whole army captive if it wasn't for the stupid order of Hitler.'

Goldensohn continued in his report of the same interview:[37]

> 'What did Kleist think of Hitler during the last few years? "I think that Hitler was more of a problem for a psychiatrist than for a general."'

The psychiatrist added:[38]

> 'I asked Kleist what occasioned his retirement at that time. "Well, on December 1 1943, I told Hitler to give up his supreme command. On March 29, 1944, I again had a very severe argument with Hitler ... I really think that the reason for my going home at that time was that I always told Hitler my frank opinions."'

These comments reveal the depth of Kleist's negative views with respect to Hitler's command abilities and appropriateness as Supreme Commander.

Field Marshal Erwin Rommel

Rommel's spectacular rise in the ranks of the army hierarchy was due to Hitler's recognition of him as a determined, resourceful and energetic leader. These characteristics had all been evident during the First World War, when he was awarded the *Pour le Mérite*, the highest award for bravery under the Kaiser's regime, and was nominated for it a second time.

Rommel's command of the 7th Panzer Division during the 1940 campaign in France received high praise, the division's tanks and other units always being in the vanguard of the offensive due to his energetic leadership. When Hitler was looking for a commander of the corps he was sending to Africa to shore up the Italian position, his choice of Rommel was vindicated by his inspired leadership. However, Rommel's experience in Africa was ultimately a dispiriting and deeply disillusioning one, causing him to view the poor leadership of the German war effort in a realistic manner and deeply embittering him because of the way his troops were treated by the high command.

Although deservedly famous for his African command, Rommel's most important role was in the defence of France. He was given command of the vital sectors covered by Army Group B, consisting of the Fifteenth and Seventh Armies, which were in the Pas-de-Calais and Normandy areas where the Germans thought that the Allies would be most likely to invade. He was nominally under the command of Field Marshal von Rundstedt, the Commander-in-Chief West (OB West), with whom he developed a good working relationship, even though they did not agree on the best strategy to defend France against invasion. Despite the pair's seniority and successful experience in operational command, ultimately it was Hitler who decided what the strategy would be, just as he decided every other aspect of the war effort. The strategy which the Fuhrer opted for was a compromise of the views of Rundstedt and Rommel, which ended up having the virtues of neither and restricted the operational employment of the reserves available to Rundstedt so that they could not be committed without Hitler's express permission. Additionally, the reserves were scattered rather than being close to the likely invasion sites, as Rommel had repeatedly stressed to Hitler was critically important so that they could be employed without delay when the Allies landed.

Hitler's strategy and operational command of the defence of Normandy led to fundamental changes in the view of the senior commanders of the German armies in the west regarding the likelihood of success in defeating the invasion, or even the chance of a stalemate leading to reasonable peace terms. Although Rundstedt was replaced by Field Marshal von Kluge, who had been one of Hitler's most loyal and redoubtable commanders on the Eastern Front, he too came to the view that an Allied victory was inevitable. This being the case, von Kluge agreed with Rommel that political action should be taken by Hitler to end the war, and if the Fuhrer would not do so then the army commanders had to take the necessary action to 'open the west front'.[39]

The question of Rommel's view of Hitler's command abilities can be answered easily and comprehensively by reference to the memorandum which he sent to Hitler on 3 July 1944[40] relating to the campaign in Normandy, which because of its importance is reproduced in summary as Appendix 1 at the end of this book.

This memorandum highlights a catalogue of incompetence and negligence of breathtaking proportions, and could only have been prepared in an attempt to convince Hitler that he should either give someone else the command of the German Army or dramatically change his *modus operandi*. Had any German general been guilty of such a record of incompetence, there is little doubt as to the judgement which Hitler would have arrived at with respect to him. The last point of the memorandum, criticizing the channels of command, must have been particularly galling to Hitler, Keitel and Jodl, who had tried but lamentably failed to provide unity of command. Little more can be added except to say that had Hitler accepted Rommel's proposed deployments, the invading Allied forces would certainly have encountered greater difficulties. In almost every case, Rommel's proposals would have led to German formations being better positioned to defend Normandy very early in the campaign, with the initial landings facing a much more severe test as they strove to secure a beachhead.

The injuries Rommel suffered on 17 July 1944 in a strafing attack by an Allied aircraft while he was returning from one of his many visits to the front meant that his role and participation in Operation *Valkyrie*, the plot to kill the Fuhrer, is still a matter of conjecture. However, if he had not been injured and had issued orders for the Western Front to be opened to allow the Allied forces to move through the German defences, it seems likely that he would have been obeyed, although what would have resulted from such an order can only be conjecture. As it was, Germany's fate was to be the complete destruction which Hitler wished for and decreed during the closing months of the Reich once he realized defeat was unavoidable.[41]

Field Marshal Albert Kesselring

Field Marshal Kesselring was involved in most of the campaigns of the war, either as a Luftwaffe Luftflotte commander or an army group commander. He finished the war as the German Army's Commander-in-Chief West, and had many meetings with Hitler from its beginning to its end. He also worked with the senior officers at the OKW and most of the leading operational commanders of the Wehrmacht. Kesselring was one of Hitler's favourite commanders, probably because he had a naturally optimistic view of operations; his nickname was 'smiling Albert'. However, he was a very shrewd and determined commander, conducting the prolonged and costly defence of the Italian peninsula with great circumspection.

Kesselring summed up the structure Hitler created and the methods he used to command the Wehrmacht in his Book *A Soldier's Record*:[42]

> 'The system adopted by Hitler of setting up organizations working on parallel lines, that is, independent of each other but active in the same field, can only be understood from the standpoint of a dictator filled with mistrust of everybody. It was fatal to the conduct of a war, the main disadvantages being mutual distrust between the army and the SS, between the Administration and the party, etc., different rules of precedence, and independent spheres of jurisdiction, etc.
>
> 'In a war which demands a unified authority and economic structure, excrescences such as the party offices were bound in some way at some time or another to be injurious. **If anyone wanted to undermine the structure of the armed forces of a nation he could not do better than apply the organization, or rather the disorganization, beloved of Hitler** [author's emphasis].'

It is impossible to disagree with this observation. Such a system could only be created by a person who was completely unaware of the most basic requirements of a military command structure.

General Hasso von Manteuffel

Manteuffel was one of the younger generals whom Hitler identified as deserving rapid promotion. Although he was of a noble background, his operational competence and direct manner made him just the type of commander Hitler preferred to advance. Manteuffel distinguished himself during the latter stages of the African campaign and was given command of the 7th Panzer Division, and subsequently in February 1944 the elite Grossdeutschland Division, both on the Eastern Front. His most important role, however, was as the commander of Fifth Panzer Army in the Ardennes offensive in December 1944. He realized from the outset that the attack had little chance of succeeding, agreeing with Rundstedt's assessment that the forces were too weak to attain the objectives specified. Manteuffel believed that it was obvious the offensive had failed by 24 December, just eight days after its launch:[43]

> 'It was now the urgent wish of the senior commanders that all our attacks be discontinued at once and the troops withdrawn from the deep salient which we had created. This desire was based on our appreciation of the situation as it existed on December 29th.'

Hitler thought otherwise and did not authorize any withdrawal until 3 January 1945, which only meant that the resulting German casualties were much higher. Manteuffel concluded:[44]

> 'There can be no question that the rigid adherence to the original objective was a mistake, as was the organization and commitment of our forces. The Supreme Command, out of touch with conditions at the front and displaying an increased and **misplaced obstinacy in its insistence that its orders be carried out to the letter, no longer displayed the necessary flexibility in adjusting operations to the situation as it developed. The ultimate fault was Hitler's** [author's emphasis].'

These comments could have been made – and often were by the other commanders concerned – regarding any of the operations which Hitler controlled after he assumed the role of Commander-in-Chief of the Army. Manteuffel summarized his view of Hitler's military capabilities in an interview with Basil Liddell Hart, which was published in the latter's book *The Other Side of the Hill*.[45]

> 'Hitler had read a lot of military literature, and was also fond of listening to military lectures. In this way, coupled with his personal experience of the last war as an ordinary soldier, he had gained a very good knowledge of the lower level of warfare – the properties of the different weapons; the effect of ground and weather; the mentality and morale of the troops. He was particularly good at gauging how the troops felt. I found I was hardly ever in disagreement with his view when discussing such matters. On the other hand he had no idea of the higher strategical and tactical combinations. **He had a good grasp of how a single division moved and fought, but he did not understand how armies operated** [author's emphasis].'

Added to Hitler's temperamental and other idiosyncratic shortcomings, Manteuffel's analysis shows conclusively that Hitler was simply not equipped to command the German Army operationally, and it was thus not surprising that his attempts at doing so led to utter disaster.

SS General Josef 'Sepp' Dietrich

'Sepp' Dietrich was one of Hitler's longest-standing followers, having been in the same regiment as him during the First World War. He had also been one of Hitler's chauffeurs. Despite having no relevant military training, Hitler promoted Dietrich to the most senior rank in the Waffen-SS, that of Oberst-Gruppenführer, equivalent to colonel general in the German Army. He was appointed to several important operational commands, most notably the Sixth SS-Panzer Army in the 1944 Ardennes offensive, which Hitler intended to have the decisive role in defeating the British and taking Antwerp. Dietrich commented on the offensive shortly after the war:[46]

> 'All I had to do was cross a river, capture Brussels and then go on and take the port of Antwerp. And all this in December, January and February, the worst three months of the year; through the Ardennes where snow was waist deep and there wasn't room to deploy four tanks abreast, let alone six armoured divisions; when it didn't get light until eight in the morning and was dark again at four in the afternoon and my tanks can't fight at night; with divisions that had just been reformed and were composed chiefly of raw untrained recruits.'

Dietrich thus maintained a realistic view of the difficulty of his assignment and did not indulge in the wishful thinking of those in the OKW who had created the plan for the offensive.

After Hitler's final offensive in Hungary failed in March 1945, he ordered that the SS divisions involved as part of Dietrich's Sixth Panzer Army – one of which was the 1st SS-Panzer Division, Leibstandarte SS Adolf Hitler (the Fuhrer's personal bodyguard) – be stripped of their divisional identity arm bands, which was the greatest military dishonour he could impose, for failing in their duty to him. Albert Speer recalled that Dietrich later told him:[47]

> "'You know" he concluded "Hitler was crazy for a long time. He simply let his best soldiers dash into the fire.'"

Coming from someone who had known Hitler for so long, it is hard to dispute such a judgement.

Reichsmarschall Hermann Goering

Goering was the highest-ranking officer in the Wehrmacht by reason of his rank as Reichsmarschall, which was plainly a reward for his loyalty and Hitler's wish to have the command of the Luftwaffe in the hands of a person he could unreservedly trust, rather than for his abilities. He was also the second person politically in the Nazi state for almost its entire duration and Hitler's designated successor in the event of his death. During the war, he lost influence with Hitler because of the Luftwaffe's failures, particularly the inability to supply the Sixth Army at Stalingrad by air and to defend Germany against the Allied strategic bombing offensive. At the very end of the war, the Fuhrer dismissed him from all his offices on 23 April 1945 as the result of an intrigue by Hitler's power-obsessed Party Secretary, Martin Bormann. Goering probably was Hitler's most loyal lieutenant, having been his follower since 1921 when he met him after an early Nazi Party rally. When he heard of Hitler's suicide, he told his wife that his greatest regret was that he would never be able to tell the Fuhrer that he had stayed loyal to him right to the end.

During the war, Goering issued many orders to the Luftwaffe's senior commanders with which they disagreed strenuously. These orders related to, amongst other matters, the tactics in the Battle of Britain, the attack on the Soviet Union and the use of the Me 262 jet. He also ordered the deployment of the Luftwaffe to support the ground forces in the defence of Normandy and in the Ardennes offensive, which on both occasions consumed the reserve of fighter aircraft which General Adolf Galland had carefully built up for a concentrated strike against the Allied bomber fleets. The senior officers of the Luftwaffe realized that these orders ultimately emanated from Hitler but expected that Goering would stand up for the correct military decisions to be taken, and were incensed at him for, in their view, failing to do so. They did not realize that on many occasions Goering did try to make Hitler see reason with such matters, but to no effect. During an interview in May 1945 with one of the most senior US air commanders, General Carl Spaatz, Goering made comments relating to these decisions by the Fuhrer:[48]

> 'Spaatz: Would you tell us something [of] the organisation of the Luftwaffe and the plans, especially the factors that went into the non-fulfilment of those plans?
>
> 'Goering: In the early years when I had supreme command of the Luftwaffe, I had definite plans, but in 1940 Hitler began to interfere, taking air fleets away from our planned operations. That was the beginning of the breakdown of the Luftwaffe efficiency.
>
> '...
>
> 'Goering: ... I was forced by Hitler to divert air forces to the east (which I always opposed). Only the diversion of the Luftwaffe to the Russian front saved England.
>
> '... I wanted to establish whether you failed to build the big bombers because you did not believe in strategic air power or because your productivity capacity was restricted to the production of tactical aircraft for the Russian campaign.
>
> 'Goering: No, I always believed in strategic use of air power. I built the Luftwaffe as the finest bomber fleet, only to see it wasted on Stalingrad. My beautiful bomber fleet was used up in transporting munitions and supplies to the army of 200,00 [sic] at Stalingrad. I always was against the Russian campaign.'

He was also interviewed by a psychiatrist acting on behalf of the tribunal during the Nuremberg trials on 15 March 1946 and stated:[49]

> 'Attack on Russia? Hitler decided that. I thought it was stupid because I believed that we first had to defeat England. Also we had to take Gibraltar. Franco was afraid to let us have it but if we had brought England to nothingness by bombing, Franco would have been agreeable. After that I had no objection – that is after the defeat of England – to attacking Russia. I felt strongly the air force was not prepared. But Hitler felt the Russian campaign would be short and then we could finish the English campaign.'

These extracts show that Goering understood that Hitler's strategy to attack the USSR and his orders relating to the deployment of the Luftwaffe entailed great risk, and that the Luftwaffe was not ready to undertake the task. He also realized that committing Germany to war with the Soviet Union before Britain was defeated was not necessary, but that destroying Britain's Mediterranean position was required before attacking the USSR. This confirms the evidence which he and Field Marshal Milch gave at Nuremberg and also the comments he made at the time relating to Operation *Barbarossa*.

Yet these observations ignore the impact of his advice to Hitler concerning the use of the Luftwaffe to supply the trapped Sixth Army at Stalingrad and in the attempt to annihilate the BEF in 1940. They are thus also self-serving to a significant degree. They do, however, show the degree of Goering's subservience to Hitler in that he did not express any misgivings relating to the orders to his subordinate Luftwaffe commanders, but supported the Fuhrer's instructions. In doing so, he may have been loyal but this did not serve Germany's best interests or assist in winning the war.

Conclusions

The views of the most senior and capable operational commanders of the German Army who had to carry out Hitler's orders show that the pattern of the Fuhrer's modus operandi when operational commander-in-chief was consistent throughout his time in the role. After he fired Field Marshal von Brauchitsch, Hitler's assumption of the operational command of the Army was seen as disastrous by almost all the most senior commanders. The only exception to this view was Jodl, whose prior operational experience was negligible and whose contribution to the loss of the war was reflected in the support he gave to Hitler during the Stalingrad operation and the defence of Normandy, both of which helped to precipitate the disasters suffered by the Germans in those campaigns.

The overwhelming conclusion, therefore, is that the German generals were aware of the disastrous shortcomings of Hitler as commander-in-chief of the ground forces but could do nothing to prevent him exercising command. This is evidenced by the result of the only serious attempt at resistance during the war by the military, the attempted coup on 20 July, 1944, which was, however, only one of many attempts made on his life. The senior generals' views lead to the following conclusions:

1. The most senior commanders of the German Army were overwhelmingly of the view that Hitler's experience and abilities were not adequate for his

exercise of operational command. Not only was this the case, but the Fuhrer was also temperamentally completely unfit to be operational commander. He did not have the patience to wait until an offensive unfolded to determine what steps were required, instead continuously chopping and changing the forces and objectives of operations, thereby upsetting timetables and supply arrangements.

2. He did not understand or did not care about the complications involved in the supply of armies and would not listen to the responsible members of the General Staff when they tried to explain how these affected the potential of the operations he planned. This was particularly apparent in the case of the Stalingrad offensive, when he was specifically told by the Quartermaster General of the Germany Army that there would be supply problems involved in the offensive Hitler planned. That Hitler went ahead anyway without any alteration to the plan is typical of his amateurish approach to military command.

3. The proof that these observations are correct is to be found in the egregious errors committed by Hitler in the most important campaigns of the war. These include the decision to halt von Kleist's armour before Dunkirk, the changes he insisted upon in the execution of the plan for Operation *Barbarossa*, the obvious weaknesses in the plan of the 1942 offensive which resulted in the Stalingrad disaster, the delays he imposed in the action proposed by Manstein relating to the 1943 Kursk offensive, his interference in the defence of Normandy – specifically not deploying the Fifteenth Army from the Pas-de-Calais when it was obvious that this was the only reserve which could reach the battlefield in time to affect the defence – and the insistence on rigid defence rather than flexible tactics which had been impressed upon him since 1941 by Manstein, Kluge, Kleist, Model and Rundstedt, among others. These flexible tactics had been shown to work in the instances when Hitler finally relented and let the field commanders use them. Particularly successful and important examples of this were Manstein's initial retreat during the Red Army's early 1943 offensive, when he was able to retake Kharkov and Belgorod, and Kleist's successful retreat from the Caucasus, due to which he was able to save the great majority of the troops and equipment from what would otherwise have been another Stalingrad, precipitating the defeat of the Germans in 1943.

4. The utterly unrealistic nature of the Ardennes offensive was pointed out to Hitler as soon as the commanders responsible for its undertaking saw his plan. Rundstedt and Model both told Hitler and Jodl that the offensive did not have a chance of reaching its objectives. The truth was that the offensive had no real military objective, being a last desperate attempt by

the Fuhrer to extend the time he had in power in the hope that the alliance against him would fall apart and he would be left to resume his war against the Red Army with no distractions from the Western Allies. That this is the case is obvious from the recorded comments he made at the time to the army and operational commanders chosen for the offensive.

5. Hitler's insistence on the offensive in Hungary and operations in Austria during March 1945 rather than concentrating all the mobile forces he could to defend the Red Army's path to Berlin is another example, among many, of the completely misguided operations he insisted upon, making the task of defending Germany even more difficult than it would otherwise have been. In effect, these orders made the defence of Germany impossible.

The following words of General Leo Geyr von Schweppenburg, an experiencd panzer corps and army commander, could hardly be more apposite:[50]

'Authority to make strategic decisions passed from seasoned soldiers, well experienced in the special conditions of their respective theatres of war, to a self-complacent and pretentious dilettante, and was affected by a combination of influences. In comparison to this system, the former Vienna Court and War Council [the body directing the armies of the Habsburg Empire from the sixteenth century onwards] was a respectable and reasonable command unit.'

In view of the examples given in the volumes of this work, these words do not seem to the author to be an exaggeration.

Chapter 5

The Effect on German Military Operations of the Attempted Assassination and Coup of 20 July 1944

From the beginning of Hitler's rule in 1933 there had been senior members of the Wehrmacht who opposed him. The reasons for their opposition varied considerably, some being of a moral nature and others stemming from their disgust at the measures taken by the regime relating to the restrictions of freedom and the sham legality of the steps taken to institutionalize its power after Hindenburg's death. The aims of these groups were also quite and 'uncoordinated', which was one of the main problems in bringing together an effective opposition to Hitler's rule. Many of these officers did not fully understand the nature of the new regime at the beginning of the Fuhrer's rule, were politically naïve and believed that they would be able to sideline or manage him once he attained power.

However, after Hitler ordered the murder of the senior leadership of the SA (Sturmabteilung) on the night of 30 June 1934 in what became known as the Night of the Long Knives, it should have been clear to all that he would stop at nothing in order to retain power and would destroy anyone who stood in his way or attempted to overthrow the state. Hitler actually said as much in a speech he made to the Reichstag on 13 July 1934, which was broadcast throughout Germany, in which he sought to justify the murder of the supposed SA opponents of the state, whom he said were intent on starting a revolution:[1]

> 'The nation should know that no-one can threaten its existence – which is guaranteed by inner law and order – and escape unpunished! And every person should know for all time that if he raises his hand to strike out at the State, certain death will be his lot.'

This speech and the murder of his own followers was undoubtedly intended to be a warning to those who contemplated opposing him or his government. It was absolutely clear from his actions and public statement that trying to overthrow the Third Reich would be a very serious undertaking which would likely cost the life of anyone who failed in the attempt.

Tracing the development of the various centres of resistance to Hitler is not necessary for the purposes of this book, which is here only concerned with the effect of the attempted assassination on the military position of the Third Reich and whether it made any material difference to the result of the war. It is enough to say that as the events of the war began to turn against Germany and it became clear that the Allies would not negotiate with Hitler, for many the necessity for the military to strike if Germany was to avoid the worst consequences of defeat became more acutely apparent. It also became more obvious that Hitler would never surrender and that therefore the defeat of the Nazi regime would inevitably involve great destruction and suffering for the people of Germany.

There were many attempts on Hitler's life, and some came extremely close to success before the most well-known attempt on 20 July 1944. Perhaps the closest of these occurred when Hitler visited the headquarters of Army Group Centre on 13 March 1943. There were actually two attempts planned on Hitler's life that day. The first was to be a simple shooting of him by a member of the army staff, but this was foiled by the closeness of the security around the Fuhrer, which made it very difficult to approach him. The second attempt was potentially the more likely. It involved placing a bomb on Hitler's aircraft which had a fuse that was timed to explode when he was on his return journey to his headquarters, flying over Poland. However, the bomb did not explode because it iced up in the cargo hold of Hitler's plane, as the plotters were able to find out when they later recovered the device from the aircraft.

Who would succeed Hitler?

A significant problem which had to be addressed was what would happen after the assassination of Hitler. The designated successor of Hitler at the time was Reichsmarschall Goering, the Commander-in-Chief of the Luftwaffe. However, Goering had lost much influence because of the Luftwaffe's poor performance in defending the Reich and had many disputes with the OKH, so the support of the army could not be taken for granted by him. The personalities at the senior level of the OKW, Keitel and Jodl, made it unlikely that they would act independently of the other power centres in the Nazi government, so they would probably not have been important in determining which government would succeed Hitler. There was also a significant question as to the attitude of Himmler and the SS to acceding to Goering's succession. Joseph Goebbels, the Reich Minister of Propaganda, was also influential, and his attitude would certainly have been to perpetuate the rule of the Nazi Party. All this meant there would most likely have been a disputed succession in the event of Hitler's death, and it was not certain who would come out on top in such a situation.

Any group undertaking the assassination of Hitler therefore had to have a plan to establish the succession in such a manner that the government which ensued would undertake policies which addressed the many difficult problems which confronted Germany and dispense with the Nazi regime. This would obviously have been a very difficult task.

The Stauffenberg group and Operation 'Valkyrie'

The group centred around Colonel Count Klaus von Stauffenberg, who carried out the attempt to kill Hitler on 20 July, sought to do so by using a plan called Operation *Valkyrie*, which had been approved by Hitler and existed ostensibly to suppress a revolt by foreign workers and slaves in Germany, empowering the German Army to take over the government to control the situation. Stauffenberg, as Chief of Staff of the Replacement Army, was required to attend Hitler's headquarters to report on matters relating to reinforcements for the army and progress on forming new army formations. The conspirators intended to use the plan to enable the Replacement Army to take over the government and to suppress the Nazi Party and the SS. The most critical part of the plan was the elimination of the Fuhrer. Stauffenberg had the opportunity to carry out the assassination several times before he attempted to do so on 20 July, but had chosen not to because Himmler and Goering were not present at the time. However, he was advised that the Gestapo was closing in on the conspirators and decided that he must finally act on 20 July.

The failure of the attempt on Hitler's life resulted from factors which could not have been foreseen by Staffenberg or anyone else when the assassination was planned. The building where the conference was held where Stauffenberg was to detonate the bomb was not the usual location, which was having repair work carried out. Because of this building's construction, the explosive force of the bomb dissipated to a greater degree than would have been the case had it been held in the normal location. Furthermore, one of the attendees at the conference moved the briefcase containing the bomb after it was put in place by Stauffenberg to a position behind the stout oak support of the table Hitler was leaning against, thereby giving the Fuhrer more protection from the bomb blast. Despite four of the attendees at the conference being killed and several others wounded, Hitler suffered only minor injuries and was able to carry on with his normal schedule, meeting with Mussolini later the same day.

The German military situation on 20 July, 1944

The military situation which faced the Reich when the attempt was carried out was all but catastrophic. On the Normandy front, Field Marshal von Kluge had been appointed to replace Rundstedt and took up his new command on 3 July. Kluge was one of Hitler's most redoubtable commanders, having presided over many critical operations on the Eastern Front, and his appointment as OB West was an indication of the favour and esteem in which Hitler held him. Kluge had been staying at Berchtesgaden and before going to Normandy was briefed by the Fuhrer to the effect that both Rundstedt and Rommel viewed the situation too pessimistically. However, he soon realized when in his new post that they were correct in their evaluation of the situation, and his reports to the OKW reflected this being the case.

Rommel was severely injured on 17 July when he was strafed by an Allied fighter while returning from one of his many trips to the front to keep in touch with developments. This was a significant problem for the Germans, as Rommel was one of the most able and energetic commanders they had. Hitler thereupon ordered Kluge to take over direct command of Rommel's Army Group B as well as the whole theatre, which further indicated his confidence in Kluge's abilities.

Rommel had sent a memorandum to Hitler on 3 July (see Appendix 1) which set out the reasons for the deterioration in the situation in Normandy, including the steps he had advised to try to defeat the invasion but which had not been authorized by the OKW. This document shows beyond doubt that Hitler's orders had significantly exacerbated the military problems the Germans faced. Rommel's last report to Hitler on 15 July had pragmatically set out the losses suffered by his command and the replacements which had been sent to Army Group B. The concluding paragraph stated:[2]

> 'The troops are everywhere fighting heroically, but the unequal struggle is approaching its end. It is urgently necessary for the proper conclusion to be drawn from this situation. As C-in-C of the Army Group I feel myself duty bound to speak plainly on this point.'

Given that Rommel had previously raised the subject of the political conclusions to be drawn from the situation at a conference with Hitler and Rundstedt on 17 June, the meaning of his memorandum could hardly be plainer.

The conspirators had made contact with both Rommel and von Kluge in an attempt to bring them into their circle. While both of them could see the writing on the wall for Germany if there was no change in the military situation or the command, neither of them totally committed to the conspiracy. As far as can be established from the evidence which exists, Rommel believed that the best solution to save Germany if Hitler would not negotiate with the Western powers for at least a truce, if not peace, was for the commanders of the field armies to allow the Western Allies' armies to reach Berlin before the Soviets did. On 15 July, Rommel met with Colonel Warning of the 17th Luftwaffe Field Division, who had been in Africa with him, and was questioned as to the best course of action for Germany's future:[3]

> "'Then,' said Rommel, 'I open the west front. There would only be one important matter left – that the Anglo-Americans reach Berlin before the Russians.'"

Rommel apparently made similar remarks to his son, Manfred, and his friend General Siegfried Westphal, who served as operations officer under Rommel in Africa and was Chief of Staff to Rundstedt in 1944. The extent of Kluge's involvement in the plot is more difficult to ascertain, but according to remarks made by Rommel, Kluge was aware of Rommel's intentions and views.

On the Eastern Front, the situation was equally disastrous for Germany at the time. Operation *Bagration* had been launched by the Red Army on 22 June and was destroying the remnants of Army Group Centre, and it appeared that nothing could arrest the progress of the massive offensive. By 20 July, the Red Army had liberated Minsk (5 July), Vilna (9 July) and Grodno (13 July), and had largely destroyed the German forces opposing it. It was a disaster on as great a scale as that looming in Normandy.

The situation facing Nazi Germany on both fronts on 20 July was therefore dire, with every indication that it would only become worse. In the air war over Germany, the Luftwaffe had been rendered virtually powerless to arrest the strategic bombing campaign or restrain the Allied tactical air forces over Western Europe.

The question of whether the attempted assassination of Hitler caused any worsening of this situation has at least two components – immediate effects and medium-term effects.

In the immediate aftermath of the attempt on Hitler's life, there were a small number of changes to the command of the army. However, Rommel had been injured and was not in a command position at the time, so the attempt on Hitler's life did not change this.

The most important change resulted from Hitler's suspicions regarding Kluge, who had been identified as having known of the plot, but not as a participant. Without advising him, Hitler sent Model to relieve Kluge, Model formally taking command of the German forces in the West on 17 August. On the same day, Hitler sent Kluge a letter in which he stated that he had worn himself out in defending Normandy and requiring him to return to Berlin. Kluge realized that this was really camouflage for his arrest and decided to pre-empt the situation by committing suicide.

Model's initial reaction on taking command was to rescind Kluge's order for the retreat of the remnants of the German armies in Normandy, but he soon realized that nothing could be done to retrieve the situation and ordered a full retreat himself. Therefore, there were no immediate consequences for German military operations on the Western Front resulting from the attempted assassination of Hitler. Neither were there any changes to the army group commanders on the Eastern Front, as none of them were implicated in the plot at the time.

There was also no change in Hitler's methods of command or the strategies and tactics he employed, which were equally ineffectual after the plot as they were before it.

Therefore, the military situation remained very much as it had been developing prior to the failed assassination, and continued to deteriorate on a daily basis.

The medium-term effects on the military command of the Nazi state were, however, pronounced. Hitler's pathological mistrust of all his generals became even more pronounced. He increased his control over the German Army through several orders which had the ultimate effect of removing the capacity for any flexibility in the carrying out of his orders and made senior officers personally responsible for their execution. The most revealing order was issued on 21 January 1945:[4]

'I [Hitler] order as follows:

'1. Commanders-in-Chief, Corps Commanders and Divisional Commanders are personally responsible to me for reporting in good time:
   '(a) Every decision to carry out an operational movement.
   '(b) Every attack planned in divisional strength or upwards which does not conform with the general directives laid down by the High Command.
   '(c) Every offensive action in quiet sectors of the front, over and above normal shock-troop activities which is calculated to draw the enemy's attention to the sector.
   '(d) Every plan for disengaging or withdrawing forces.

'(e) Every plan for surrendering a position, a local strong-point or a fortress.

'They must ensure that I have time to intervene in this decision if I think fit and that my counter orders can reach the frontline troops in time.'

Hitler went on to threaten 'draconian punishment' for infringements of this order, the effect of which can easily be imagined.

Other high-ranking members of the Army were identified as being involved in the plot and were dealt with as they came to light. One immediate casualty was General Eric Fellgiebel, who was in charge of the communications network at Fuhrer Headquarters and was able to temporarily isolate it from the rest of the Wehrmacht to give Operation *Valkyrie* a chance of success. Hitler had long believed that there was a traitor at Supreme Headquarters who was providing information to the enemy, and when told of Fellgiebel's arrest immediately assumed that he was the highly placed traitor, which was in fact not correct. He was executed on 4 September.

The Military Governor of France, General Carl-Heinrich von Stulpnagel, was a member of the conspiracy and had arrested all the Gestapo and SS operatives in Paris when he was told that Hitler had been killed. When the plot failed, he attempted suicide unsuccessfully and was executed on 30 August.

Warlimont described how the atmosphere in Supreme Headquarters worsened further after the assassination plot failed:[5]

'Hitler seemed to feel that even among those who stood round him there were some who had perhaps not been unmasked.'

Such an atmosphere would have made meaningful work all but impossible.

Conclusions

1. The immediate effects of the failed 20 July 1944 attempt on Hitler's life on the military situation of the Reich were inconsequential. As a result of luck, the Fuhrer suffered only minor injuries, which did not incapacitate him or upset his schedule to any significant degree.
2. There were no immediate wholesale changes in the highest level of the command of the German armies in either the Eastern or Western Front, so Hitler's orders continued to be issued and obeyed. The main victims of Hitler's revenge for the bomb plot were Kluge and Rommel, both of whom elected to commit suicide.

The Effect of the Attempted Assassination and Coup of 20 July 1944

3. The effects which were felt in the medium term, however, fundamentally affected the way in which the command of the German Army was carried out. Hitler's orders relating to matters which had to be reported to him made it impossible for any senior commanders to exercise any flexibility in implementing them, which meant that all operational initiative was totally stultified. This development ended the process which Hitler had been trying to impose operationally since the beginning of his rule in 1934.

Chapter 6

Hitler As Warlord – Final Conclusions

As has been related in detail elsewhere in the three volumes of this work, Hitler arrogated to himself the roles which had previously been undertaken by the President, Chancellor, Minister of War, Supreme Commander of the Armed Forces and Commander-in-Chief of the Army under the Weimar constitution. At one stage he even appointed himself to be an army group commander after he sacked Field Marshal List during the 1942 Stalingrad campaign. He also personally closely supervised the foreign policy of Nazi Germany and the research for and manufacture of all weapons for the Wehrmacht.

In these roles he made all the most important decisions relating to military and diplomatic strategy, operational deployment of the Wehrmacht, production priorities, weapons development and personnel appointments for the whole of the German war effort. Analysis of his decisions in these capacities explains the development of the war and its outcome. This concluding chapter provides a final review of these decisions and their impact.

Diplomatic strategy

The noted German strategist Carl von Clausewitz famously stated:[1]

> 'War is not merely a political act, but also a real political instrument, a continuation of political commerce, a carrying out of the same by other means.'

His contention, in summary, is that war cannot be divorced from other forms of political activity, that it is a continuation of that activity. One of the most important types of political activity undertaken by any state is of course its diplomatic strategy and relations with other countries. Hitler was a great devotee of Clausewitz, even if it is apparent that he did not properly understand much of his meaning, and there is no doubt that his diplomatic methods and strategy should be regarded as the starting point of any analysis of his war strategy. When Hitler's diplomacy and its results prior to the outbreak of war are viewed as a whole, it is also clear that he attempted to practice this main dictum of Clausewitz. Paul Schmidt, who was Hitler's interpreter and was present at almost all the important meetings relating to his foreign policy for the whole period of the Third Reich, gave the following evidence at the Nuremburg trials:[2]

> 'The general objectives of the Nazi leadership were apparent from the start, namely, the domination of the European Continent, to be achieved, first, by the incorporation of all German speaking groups in the Reich, and secondly, by territorial expansion under the slogan of "Lebensraum". The execution of these basic objectives, however, seemed to be characterized by improvisation. Each succeeding step apparently was carried out as each new situation arose, but all consistent with the ultimate objectives mentioned above.'

The early successes Hitler enjoyed relating to the reoccupation of the Saar and the remilitarization of the Rhineland were achieved with no interference by the victor states of the First World War, which was a diplomatic success for Hitler because Germany was not strong enough to resist them at the time if they had done anything to dispute Germany taking back control of the territories. He gained great prestige domestically and internationally by these moves not resulting in war. When Hitler took these initial steps there was a feeling, especially among many in the British government, that they were only instances of the Germans 'moving back into their own backyard', which was not unreasonable and to be expected.

The Anschluss with Austria was the last time Hitler achieved his aim without the open diplomatic interference of the Western democracies, despite it being a clear breach of the terms of the treaties which ended the First World War. These successes encouraged the Fuhrer in his subsequent use of tactics including the threat of force to achieve his aims because he believed that the Western democracies would not oppose him. The next objective in his programme of expansion was the Sudetenland, which was located on the border of Czechoslovakia and had never been part of Germany. It did, however, have a majority of ethnic Germans who had been subjects of the Austro-Hungarian Empire. Although Hitler eventually achieved the ceding of this territory to Germany, the Western democracies came very close to war with Germany over the issue; it was only the last-minute intervention of Italian dictator Mussolini, who offered to mediate the dispute at the infamous Munich conference, which prevented war occurring in 1938. While achieving an understanding with Hitler which avoided war was very popular in the Western democracies when it occurred, there was a backlash in Britain and France which reflected a dawning understanding that the terms of the settlement were dishonourable and had thrown Czechoslovakia to its fate despite it having had treaties of alliance with the Western powers. There was growing regret at the contemptuous way with which the Czechs had been treated. The settlement terms included a provision to the effect that the signatories, including Germany, guaranteed the future integrity of Czechoslovakia, but it proved to count for nothing. The acquisition of the Sudetenland had the effect of further increasing the prestige of Hitler's government both within Germany and externally. There were very senior generals in the Wehrmacht who were opposed to Hitler's ambitious foreign policy and wanted to overthrow him as they believed that he was leading the country to war, but following the Munich agreement they were no longer confident of having enough broad support in the army to do so.

The event which finally caused the Western democracies to lose all faith in Hitler's assurances of pacific intent was the occupation of the remainder of Czechoslovakia on 15 March 1939, which was a clear breach of the guarantee given by Hitler in the settlement of the Sudeten crisis in 1938. Hitler had a dim view of the other European statesmen he dealt with at Munich:[3]

> 'Our enemies are men below average, not men of action, not masters. They are little worms. I saw them at Munich.'

He felt that he could threaten and manipulate the Western politicians at will and consequently believed that taking over the rest of Czechoslovakia would not lead to war, as had been the case previously with respect to the Rhineland, Anschluss and Sudetenland when the other European statesmen did not stand up to him. When he did sieze the rest of Czechoslovakia and there was no war, the Fuhrer seemed to have been proven right yet again. However, the damage to his credibility with the West was complete, particularly in Britain:[4]

> 'The day after [the occupation of] Prague the Conservative Foreign Affairs Committee called for national service, all party government and **a Russian alliance** [author's emphasis]. The first two of these had long been championed by Halifax, who was also swiftly coming around to the third. For a great many Britons Prague marked the point at which war began to seem inevitable.'

For the British Conservative Party to call for an alliance with the USSR was an extraordinary event, comparable to seeking an alliance with the devil for many conservatives of the time. It was actually a last opportunity to use the structure created by the League of Nations to halt the slide toward war.

Hitler then found that his attempts at intimidating the Poles and the Western allies rebounded when he tried the same tactics he had used with respect to Czechoslovakia. The allies were determined that they would not allow Hitler to take over or invade any other country, which led to the British and French guarantee of Poland on 31 March 1939 and the pact for mutual assistance in the event of war. Hitler's failure to understand that the Western leaders meant what they said during the Polish crisis was a fatal error of diplomacy for which he alone bears responsibility. It is possible – but unlikely – that he would have been able to achieve his aims if he had allowed the diplomatic efforts in place at the time to progress, but his peremptory demands and overweening arrogance ensured that the Poles and Western allies would not accede to his unilaterally imposed timeline and conditions.

The only major ally that Germany had during the war was Fascist Italy, whose assistance at the Munich Conference had been crucial to the advantageous outcome for Germany. The Foreign Minister of the Italian regime, Count Galeazzo Ciano – who was also Mussolini's son-in-law – recorded his view of German diplomacy leading up to the invasion of Poland in his diary entry on 13 August 1939:[5]

'I report to the Duce at the Palazzo Venezia. And, in addition to reporting to him what happened, I make known also my own judgment of the situation as well as of the men involved and of events. **I return to Rome completely disgusted with the Germans, with their leader, with their way of doing things. They have betrayed us and lied to us. Now they are dragging us into an adventure which we have not wanted and which might compromise the regime and the country as a whole. The Italian people will boil over with horror when they know about the aggression against Poland and most probably will wish to fight the Germans. I don't know whether to wish Italy a victory or Germany a defeat. In any case, given the German attitude, I think that our hands are free, and I propose that we act accordingly, declaring that we have no intention of participating in a war which we have neither wanted nor provoked** [author's emphasis].'

Coming from Germany's ally, this view is a devastating indictment of the Nazi government and its diplomatic policy.

As a prelude to the invasion of Poland, Hitler concluded the Non-Aggression Pact with the USSR on 23 August 1939, which was a major diplomatic achievement. However, he undoubtedly saw it as a temporary means by which he would nullify the threat from the Soviets while he conquered Poland and make it impossible for the Western allies to fulfil their guarantees to Poland. He expected that by presenting the Western powers with a fait accompli with respect to Poland, they would once again demur before the strength of his position. In this assumption he was fatally incorrect, which is indefensible given the crystal-clear content of the communications made on behalf of the British and French governments by Chamberlain and Daladier in late August and early September 1939, as set out in the chapter 'Hitler Roles the Dice for War' in Volume 1 of this work. This was arguably the single greatest error of judgment that Hitler made in the whole period of the Third Reich.

After the defeat of Poland, Hitler again thought he could make a peace deal with the Western allies that would leave him free to do what he wished in Eastern Europe, but once more was proven wrong. After the invasion and defeat of France, Hitler made the famous so-called 'Peace Offer' in a speech to the Reichstag on 19 July 1940, in which he stated:

> 'In this hour I feel it to be my duty before my own conscience to appeal once more to reason and common sense in Great Britain as much as elsewhere. I consider myself in a position to make this appeal, since I am not the vanquished, begging favors, but the victor speaking in the name of reason. I can see no reason why this war must go on.'

But once again he was wrong if he expected that the British would sue for peace, as he said privately and publicly that they would. The response from the British was to rally around Churchill as Prime Minister, the man Hitler most loathed in the whole British Empire.

In his diplomacy after the defeat of France, Hitler did not bring Spain into the war because he said that their price was too high, although he met with fellow Fascist dictator Franco only once and did not make any further attempt to achieve a deal with him. Franco was ideologically aligned with Nazi Germany and was indebted to Hitler and Mussolini for the military assistance provided to the Nationalist cause during the Spanish Civil War. Spain would have been an invaluable ally as it could have facilitated the occupation of Gibraltar, thereby closing the Mediterranean and rendering the Suez Canal irrelevant, which would have meant Britain's position in the Middle East and Asia being seriously imperilled. Grand Admiral Raeder tried to get Hitler to see the advantages of such a strategy as an alternative to the invasion of the Soviet Union, but to no avail.

Apart from not attempting to negotiate any involvement of the Spanish in the war, Hitler made no moves to create a broader and closer co-operation alliance between Germany, Italy, Spain and Vichy France, which could have been possible, especially after the Royal Navy attacked the French fleet in its base at Mers-el-Kebir on 3 July 1940, during which some 1,300 French sailors were killed. Thereafter, the Vichy French government severed diplomatic relations with Britain, bombed Gibraltar and could probably have been induced to declare war on Britain if they were offered serious enough incentives to do so. Instead, Hitler decided to pursue his dream of conquering the USSR, against the advice of his military commanders, including on this occasion Goering, who wanted some respite for the Luftwaffe to be re-equipped after the losses suffered in the French campaign and Battle of Britain. Goering also pressed for Britain to finally be dealt with before attacking the Soviet Union.

Similarly, Hitler did not attempt to involve the Japanese in Operation *Barbarossa*, although they were in the process of working out their war strategy at the time the invasion of the USSR was being planned. Evidence from conversations Hitler had with the Japanese Ambassador, General Oshima, indicates Japan would probably have been very interested in any proposal regarding the Far Eastern territories of the Soviet Union. It must also be remembered that the Japanese had two border wars with the USSR during the 1930s, and the generals of the Japanese army in Manchuria were thirsting for revenge at the time. Warlimont commented on the German attitude to their Japanese allies:[6]

> 'Even after the opening of the campaign against Russia little thought was given to the possibility of direct Japanese assistance as proved by the fact, that after a period of disillusionment, the old confidence in the imminent collapse of the Soviets revived in the autumn of 1941. The overweening self-assurance in German headquarters was illustrated by the phrase coined when Japan was thought to have made an offer of assistance: **"we don't need anyone just to strip the corpses"**! [author's emphasis]'

There is another illuminating quote from Warlimont regarding Hitler's attitude to the Japanese:[7]

> 'Hitler: You mustn't believe what the Japanese say. I don't believe a word of it.
> '...
> 'Hitler: They lie to beat the band; everything they say has always got some background motive of deception.'

An attack by Japan was certainly an event feared by Stalin, who kept powerful forces in the Soviet Far Eastern territories until he was sure there would be no invasion from that quarter. The forces he later transferred from the Far East to the Moscow front were a crucial part of Zhukov's counter-offensive which defeated the German attempt to take Moscow in December 1941, as related in Volume 2 of this work. So this too was a major diplomatic and strategic error by Hitler. Had Japan attacked the USSR, it is almost certain that it would not have attacked the USA. This would have meant there would not have been war between the USA and Germany unless Roosevelt was able to prevail upon Congress to declare war without any aggressive act against it, which would have been very difficult.

The Fuhrer's declaration of war against the United States on 11 December 1941 occurred without any consultation with the senior members of his government or any of the high command of the Army or the OKW. General Warlimont, the Deputy Chief of Operations at the OKW, relates that General Jodl then called him from Berlin, which led to the following 'memorable telephone discussion':[8]

'Jodl: You have just heard that the Fuhrer has just declared war on America?
'Myself: **Yes and we couldn't be more surprised** [author's emphasis].
'Jodl: The staff must now examine where the United States is most likely to employ the bulk of her forces initially, the Far East or Europe. We cannot take further decisions until that has been clarified.
'... This and no more was the beginning for our headquarters of German strategy against America which was to reach its end on the banks of the Elbe in May 1945.'

As previously mentioned, obtaining a declaration of war against Germany would not have been straightforward for President Roosevelt in 1941; such was the case even after the attack on Pearl Harbor. Without the declaration by Hitler, there would have been very great pressure for the whole emphasis of the United States' war effort to be solely directed against Japan.[9] Without the involvement of the United States, there would have been no threat of invasion for German-occupied Western Europe and Hitler would have been free to concentrate all the forces he had on Operation *Barbarossa*, giving him a much greater chance of victory. His dream of an Eastern empire would have been more likely to come true and the whole course of the war – and subsequent world history – could certainly have been significantly different.

In December 1942, and again in June 1943, the Soviets made it known to the Germans through their ambassador in Stockholm that they were willing to negotiate a separate peace.[10] This approach resulted from Stalin's fear that the capitalist Western Allies were watching from the sidelines while the two dictator powers fought a war of annihilation which they would allow to continue until both were exhausted and they could then profit from. Stalin had come to this conclusion because he did not properly understand the difficulties associated with the seaborne invasion of Western Europe, concluding from the delays which occurred that his allies were not truly committed to carrying out the invasion of France, a conclusion for which there was no evidence. In rejecting these offers, Hitler is again shown to have been completely deluded. His attitude to a separate peace with the Soviet Union is illustrated by the following statement he made to his incompetent and vainglorious Foreign Minister, von Ribbentrop:[11]

'You know Ribbentrop, if I came to an agreement with Russia today, I'd attack her again tomorrow. I just can't help myself.'

These facts show that Hitler had no diplomatic strategy other than to pursue his ultra-nationalist and racist expansion of Germany into the territories of the USSR, as he had outlined a long time prior to the war in *Mein Kampf*:[12]

'We terminate the endless German drive to the South and West of Europe and direct our drive to the land of the East. We finally terminate the colonial and trade policy of the pre-war period and proceed to the territorial policy of the future. But if we talk about new soil and territory in Europe today we can think primarily only of Russia and its vassal border states.'

It is hard to think of a clearer statement of intent or to understand how his intentions could possibly have ever been misunderstood. Hitler confirmed his ambitions regarding the Soviet Union on the eve of war, stating on 11 August 1939:[13]

'Everything that I undertake is directed against Russia. If those in the West are too stupid and too blind to understand this, then I shall be forced to come to an understanding with the Russians to beat the West, and then, after its defeat, turn with all my concerted force against the Soviet Union.'

Hitler's diplomatic strategy once the initial victorious stage of the war had turned sour was best stated by him during a meeting at his Wolf's Lair headquarters in East Prussia on 31 August 1944:[14]

> 'The moment will arrive when disagreements between the Allies will be so great that the break will come. Coalitions have always failed right throughout history; you just have to wait for the moment, however difficult that may be. It's been my particular job ever since 1941 never to lose my nerve and whenever something collapses always to find ways and means of patching it up somewhere.'

It should be pointed out that many coalitions have been very successful in prosecuting wars, the obvious examples being the Allies of the First World War and the coalition which defeated Napoleon in 1815. Hitler was fond of referring to the 'Miracle of the House of Brandenburg', when Frederick II ('the Great') of Prussia averted defeat following the death of the Czarina Elizabeth in 1762 and the breaking up of the alliance between Russia and Austria. Such was the hollowness of Hitler's strategy, which was essentially just an attempt to extend his rule based on the possibility of the Allies falling out, which in the circumstances was a fantasy.

Thus, the evidence overwhelmingly confirms that the dream of a Germanic Empire in the East was the supreme goal of Hitler's diplomacy, in the pursuit of which he never wavered. While he did achieve some early successes in his seeking of this chimera, ultimately his diplomatic strategy can only be regarded as a total and abject failure.

Crucial operational military decisions

There were a small number of climactic military events which determined the outcome of the Second World War. Individually, these turning points may have determined the result of the war by themselves, but in combination they certainly did. There were also a very small number of German witnesses to the decisions made by Hitler concerning these turning points. As these decisions have been dealt with in detail in previous volumes of this work, I will here only summarize the most important crises caused by Hitler's military decisions during the most critical campaigns of the war.

France, 1940

It is fair to say that Hitler's use of the strategy proposed by Field Marshal von Manstein, which led to the rapid defeat of the French, British, Dutch and

Belgian forces in 1940, was the best military decision which he made during the war. There is no doubt it was a bold decision to attack in the West at all, and the credit for the victory which was gained must be largely attributed to Hitler, who did not allow the arguments of many of his generals to deter him. However, while the decision to attack and the strategy which was used were exceptional and justified by the result of the campaign, the implementation of the strategy was faulty to such a degree that the result was not a complete strategic victory but an inconclusive one, with Germany failing to defeat the British decisively.

There is no doubt that the reason why the Germans did not attain a strategic victory against the British was Hitler's two 'halt' orders of 17 and 24 May. The first of these orders slowed the advance of the panzer divisions while infantry units were brought forward to form a defensive flank on the southern arm of the offensive, when there was no actual threat from that quarter. This order did not lead to any significant practical consequence, however, mainly because the commanders on the spot allowed Guderian to press on under the guise of 'reconnaissance', which he interpreted to mean sending strong elements of his forces as fast as possible to secure the objectives he was assigned. This order was superseded on 18 May and the main attack then developed as planned.

The second 'halt' order, however, was of much greater importance. Issued on 24 May, it halted von Kleist's armoured divisions when they were poised to encircle the British forces and prevent them withdrawing into Dunkirk, the last Channel port remaining to them. There is little doubt that this encirclement could have been achieved. The reason for this order seems to have involved Hitler deciding that the army generals would obtain too much prestige from the victory if they were seen to have won it themselves, and he therefore accepted Goering's suggestion to allow the politically more reliable Luftwaffe to 'finish off' the retreating British and French forces. Additionally, Rundstedt indicates that Hitler told him that he wanted to negotiate peace with Britain as soon as possible, and sparing their forces from complete defeat would make this easier. It is difficult to understand this line of reasoning, but there is no reason to doubt Rundstedt's evidence, which is contained in a letter from him to General Warlimont in 1949,[15] when the latter was preparing his book *Inside Hitler's Headquarters, 1939–1945*. This episode is dealt with in detail in Chapter 10 of Volume 1 of this work.

It is incontestable that because of this order, the British Expeditionary Force and tens of thousands of French troops were able to escape. Hitler was therefore responsible for the 'miracle of Dunkirk', and in allowing this to occur ensured that the war would continue, ultimately leading to his own demise.

Operation Barbarossa, 1941

The attack on the USSR is widely accepted to be the single most important factor in the ultimate demise of Nazi Germany. The reason Hitler attacked was the result of his long-standing ideological and racial dogma, together with his belief that he was destined to be the destroyer of communism, which he asserted was an integral part of the 'world Jewish conspiracy' to destroy the German and Aryan races. He had stated many times that he would not commit the mistake of waging a 'two-front' war, but by attacking when he did he created exactly this situation. His decision also involved a grotesque underestimation of the military potential of the Soviet Union. He took this decision against the advice of virtually all his generals, including Reichsmarschall Goering. The decision was a cardinal error on Hitler's part, which he aggravated by his interference with the operations of the armies in carrying out the plan for *Barbarossa*.

There were three imperative necessities if victory over the USSR was to be achieved: concentration of the attacking force, relentless speed of exploitation of the attack and clear operational objectives from which the attack should not be distracted.

The geographic configuration of the Soviet Union in 1941 was such that any attacker from the west was confronted by the problem that the area of operations became larger the further east that the invaders went. This led to the attacking force becoming less concentrated, a problem which had to be overcome through achieving the most important objective of the campaign, which was to overwhelm the Red Army as quickly as possible and thereby to achieve a strategic victory before the onset of the winter, and not to allow a second campaigning season to occur. This aim was made more difficult by the lack of modern roads and other infrastructure in the USSR, which inhibited the movement of the mobile German formations. The composition of the panzer and mechanized divisions of the Wehrmacht was not ideal for Operation *Barbarossa* because most of their vehicles were wheeled and not tracked. The limitations this imposed in the Soviet landscape, even during periods of good weather, was a major restriction to the necessity for speed. This problem had not existed in the previous campaigns because the road systems in Western Europe were modern and allowed for the easy movement of wheeled vehicles. The other significant geographical problem not previously encountered by the Wehrmacht was the sheer distances involved to the objectives within the USSR, which were much further from the borders of the Reich than its previous campaigns. For example, Moscow was over 1,000km from the Polish border with the Soviet Union.

The original plan of operations for *Barbarossa* developed by the General Staff of the Army, the OKH, made the primary objective of the campaign Moscow. It was obvious that the Soviet government would have to defend its capital, and therefore the Germans would find the Red Army there, providing the opportunity to defeat it comprehensively and achieve a strategic victory. It is very difficult to find any fault with this strategy; indeed, the Red Army's deployment conformed to this expectation. However, Hitler saw the situation differently and ordered that the priorities of the attack be the taking of Leningrad and defeating the Red Army concentration around Kiev when the opportunity presented. These aims involved moving the forces required to the extremities of the area of operations, which took too much time and meant that the vital operation to precipitate the strategic defeat of the Red Army could not be completed before the winter weather became a major factor in the campaign.

Hitler was unquestionably responsible for these changes, which were the primary causes for the ultimate failure of Operation *Barbarossa* if it is assumed that it could ever have been successful.

The Stalingrad disaster, 1942–43

The 1942 summer campaign in the USSR occurred because Hitler could not acknowledge the failure of Operation *Barbarossa*, seeing the only alternative to a defensive posture which was recommended by his generals as the renewal of offensive operations to destroy the Red Army. However, the forces necessary to resume the offensive could not be provided from the Wehrmacht alone. Therefore, Hitler cajoled the Axis partners – Hungary, Romania and Italy – to significantly increase their contributions to the campaign in the Soviet Union. The Germans knew that these troops were not equal to those of the Red Army and were not equipped or trained to withstand any attack by them. However, according to Zeitzler, 'Hitler was intoxicated by numbers, and saw only the vast increase in divisions which now appeared upon his staff maps.'[16]

The plan of operations involved taking objectives on the Volga River at Stalingrad as well as Baku in the Caucasus, both of which were very long distances from the starting points of the offensive and hundreds of kilometres apart. The objectives were primarily economic in nature, as Hitler believed that taking them would cripple the economy of the USSR and enable the Germans to be self-sufficient for a war of long duration, which was the opposite of the type of conflict he had intended.

The plan which Hitler devised was defective because 'as in the previous year, the objectives were divergent. The blow was struck, *not with a clenched fist, but with an open hand and the fingers extended.*'[17] It also failed to take into account the dependence of the German forces on a single bridge at Dnepropetrovsk for the supply of all the attacking forces and the drastic limitations this imposed,[18] although Hitler was warned of this prior to the offensive by General Eduard Wagner, the Quartermaster General of the German Army. Hitler also dispensed with the normal practice which the General Staff had always undertaken on all new operations, which tested through various virtual scenarios the adequacy of supply arrangements and the likely course of the battles involved.[19]

When the offensive began on 28 June, the initial results seemed to be very promising. However, the Red Army withdrew rather than fight and be encircled, as it had in 1941, and comparatively few prisoners were taken. The Fuhrer interpreted the withdrawal as indicating that the Soviet forces were on the verge of defeat, but the Soviet High Command was actually carefully harbouring its forces to fight another day. Acting on his assumption that the Red Army was on the brink of collapse, Hitler ordered alterations to the plan of operations which had the effect of further splitting the power of the German attack, committing forces to areas where they were not required. An egregious example of this was the commitment of the Fourth Panzer Army to the drive for the Caucasus when it had previously been assigned to the attack on Stalingrad, only later to be recommitted to Stalingrad when Hitler belatedly accepted that it was not needed in the Caucasus, as Kleist and Halder had warned him when he first made the change. The change of deployment occurred at a time when Stalingrad was lightly defended and could probably have easily been taken by the Fourth Panzer Army. This was reminiscent of the problems Hitler caused through his interference in the execution of Operation *Barbarossa* the previous year and had the same result, causing even greater supply problems than already existed and complicating the operational deployment of the German forces.[20]

The salient forced into the Red Army's front by the offensive towards Stalingrad meant that Hitler had to cover a very long northern flank for which there were insufficient German troops. To deal with this situation, the Fuhrer had to commit his allies' armies to the flank, despite his knowledge of their limited operational value. Halder advised Hitler on numerous occasions that these dispositions were very risky, but the Fuhrer dismissed his concerns. Halder and Hitler repeatedly argued during the offensive over the deployment of the army, Halder describing Hitler's unrealistic underestimation of the Red Army as 'grotesque' in his diary entry on 23 July. Halder continued:[21]

Hitler As Warlord – Final Conclusions 185

'There is no room for any serious work. This so-called leadership is characterized by pathological reacting to the impressions of the moment and a total lack of understanding of the command machinery and its possibilities.'

These arguments finally led to Halder being fired as Chief of the Army General Staff on 24 September, his place being taken by Colonel General Zeitzler. Warlimont recalled what he heard Hitler say after Halder's departure:[22]

'[I]n view of the tasks now facing the Army, rather than relying on technical competence, **it must be inspired by the fervour of belief in National-Socialism** [author's emphasis].'

This statement of Hitler's is an indication that his understanding of military command was governed by political and not strategic or any other recognizable military considerations. It is impossible to assign any rational meaning to it, the only possible way to arrive at any understanding of it being to assume that it had been confected for posterity.

Zeitzler was quite junior, being only a major general prior to being appointed as Halder's successor. His reputation was built as an expert in the command of mobile operations, especially their maintenance and supply arrangements. He was crucial to the success of the campaigns in France, Yugoslavia and Greece as Chief of Staff to Field Marshal von Kleist's First Panzer Army, and in the initial stages of Operation *Barbarossa*. His star had also risen with the successful repulse of the Allied raid on the French port of Dieppe in August 1942, when he was the Chief of Staff of Army Group West under von Rundstedt. The timing of his appointment as Chief of the General Staff in the prelude to the major crisis of the Stalingrad campaign could hardly have been worse from his perspective. He wrote a treatise on the Stalingrad campaign in *The Fatal Decisions*[23] which is indispensable reading for any considered review of the campaign.

Despite Hitler's dismissal of the strength of the Red Army, the campaign developed very much as he was told it would by Halder before he relieved him of his position. Stalingrad became a slaughterhouse, into which Hitler poured all the offensive forces he could muster. This reduced the strategy of the Germans to the kind of warfare which best suited the Red Army while minimizing the advantages the Germans still had in operational flexibility. The Red Army thus just managed to hold onto its positions on the west bank of the Volga within Stalingrad. The Soviet counter-offensive began on 19 November with a major attack north of the positions occupied by the Sixth Army and the other units in Stalingrad, followed shortly after by another to the south. These attacks concentrated on the weak allied contingents and swept them aside, and within a matter of days had cut off the Sixth Army in Stalingrad, as Halder and Zeitzler had both continually warned Hitler. The problem that urgently needed addressing now was whether the Sixth Army could be saved, the only realistic option to do so being for it to break out through the Red Army forces encircling it as soon as possible, in co-ordination with a relieving force. Zeitzler advised Hitler to order the breakout immediately that the Soviet offensive began, but in vain. He repeatedly advised the same course of action, with the same result.

Speer was at Fuhrer Headquarters on 24 September and witnessed the decision which sealed the fate of the Sixth Army in Stalingrad, Hitler accepting Goering's assurance that it could be supplied in situ by the Luftwaffe following a discussion that also involved Zeitzler.[24] This ruinous decision was merely based on Goering's braggadocio but led to the loss of over 200,000 German troops and all their equipment. Speer later related:

'[T]he fate of the encircled army was finally sealed. For Goering appeared in the situation room, brisk and beaming like an operetta tenor who is supposed to portray a victorious Reich Marshal. Depressed, with a beseeching tone in his voice, Hitler asked him: "what about supplying Stalingrad by air?" Goering snapped to attention and declared solemnly: "My leader! I personally guarantee the supplying of Stalingrad by air. You can rely on that." As I later heard from Milch, the Air Force General Staff had in fact calculated that supplying the pocket was impossible. Zeitzler, too, instantly voiced his doubts. But Goering retorted that it was exclusively the business of the air force to undertake the necessary calculations. Hitler ... revived at Goering's mere words, and had recovered all his old staunchness. Then Stalingrad can be held! It is foolish to go on talking any more about a breakout of the Sixth Army. It would lose all its heavy weapons and have no fighting strength left. The Sixth Army remains in Stalingrad.'

Zeitzler's account of this episode is materially the same as that of Speer. After Goering's avowal that the Luftwaffe could supply Stalingrad by air and Hitler's decision to leave the Sixth Army where it was, Zeitzler recalled he said:[25]

"'I should like to make another request." Hitler said: "What is that?" I said: "May I submit a daily report to you giving the exact tonnage of supplies flown in to the Sixth Army during the previous twenty-four hours?"'

Although Goering objected to this procedure, Hitler agreed. It is established by many sources that the amounts delivered by the Luftwaffe did not reach anywhere near the level required to maintain the Sixth Army and its attendant formations. Hitler's acceptance of Goering's assertion was reckless in the extreme and reflects, at best, his propensity for grotesquely wishful thinking in place of rational evaluation, for which there can be no place in higher military command decisions.

In an attempt to relieve the Sixth Army, Hitler brought together Army Group Don under Field Marshal von Manstein. Manstein immediately told the Fuhrer that the forces provided were insufficient to relieve those trapped in Stalingrad and that any attempt to do so must be combined with a breakout by the Sixth Army. Hitler would not agree to such a proposal unless the Sixth Army simultaneously held onto its position on the Volga while linking up with the relieving forces, which was impossible. The attacks to relieve Stalingrad subsequently failed, as Hitler was told they would, and the Sixth Army was destroyed in situ by the Red Army, the last remnants surrendering on 2 February 1943.

Hitler's performance during the Stalingrad campaign combines all the elements of his version of military command. Firstly, the operational plan for which he was responsible did not sufficiently concentrate the forces used for the tasks involved and had not been tested, as would have been the case if the General Staff had been in command of the process.[26] General Westphal's description of the campaign as being made 'not with a clenched fist, but with an open hand and the fingers extended' is perfectly apposite. Secondly, the objectives were too far apart from each other and thereby lost the possibility of concentration of force. Thirdly, the changes Hitler made during the campaign did not contribute to the achievement of any of its objectives, merely complicating the serious problems which already existed relating to the supply of the forces involved.[27] Fourthly, when he was told of the obvious danger which existed on the northern flank of the Stalingrad front, he dismissed the concerns without due regard to the evidence, despite being warned by Halder and Zeitzler[28] of the preparations being made by the Red Army to take the offensive against the exposed flank. Furthermore, once the Red Army offensive began, the Fuhrer refused to take the only rational decision available, which was to withdraw the Sixth Army and combine its breakout with the relief forces under Field Marshal von Manstein.[29] Finally, Hitler's acceptance of Goering's assurance that the Luftwaffe could supply the forces surrounded in Stalingrad was reckless in the extreme, especially as he took no steps to determine whether the Luftwaffe could make good on Goering's promise.[30]

The result of these decisions, for which Hitler was solely responsible, was a strategic defeat of catastrophic proportions. While there is no question that the timely withdrawal of the troops from Stalingrad would still have represented a defeat, by adopting such a course the human and materiel losses would have been greatly minimized.

The defence of France, 1944

The German defence of France in 1944 exhibited in great clarity the faults of the strategy Hitler followed, the system of command he created and his shortcomings as operational military commander.

The strategy for the defence of France which Hitler sought to implement was anchored around extensive fortifications known through German propaganda as the 'Atlantic Wall', the strongest sections of which were located around the Pas-de-Calais. The Fuhrer also ordered the fortification of the Channel Islands, which were heavily garrisoned and had extensive anti-aircraft and artillery emplacements constructed. The reasoning behind locating the main fortifications in the Pas-de-Calais area was that Hitler and the German command took a very conventional view of how the Allies would determine where to land their invasion forces, based on the distance from the main British embarkation ports and the closest locations for air force support. They also had regard to their own intended jump-off points for the proposed *Sea Lion* invasion of Britain in 1940 and expected that the Allies would use the same logic to determine the location of their invasion. This area was also where most of the V-1 flying bomb launch sites were located at the time, and it was thought that destroying these would also be a major factor in Allied offensive plans.

The massive fortifications here, however, were ultimately of no value to the Germans as the Allies actually invaded in Normandy, where comparatively few large-scale defences existed. The other factors which Hitler had thought important were also shown to be irrelevant by the choice of this landing area.

The German forces in the west consisted mainly of a combination of semi-mobile and immobile infantry divisions, the majority of which were deficient in training, combat experience and equipment. Many of the troops were overage, had been previously wounded, or suffered from medical conditions which meant they were not used in regular Wehrmacht formations. There were also 'volunteers' from ethnic Germans in the conquered territories and from amongst Red Army prisoners. Additionally, there was a pronounced shortage of experienced non-commissioned officers and junior officers, with approximately 30 per cent of these command positions not filled on D-Day.

Hitler and the German High Command believed that there would be more than one landing and that the first one would probably be a feint. This view was deliberately encouraged by the Allies as part of an elaborate deception plan called Operation *Fortitude*, through which misinformation was passed using several German spies in England who had been turned by the British to work in the Allies' interest. It was imperative for the Germans to defeat the invasion as soon as possible, for the simple reason that if the first landing succeeded there would be no need for any second landing. Therefore, everything that the Germans could muster had to be committed against the invasion, no matter where it landed, and this was recognized by Hitler's Directive 51, which set out his plan for the defence against an Allied invasion.

The only real prospect for a successful defence of the German position in France depended on the speedy deployment at the invasion point of the mobile reserves which had been accumulated. This reserve consisted of ten Army and SS panzer and mechanized divisions, which included some of the best formations in the Wehrmacht. However, these units were dispersed, and their use was affected by Hitler's instructions which limited the ability of the battlefront commanders to deploy them.

The command structure which Hitler created was far too fragmented and complex, even by his byzantine standards, to be efficient. The defence of France was part of OB West (Commander-in-Chief, West), which included the Netherlands, Belgium and Luxembourg together with occupied France. It was designated as an OKW theatre, which meant that Hitler commanded through his personal staff in the armed forces high command, which did not have the resources to perform its duties supervising all theatres of war except the Eastern Front.

Operationally, there were several unusual anomalies resulting from the bizarre command structure. For example, the heavy artillery which was expected to repel the invasion was under the command of the Kriegsmarine until the invasion forces landed, when it would come under the control of the Army. The Flak artillery, meanwhile, was part of the Luftwaffe but under the operational command of the Army. Army Group West was the responsible army group command, with Field Marshal Rundstedt designated as overall theatre commander, but its largest grouping of forces was Army Group B, under the command of Field Marshal Rommel, who had a direct line to Hitler and was almost independent of OB West.

Additionally, there was no agreement as to the strategy to be employed with the mobile reserve once the invasion forces had landed. Rundstedt favoured keeping the mobile reserve at a central point in one powerful grouping far enough inland not to be affected by Allied air superiority and heavy naval ordnance support. Rommel preferred committing all the reserves at the invasion point as soon as the landing occurred to defeat it as close to the beaches and as quickly as possible. Hitler imposed a compromise strategy which managed to achieve the virtues of neither and had the effect of weakening the German forces which could respond, so that the defeat of the invasion was ultimately rendered less likely. He did this by keeping part of the mobile forces in OKW reserve and deploying some of it in locations near the potential invasion points, but not as close as Rommel requested or in enough strength to overwhelm the invasion forces without further reinforcement. The OKW reserve could also only be committed with the Fuhrer's consent, which further complicated the situation and made its speedy commitment less likely.

The deployment of forces prior to the invasion was adversely affected by the continuous interference of Hitler, who became involved in the siting of all troops and their support equipment. His changes from the deployments made and intended by Rommel were almost invariably shown to have detracted from the power of the defence when the invasion occurred. Rommel's report to Hitler of 3 July 1944 is completely reproduced in this volume in Appendix 1 and is enough in itself to establish the incompetence of Hitler beyond reasonable doubt.

When the Allied airborne troops landed to commence the invasion shortly after midnight on 6 June 1944, the Germans were unsure of how to react and whether this signalled the actual landings or were merely the feint they had expected. This doubt remained for some hours, but when he heard of the landings, Rundstedt wished to immediately send the armoured reserves from their positions around Paris to be closer to Normandy so that they could be deployed as quickly as possible when required. Hitler was asleep, so Rundstedt's request for the redeployment was taken by Jodl, the OKW Chief of Operations. Jodl was unwilling to wake Hitler to transmit the request and therefore the reserves stayed where they were. The importance of this decision does not necessarily lie in the question of whether the invasion would have been defeated by these troops being deployed as requested, but that it shows the absolutely ridiculous situation which had developed whereby the judgement of Rundstedt, one of the best commanders the Germans had, could be thwarted by Jodl, who had no operational command experience and no authority to countermand the orders of Rundstedt. This situation exemplifies the defective command structure under which the German commanders laboured. It is also worthwhile pointing out that Rundstedt's view was, of course, shown to be correct; had the reserves been moved when he requested, they may well have made a difference to the development of the battle, even though the invasion may not have been defeated.

There was another reserve which did have the potential to defeat the Allies, but which Hitler also would not allow to be moved. This was the nineteen divisions of the Fifteenth Army, which were concentrated around the Pas-de-Calais, a comparatively short distance from the battlefield. These divisions were not of particularly high quality, being only partially mobile or essentially immobile, but would have been capable of filling out the German line and allowing the higher-quality panzer and mechanized divisions to be withdrawn and concentrated for attack. Warlimont commented:[31]

'Rommel and the OKW Operations staff, **with the significant exception of Jodl** [author's emphasis], independently reached the conclusion that **every risk must be taken** [author's emphasis] and all available forces concentrated for a rapid counter-attack against the enemy who had just landed – as indeed Directive 51 laid down; no one else reached this conclusion. The most important step was to move from the Straits to Normandy **the bulk of the Fifteenth Army** [author's emphasis], then to collect all forces which could be made available rapidly from the other parts of France, and so be in a position to launch a decisive counter-attack.

'This was too bold a decision for Hitler. He would allow no reduction in the strength of the Fifteenth Army. **Any other possible reinforcements however could not arrive for days or even weeks** [author's emphasis].'

General Omar Bradley, who was in command of the US 12th Army Group committed to the Normandy beachhead, commented:[32]

'Hitler and his generals had one last chance to defeat us. The nineteen divisions of the Fifteenth Army in the Pas de Calais (120 miles away) and von Rundstedt's five panzer divisions of armoured reserve were still uncommitted. Had Hitler thrown these forces against us within the first few days or within the first week, he might well have overwhelmed us.'

The Allies were thus fully aware of the threat posed by the Fifteenth Army, but Hitler was completely unwilling to commit it to battle because he still expected another invasion in the Pas-de-Calais. The Germans were therefore incapable of defending Normandy effectively because the Allies were able to build up their forces more rapidly and had far greater firepower available through the use of their air forces and the heavy naval guns of their fleets, which could reach targets up to 40km inland. Warlimont recalled the following incident:[33]

'Hitler might now have thought back to his statement that an allied success in the West would decide the war and have drawn the necessary conclusions from it; but instead he was to be seen in front of the assembled company at a briefing conference, using ruler and compass to work out the small number of square miles occupied by the enemy in Normandy and compare them to the great area of France still in German hands. One's thoughts went back to those early days of the Polish war. **Was this really all he was capable of as a military leader? Or did he think that this elementary method would have some propaganda effect on his audience? It was a sight I shall not readily forget** [author's emphasis].'

The report Rommel sent to Hitler on 3 July setting out the reasons for the problems which had occurred in the defence of Normandy, and the steps which he had tried to take but which had been blocked by the OKW, is a catalogue of disastrous decisions by Hitler which fully explain the defeat which ensued.

This catalogue of errors and negligence in command can only be marvelled at for its breadth and comprehensive nature. It is hardly possible to envisage how the situation could have been more mismanaged from the German point of view. If these decisions had been the responsibility of any other person in the German command structure, Hitler would have eagerly sacked and blamed them for the disaster which occurred as the direct result of them.

Rundstedt reached the only militarily sound conclusion when he told Keitel in a phone conversation on 3 July, in answer to his question 'what shall we do?', that 'You should end the war!'[34] Hitler had briefed Kluge that Rundstedt and Rommel had been too pessimistic regarding the position in Normandy, but when he took command he soon realized that they had not exaggerated the position and that the front was near to collapse.

While he was recuperating after having been injured when strafed by an Allied aircraft on 17 July, Rommel spoke with his son, Manfred:[35]

'My functions in Normandy, he said, were so restricted by Hitler, that any sergeant-major could have carried them out. He interfered in everything and turned down every proposal we made. The British and Americans only had two bridgeheads to begin with, a weak one on the Cotentin peninsula and a somewhat stronger one near Bayeux. Naturally, we wanted to attack the weak one first. But no; Hitler thought otherwise. The half-hearted dispersed attack which resulted was simply nipped in the bud. If we pulled a division out, Hitler ordered us to send it straight back. Where we ordered "Resistance to the last round" it was changed from above to "Resistance to the last drop of blood". When Cherbourg finally surrendered, they sent us a court martial adviser. That was the sort of help we got.'

When the breakout by the US Third Army occurred on 25 July, Kluge was instructed by Hitler to mount an offensive against the US forces at Mortain in order to cut them off. This offensive could not be mounted in anything like sufficient strength, although Kluge scraped together every formation he could to undertake it. Warlimont, who happened to be at Kluge's headquarters when the offensive was being arranged, reported to Hitler when he returned to the Fuhrer HQ:[36]

> 'I concluded by commenting that the failure of the counter-attack was certainly not due to any lack of preparation. This drew from Hitler his only comment; with a harsh edge to his voice he said: "the attack failed because Field Marshal von Kluge wanted it to fail."'

By this stage of the war, and with the attempted coup in the very recent past, Hitler's paranoia regarding his generals was virtually all-embracing. Although Kluge was suspected of being inclined toward the aims of the coup, there is no direct evidence that he was willing to give his blessing to any attempt to kill Hitler. Nevertheless, the suspicion was enough to convince Hitler of his guilt. The same suspicion was also enough to ensure Rommel's forced suicide.

Field Marshal Model, who succeeded Kluge to the command of what remained of the German forces in the West on 17 August, soon realized that there was nothing he could do to redeem the situation except to order the retreat of the remnants of the German formantions as quickly as could be arranged. Hitler acquiesced in the retreat, but ordered that the Channel ports and those in Brittany and southern France be maintained as fortresses. This tied up tens of thousands of troops which could have been used to shore up the main German defence.

According to a report of 28 September 1944 by the Commander-in-Chief West and the Chief Surgeon of the German Army, the approximate German losses in the West from 6 June to 31 August were 30,000 killed, 80,000 wounded and 210,000 missing.[37] The heavy equipment of almost all the German divisions involved in the defence of Normandy had been destroyed or left behind in the retreat.

The elite German Army divisions which were virtually destroyed in the Normandy campaign included the 2nd Panzer, 9th Panzer, 11th Panzer, 21st Panzer, 116th Panzer and Panzer Lehr, while the Waffen-SS divisions decimated included the 1st SS-Panzer, 2nd SS-Panzer, 9th SS-Panzer, 10th

SS-Panzer and 12th SS-Panzer, as well as the 17th SS-Panzer Grenadier Division. The loss of these formations represented a crisis involving the most experienced and best-equipped divisions of the Wehrmacht, which could not be replaced with respect to their personnel or equipment.

Once again, Hitler's contribution to the defence of the German position was almost totally negative. His interference with the deployment of the forces in Normandy prior to the invasion was shown by Rommel's memorandum of 3 July to have been wrong in virtually every detail. The strategy which he imposed on Rundstedt and Rommel regarding the use of the mobile reserves in France managed to establish the worst of both worlds because it did not commit enough power to either strategy to enable the defence to succeed.

The fact that Jodl was able to delay the commitment of the reserve on the first morning of the invasion is enough to show how ludicrous were the command arrangements under which the commanders in OB West laboured.

Hitler's delay in committing the Fifteenth Army, which was relatively close to the Normandy battlefield, was a major mistake and effectively meant that there was no hope of building up sufficient forces to defeat the invasion. It should have been obvious that it did not matter if another invasion was planned, because if the first one succeeded, the second would not be necessary. Therefore, everything had to be concentrated to defeat the Normandy landings as soon as possible; Hitler was advised that this was the case but refused to act on that advice.

The Mortain counter-attack was a case of too little too late, a desperate measure which had no realistic chance of success. It merely made the defeat of the German forces worse than would otherwise have been the case by ensuring more of them were trapped in the Falaise pocket.

It is thus obvious that Hitler's interventions in the West made the defeat of the German forces there certain, rather than a real possibility.

Operation *Citadel*, 1943

During the winter of 1942–43, Field Marshal von Manstein conducted a series of defensive battles after the defeat at Stalingrad which, together with the withdrawal of most of the German forces from the Caucasus region, stabilized, momentarily at least, the German front. In doing so, he used, as far as Hitler's interference would allow, the tactics in which the Germans still had an advantage, namely flexible defence. During the Soviet winter campaign, and despite Hitler's interference, he avoided several attempts by the Red Army to cut off and encircle German formations and was able to largely minimize the effect of the offensive by much larger Red Army forces. When the Soviet offensive outran its supplies, Manstein was also able to mount a riposte which resulted in Kharkov and Belgorod being retaken in March 1943.

During February 1943, Manstein had proposed to Hitler that plans be developed to anticipate the Red Army offensive which would occur once they had resupplied themselves following the winter offensive. The possibilities he raised included waiting for the offensive and destroying the Soviet formations through concentrating all the panzers forces available, which he called the 'backhand' option, or attempting an offensive attack before the Red Army had established itself to destroy its concentration in the salient around Kursk. Of these options, he recommended the 'backhand' option. If the offensive was to be taken by Germany, he stipulated that it must occur no later than April to ensure that the Red Army had not been able to fully establish itself in the positions around Kursk. Hitler and Zeitzler both accepted that this was a real opportunity to achieve a significant victory, which might perhaps even restore the initiative to the Germans. The crucial point in Manstein's proposal, however, was the timing, which he said was critical to its success and meant that the attack had to be made before the Red Army was able to restore its losses and deploy defensively around Kursk. He stipulated this must be carried out as soon as possible, and definitely before May.

Manstein also indicated that he preferred to wait for the Red Army to attack and then to use the concentrated power of all the German panzer forces, which could be gathered to impose a significant defeat on the attacking formations. The Fuhrer, however, did not accept this proposal and decided to mount an attack on the Soviet positions. He also decided on several occasions to delay the attack in order to increase the forces for the offensive to give it as much weight as possible. This included waiting for the first production run of the new Panther medium tanks and the first deployment of the Ferdinand heavy tank destroyers. The forces which Hitler committed to the offensive, which was codenamed Operation *Citadel*, involved virtually every panzer and mechanized division which the Germans could spare from all fronts, and were concentrated at the northern and southern shoulders of the Kursk salient. The two army groups were commanded by Model, attacking from the north, and Manstein, attacking from the south – there could hardly have been better commanders or more force concentrated by the Germans. In total, the Germans amassed twenty-three regular infantry divisions, twelve panzer divisions, three panzer grenadier divisions, two regiments of Ferdinand tank destroyers, two battalions equipped with Tiger tanks, one brigade of Panther tanks, one SS panzer division and two SS panzer grenadier divisions. The Luftwaffe, meanwhile, contributed approximately 1,700 aircraft of all types. Regardless of the time constraints stipulated by Manstein or the evidence of the Red Army's defensive efforts, the size of the forces committed gave rise to Hitler's confidence that the attack would be successful.

Prior to the date of the attack, the Fuhrer convened a final conference attended by Field Marshals Manstein and Model, together with Generals Guderian and Zeitzler. Hitler asked each of them if they were still in favour of the attack going ahead. Manstein said yes, but that he needed more infantry to achieve victory, which wasn't available. Model said no, because he had aerial reconnaissance photography which showed that the Red Army had entrenched itself in formidable positions precisely in the areas where the attack was to be made, and this indicated that they knew of the German plan. Guderian was not in favour of the attack going ahead, because in his view the Wehrmacht should husband its resources and defeat the Soviet offensive which he was sure would come shortly. Zeitzler was in favour of proceeding.

Yet despite the fact that both the operational commanders, whom he had himself selected to command the troops involved in the offensive, were not in favour of the attack proceeding or stated that it needed additional force to guarantee success – which amounted to the same thing – Hitler ordered that it be undertaken anyway.

The attack commenced on 5 July, which was three months after Manstein had stated was the limit of when the offensive should be made. The Red Army had prepared defences of unprecedented depth and strength and had mobile reserves available which were significantly larger than those of the Germans. Model's attack made little headway, and by 9 July his formations had been involved in costly battles for little gain. When he was ready to recommence the attack on 12 July, he was pre-empted by the Red Army, which mounted its own offensive from a bridgehead at Orel against Army Group Centre to the immediate north of Model's army group, which meant that his mobile forces had to be detached to assist in defending against this new Soviet attack. Consequently, the German attack from the north was effectively over.

Manstein's southern attacking force had made better progress, but when he requested reinforcements to exploit the advance made on 6 July – and twice subsequently – Hitler refused. On 13 July, Hitler decided to halt the southern offensive as a result of the Allied invasion of Sicily on 9 July. The Fuhrer explained that he had to send forces to defend Sicily, and the only ones available were on the Eastern Front. Nevertheless, the forces which were sent did not arrive in time to make any difference to the defence of Sicily, and the island was lost.

Hitler's management of the *Citadel* offensive was another example of his unfitness to be a senior military commander, let alone the operational Supreme Commander of the Wehrmacht. The first and most important factor to remember is that Manstein's proposal was for the offensive to occur before the Red Army had time to consolidate its position around Kursk. Hitler delayed the offensive's commencement twice, in May and June. Both times were later than Manstein had stipulated, but launching the offensive in July was well outside the window of opportunity and therefore lost the prime element which he had intended to take advantage of – to strike the Soviets while they were off balance. Secondly, Manstein had told Hitler that he favoured allowing the Red Army to attack and then to use German forces to mount their own offensive to destroy the Soviets, once the Red Army was committed. Hitler thus adopted the option which Manstein did not favour. Thirdly, Hitler's delaying of the offensive to obtain further weight was counterproductive because the Soviets were out-producing the Germans; indeed, the Fuhrer had been given production figures showing this to be the case. But Hitler chose to ignore this data, and by delaying the commencement of the offensive actually caused the disparity between the forces to increase in favour of the Red Army. Fourthly, Model had photographic reconnaissance evidence that the Soviets had constructed defences of great depth, which also existed on the southern shoulder of the salient. Hitler chose to ignore this evidence.

Characteristically, when the offensive failed, Hitler chose his usual path of shifting the blame onto the General Staff, saying: 'This is the last time I will listen to the council [*sic*] of my general staff.'[38] This was despite the fact that at the last conference prior to the offensive, the majority of his generals had advised him either not to go ahead with the operation or that it needed greater force to succeed, which was tantamount to the same thing.

The final analysis must conclude that Operation *Citadel* again exhibited all the weaknesses of Hitler's amateurish methods of high command. The result was another disaster, one from which Germany now did not have the resources to recover.

The Ardennes offensive, 1944

It is hard to see how the 1944 Ardennes offensive can be categorized as a serious operation of war. This comment is not intended to disparage the bravery of the Allied troops involved or the tactical complications it caused. Objectively looked at, however, the offensive amounted to nothing more than a figment of Hitler's imagination, a last desperate attempt by him to cling to power for as long as possible in the hope that the coalition against Nazi Germany would fall apart.

None of the German commanders involved thought it had any chance of success. Rundstedt stated that he was 'staggered' when he saw the plans, realizing at once that there were insufficient forces committed to have any chance of reaching the objectives envisaged. Model commented that the plan 'didn't have a damned leg to stand on'.

The timeframe for the German forces to reach the Meuse River was ridiculously short – only 48 hours. In 1940, Guderian's tanks had taken three days to reach the Meuse, when Germany's operational situation was completely different.

The picture regarding the Luftwaffe was also entirely different than had been the case in 1940, when it had enjoyed air superiority over the battlefield. In 1944, it was virtually incapable of influencing the development of the battle, and had been so since well before the Allies landed in Normandy.

The plan anticipated that the Americans would not be able to put up a strong defence, which was typical of Hitler's underestimation of his enemies. It also relied on the Germans being able to capture large US supply bases, which did not occur. The primary reason why neither of these expectations was correct and for the consequent defeat of the offensive was the stout defence of the US soldiers.

Hitler's disposition of the forces involved were made so that the Waffen-SS, representing the Nazi government, would garner the credit for the success which he was sure would occur, further degrading the position of the regular army's generals. The dispositions themselves were amateurishly arranged, involving the main forces attempting to push their way through defensive bottlenecks and in territory very much in favour of the defenders.

Hitler's plans were proven operationally to be wrong in almost every respect.

The Supreme Headquarters Allied Expeditionary Forces (SHAEF), in the person of Eisenhower, reacted very quickly to the offensive and ordered two armoured divisions, together with the US 82nd and 101st Airborne Divisions, to the battlefield on its first couple of days. Further reinforcements were found in France and Britain and sent speedily to shore up the Allied position. Furthermore, command of the Allied forces was readjusted so that the northern section of the battle area was assigned to Field Marshal Montgomery and the southern part to General Bradley, which conformed to the communications and other resources available to the commanders. These steps had been taken by the second day of the offensive and guaranteed that it had no realistic chance of success. In the view of the author, General Eisenhower has never been given due credit for these timely and well-thought-through responses.

Characteristically, Hitler pressed the offensive for too long, which resulted in unnecessarily high casualties for the Germans which could simply not be replaced. The utter defeat suffered was a fitting end to Hitler's operational offensives, epitomizing the inept leadership which the Fuhrer exercised throughout his time as Commander-in-Chief of the German Army.

The Soviet winter offensive, 1944, and final offensives of January–April 1945

During the latter part of 1944, the Red Army winter offensive rolled on into Poland, Romania, Hungary and finally East Prussia, apparently unstoppable. Colonel General Guderian, who had been appointed as Chief of the General Staff on 21 July 1944 in the aftermath of the failed assassination attempt, realized at once that there was no hope of resisting the Red Army with the forces available. He repeatedly pressed Hitler for reserves to be committed to the Eastern Front, but only the smallest improvements were made while all the new formations and all tank production were committed to the Ardennes offensive. Guderian observed:[39]

> 'All attempts to assemble reserves behind the most immediately threatened sectors of the very tense Eastern Front foundered on the rocks of **Hitler's and Jodl's incomprehension** [author's emphasis]. The attitude of the OKW was based principally on a vague hope that our very precise intelligence to the great forthcoming Russian attack might be based on nothing but bluff. The men at headquarters were only too anxious to believe what they wanted to believe, and they closed their eyes when confronted by the ominous truth. Ostrich politics were combined with ostrich strategy. To console me Hitler said: "The Eastern Front has never before possessed such a strong reserve as now. That is your doing. I thank you for it." I replied: "The Eastern Front is like a house of cards. If the front is broken through at one point all the rest will collapse, for twelve and a half divisions is far too small a reserve for so extended a front."

It is apparent that Jodl misread the operational position in the same way that Hitler did, or that he professed to do so. Guderian states that when it was obvious that the Ardennes offensive had failed, Jodl continued to contend that the attacks in the West must be continued to take advantage of the initiative which he believed had been recaptured and because the German attacks had upset the Allies' plans and operational timetable.[40] That these results were patently not the aims which had been repeatedly stated as those of the offensive and which spelt the doom of its chances, was not noticed by either Hitler or Jodl. The atmosphere of delusion seems to have completely taken control of both of them. This confirms Jodl's unsuitability for his position in the OKW, which required above all complete objectivity in analysing any given military situation, not just agreeing with Hitler so that he could have an easy existence.

Hitler did eventually concede on 15 January 1945 that the Ardennes offensive had failed, ordering that the forces in the West revert to the defensive and that all armoured reserves which could be gathered be sent to the Eastern Front. In doing so, he ordered that they be used in two offensives – in Hungary and eastern Germany – thus splitting their power, whereas Guderian wanted to concentrate them and attack the Red Army bridgehead across the Oder River before it was fully established. Hitler personally ordered that the Sixth SS-Panzer Army be used to attack in Hungary, ensuring that the operation against the Oder bridgehead did not have the power to succeed. Indeed, by splitting the forces to the two operations, neither had the power to achieve success. These orders were typical of Hitler's desire to attack everywhere and show that he had learned nothing from his experiences while in command of the German Army.

I do not intend to examine in detail the course of the last months of the war in the East, not because developments in the situation there were not important, but due to there being no evidence of any change in Hitler's strategic views, tactics or methods of command that illustrate his unfitness for command any better than the examples which have already been given.

Key personnel appointments

Hitler's appointments to key positions in the armed forces betrayed his inability to trust all but a small group of commanders, although he did tolerate some whom he did not fully trust because of their outstanding ability, including Manstein, Guderian, Kleist, Rundstedt and Halder. From 1942 onwards, however, his appointments became more overtly based on his perception of the political reliability of candidates for senior positions, as is illustrated by the circumstances related earlier surrounding the dismissal of Halder.

The sacking of Blomberg, Beck and Fritsch (respectively Minister of War, Chief of the General Staff and Commander-in-Chief of the Army) in 1938 was based on their resistance to his wishes to expand the German Army to thirty-six divisions, which was much higher than the Army's estimate (twenty-one divisions) that could be properly trained, and their reluctance to undertake any actions which could involve increased tension with the victors of the First World War. These sackings show that Hitler's reluctance to work with anyone who opposed his wishes was a factor which existed from the very beginning of his dictatorship. It was a charcter trait which became more pronounced the longer he remained in power.

The first time during the war that he sacked a senior army commander was on 1 December 1941, that is to say before he assumed the role of the Army's operational commander-in-chief, when he sacked Rundstedt. This was done because Rundstedt had told him that Rostov could not be held against Red Army counter-attacks and that if he didn't trust his judgement he should get someone else to command his army group. Hitler replaced Rundstedt with Field Marshal von Reichenau, but Rundstedt's prediction that Rostov could not be held was shown by subsequent events to be correct, as although the Fuhrer emphatically ordered that Rostov be held, German forces had to retreat from there later the same day. Hitler subsequently admitted that he had been wrong on his ocasion, something which did not occur often in the future. Halder's diary entry of 3 December 1941 confirms this rare event. Nevertheless, there is no evidence that Hitler drew any conclusion which required him to change his mode of command.

Brauchitsch, Halder, Leeb, Bock, List, Manstein, Kleist, Rundstedt and numerous others were all sacked by the Fuhrer because they did not act in accordance with his wishes, although he frequently refrained from giving any reasons for the dismissals. This list reads like a 'Who's who' of the best commanders in the German Army. In all these instances, the real reason for the sacking was not the incompetence of the commander, but Hitler's inability to understand that military command ability does not equate to acquiescence to every order which is given. Keitel made the following general remark relating to Hitler's method of command:[41]

> 'It was Hitler's wont to find a scapegoat for every failure, and even more so if he could hardly fail to see that he himself was to blame for the failure's origin at least.'

Coming from Keitel, who is widely regarded as Hitler's most subservient lackey, this view must be accorded real weight.

With respect to the sacking of Brauchitsch on 19 December 1941, Keitel made the following observation:[42]

> 'Only the real reasons for the reverse were supressed, evident though they were; he [Hitler] had underestimated the enemy's ability to resist and the risk of winter closing in early that year and expected too much of the troops' fighting capacity in the endless battles from October onwards; and finally they lacked sufficient supplies. ... the guilty party would soon be looked for, and his name would not be Hitler.'

Keitel shows in this passage that he really understood how Hitler operated, but that he probably supressed his views and conclusions because of a misguided sense of duty or was too weak to press them on Hitler. He also realized that if he annoyed Hitler by arguing against his decisions, he would simply be replaced.

Field Marshal Fedor von Bock's sacking is another perfect example of Hitler's modus operandi. Bock was never given a clear-cut reason by Hitler for his dismissal. Warlimont recorded:[43]

> '[Bock] was dismissed a second time with "expressions of the utmost indignation"; his Chief of Staff was only saved from the same fate by the intervention of Halder. Hitler justified his decision by quoting a previous "unfortunate proposal" by the Army Group, which however, had never been carried out; he never failed subsequently to ascribe the failure of the entire offensive to Bock's dilatoriness at Voronezh.'

Halder's dismissal is yet another example of Hitler's capricious and duplicitous mode of dealing with people. Warlimont gave a very powerful description of the scene that he believed caused Hitler to sack Halder on 24 August 1942. Halder had been trying once again to obtain Hitler's approval for the Ninth Army, which was fighting at Rzhev, to be allowed freedom of movement to redeploy so that it could minimize its casualties and maximize its defensive power. This led to a serious argument in which Halder answered back to Hitler's insinuations that he did not have the same toughness as the troops at the front. Warlimont concluded that 'it was now clear that the final breach between these two men, who were as different as chalk from cheese, could not be far off'.[44]

List, meanwhile, was sacked because he *did* comply with Hitler's orders, as Jodl himself confirmed. The circumstances around his dismissal were even more extraordinary than usual. Hitler was extremely displeased by the lack of progress being made by List's army group, which he had sent to the trans-Caucasus region to take the oilfields of Baku as part of the 1942 summer offensive. Although the offensive began with good progress, it stalled, primarily through a combination of lack of supplies and stronger-than-expected Soviet resistance. To get the offensive moving again, Hitler sent Jodl to List's headquarters with an imperative directive that the attacking momentum must be resumed. When Jodl returned he told Hitler that he agreed with List that the offensive could not be resumed, adding that List had carried out all of the Fuhrer's orders. This episode, according to Jodl, led to Hitler refusing to take his meals with his OKW staff or any other general for the rest of the war. Hitler also refused to shake the hand of any general, as noted by Zeitzler.

These childish manifestations in Hitler would be unbelievable if they were not attested to by the recollections of many senior military personnel.

Keitel stated:[45]

'[This episode illustrated Hitler's] pathological delusion that his generals were conspiring against him and were trying to sabotage his orders ... What he did not seem to want to understand was that the very great supply and logistical difficulties entailed by the mountain paths made the operation absolutely impracticable.'

Once again, coming from Keitel, widely seen as Hitler's most subservient disciple in the military hierarchy, this assessment must be given credence.

In addition to those who were dismissed or demoted, there were others who were executed for involvement – or suspected involvement – in the assassination plot of 20 July 1944. These included Field Marshals Rommel, Kluge and Witzleben. Erwin von Witzleben was shown to have been in league with the plotters and was subjected to the most humiliating trial that Hitler and his judicial myrmidon, Roland Freisler, could inflict. There was no direct evidence of Rommel or Kluge having approved of any decision to assassinate the Fuhrer, but the suspicion was enough for Hitler to assume that they were full parties to the attempted coup. Rommel was given the choice of taking his own life or having his family included in any steps taken against him, and chose suicide. Kluge realized the fate which awaited him because he had flirted with the conspirators, although he did not act against Hitler. The fact that the people Hitler pursued for revenge included two of the best and hitherto most formidable military commanders in the Nazi state did not seem to cause him to question his policies or methods in any regard.

There is no doubt that Hitler had commanders who he favoured, some of whom were very good in that role. Kesselring and Model were in this category, but they were in a distinct minority. Kesselring wrote a biography after the war entitled *A Soldier's Story*,[46] in which he related the substance of a meeting with the Fuhrer on 15 March 1945 after he had been appointed as Commander-in-Chief West:[47]

'As I drove back in the night of 15–16 March I had the impression that Hitler stubbornly believed we could defeat the Russians in the east, and that what was happening in the west neither surprised nor particularly worried him. He took it for granted that once the Russian front had been consolidated he would be able with the forces so released and his newly created divisions to clean up in the west. He was equally convinced that his orders to increase supplies would be carried out to the letter.

'It was very different in fact.'

This was after the Ardennes offensive had been comprehensively defeated and the Red Army had taken parts of East Prussia and was menacing Berlin. For anyone – let alone Hitler, who was fully aware of the dire strategic situtaion faced by the Reich – to hold these views seriously shows that they were completely delusional.

Model committed suicide on 15 April, less than a month before the surrender occurred, and destroyed all his personal papers before doing so. He thus did not leave any written views on the command structure or Hitler's abilities in that role. However, although he had been a strong supporter and trusted commander of Hitler, he did not carry out his orders that Army Group B, which Model commanded, should defend the Ruhr to the end when they were surrounded by Allied forces. Model instead discharged the army group's men so that they could either go on leave or surrender. Subsequently, the whole of Army Group B was denounced as traitors through a proclamation on the German radio network. For Model to disobey an instruction from Hitler was unheard of, and evidence enough of his view of that order.

Hitler also made appointments which were beyond rational understanding. Perhaps the worst was the elevation of Himmler to command Army Group Vistula on 24 January 1945. Himmler had no military command experience at all and did not even serve in the First World War, having been too young, although he did undergo some military training. His appointment to this vital post was viewed with astonishment by Guderian, who later commented:[48]

> 'This preposterous suggestion appalled me and I used such argumentative powers as I possessed in an attempt to stop such an idiocy being perpetrated on the unfortunate eastern front. It was all in vain.'

The appointment inevitably led to Guderian having a major dispute with Himmler and Hitler regarding the way in which Himmler attempted to manage an offensive. The starting point was the appointment of a competent and experienced senior officer to command the attack, Guderian insisting that General Walther Wenck be attached to Himmler's staff to manage the attack, which was not in accord with Hitler's wishes. This led to an argument with Hitler that was described by Guderian:[49]

'And so it went on for two hours. His fists raised, his cheeks flushed with rage, his whole body trembling, the man stood there in front of me, beside himself with fury and having lost all self-control. After each outburst of rage Hitler would stride up and down the carpet edge, then stop immediately before me and hurl his next accusation in my face. He was almost screaming, his eyes seemed to pop out of his head and his veins stood out on his temples. I had made up my mind that I would allow nothing to destroy my equanimity and that I would simply repeat my essential demands over and over again. This I did with icy consistency.

'... Suddenly Hitler stopped short of Himmler and said: "Well Himmler, General Wenck will arrive at your headquarters tonight and will take charge of the attack." Then he walked over to Wenck and told him that he was to report to the army group staff forthwith. Then he sat down in his usual place, called me over to him and said: "Now please continue with the conference. The General staff has won a battle this day." And as he said this he smiled his most charming smile.'

It is not possible to assign rational explanations to this episode on Hitler's part. It paints an extremely disturbing picture of the man who had the fate of Germany in his hands and was responsible only to himself. The timing of the appointment was crucial, and speed was necessary to ensure that the opportunity to attack the Red Army while it was off-balance was not lost. Equally crucial was the ability of the executant of the proposed attack, so engaging in such a time-wasting and enervating argument was contrary to every rational consideration which the situation required. It is a fitting episode to end this chapter, perfectly illustrating Hitler's quixotic and unrealistic methods and attitudes to the appointment of commanders to senior positions in the military hierarchy of the Third Reich.

Conclusions

1. There is more than enough evidence in the forgoing material and the detailed chapters of Volumes 1 and 2 of this book to show that Hitler was completely out of his depth in attempting the operational command of the German Army.
2. His inability manifested itself through, among other matters, his chronic underestimation of his enemies. There are numerous examples of this on the Eastern Front, as well as his underrating of the American forces as expressed to Speer prior to the Ardennes offensive. No-one acting under

these delusions could effectively manage a military campaign where absolute objectivity was necessary in a senior commander.
3. Hitler's inability or unwillingness to understand issues relating to the relationship of force and space are evident throughout the time he commanded the German Army. A particularly egregious example was the offensive prior to Stalingrad, which is commented upon by Zeitzler in his treatise *The Fatal Decisions*.
4. The Fuhrer's apparent ignorance of the importance of supply of operations is commented upon by Manstein and others. Once again, this is illustrated by the lack of adequate preparations made for the 1942 Stalingrad offensive which resulted in the loss of the Sixth Army. The fact that he dispensed with the testing of his plans, as had been the case by the OKH whenever new offensives were undertaken, as related by Warlimont, is further evidence of his amateurism in the field.
5. His constant chopping and changing of plans is obvious to anyone who takes the time to analyse the operations Hitler commanded. These changes resulted in unclear operational objectives and reduced the chance of success of the operation affected. This was most apparent during the early stages of Operation *Barbarossa*, when he ordered changes to the OKH plan which required the redeployment of major forces to the extremities of the operational theatre of the campaign, around Leningrad in the north and Kiev in the south. This was a major feature of all the operations he commanded. The most obvious problem this caused was that it reduced the time available to achieve the objectives required to gain success.
6. The Fuhrer's objectives were almost always selected for political or economic factors which had little to do with military realities. This is epitomized by the selection of the objectives for the 1942 Stalingrad campaign, which were to cut off the flow of supplies to Soviet industry along the Volga and to obtain the oil resources of the Trans-Caucasus region. As Manstein pointed out, these were important objectives, but in order to attain them Germany had first to destroy the military forces of the USSR.
7. Hitler's 'strategy' of inflexible defence reduced the German forces during the winter of 1941, and afterwards, to fighting in which they minimized their own advantages and maximized those of the Red Army. During the winter of 1941, he forbad any redeployment of German forces, which meant that in many cases they were fighting in geographically disadvantageous positions. He apparently did not understand that the senior German field commanders – who included Rundstedt, Kluge, List and Leeb – were not proposing wholesale retreat from every position, but a considered readjustment of the German forces to take advantage of their defensive

power. That this was within the capability of the German formations and would not have led to a rout of the kind suffered by Napoleon's army of 1812 is illustrated by the actual course of the fighting which occurred. Despite the disadvantageous position of the German forces, they held on – how much better they could have done if an intelligent rearrangement of their positions had occurred is surely not an arid enquiry.

8. His method of command led to the stultification of initiative in the operational levels of formations because he did not understand the importance of allowing flexibility in the implementation of orders by lower-level commanders where they could see opportunities not apparent to those not on or close to the battlefield. The reason he did not wish to allow this was because he believed that he alone possessed the ability to determine all issues relating to the best deployment of the German Army.

A Note on Sources and Further Reading

Witnesses

The generals who were with Hitler on a day-to-day basis during the war and were therefore direct witnesses of his attempts to command the Wehrmacht were the three Chiefs of the General Staff, Colonel Generals Halder, Zeitzler and Guderian, and those who formed the highest command of the OKW, Field Marshal Keitel, Colonel General Alfred Jodl and General Walter Warlimont. Halder and Guderian both wrote important books after the war, while Halder's diary provides unique insights into the operation of the supreme command. Zeitzler wrote some commentary for published books and articles, the most important of which is his thoughts on the Stalingrad campaign, in which he was probably the principal military participant after Hitler himself.

Halder's book, *Hitler as Warlord*, is a reasoned, trenchant description and review in general terms of Hitler's command of the German Army. It is a relatively short work, but no less valuable for that.

Halder's published diary of the period while he was Chief of the General Staff has been described as 'the most significant personal document of World War 2 from the German side'. Reading it, it is quickly apparent why he and Hitler were ultimately not able to work together – their intellectual approach was poles apart. Halder reflects the approach of an intelligent, thoughtful person, being evidence based and analytical, whereas Hitler's approach was the polar opposite, mainly based on intuition and wishful thinking.

The fact that Guderian's book *Panzer Leader* has been in print continuously since it was first published is an indication of its interest and relevance. His many operational commands give his observations particular force and importance, while his experiences working with Hitler and the OKW perfectly reflect the difficulties involved in attempting to manage the German war effort rationally.

Zeitzler's recollections of the Stalingrad disaster and his comments on the campaign in general are indispensable to any review of its course and the steps taken. These are brought together in his treatise as part of *The Fatal Decisions*, a book which deals with several campaigns through the recollections of the

German commanders involved. I have cross-checked his recollections with other participants, and they are consistent. Equally relevant are his observations relating to wider strategic questions. Zeitzler's dismissal by Hitler occurred in the aftermath of the assassination attempt of 20 July 1944 and was marked with every sign of disapproval. For example, he was stripped of his pension rights and entitlement to wear the uniform, even though he was not regarded as having been implicated in the assassination plot. Zeitzler apparently simply could not work with Hitler any longer and had some form of breakdown.

Keitel and Jodl were both executed following the trial of the major war criminals at Nuremburg, but Keitel was able to write a draft memoir which has been published. Entitled *The Memoirs of Field Marshal Keitel*, it was edited by Walter Gorlitz. Keitel comes across as having finally realized his fault in serving Hitler so slavishly, and is ultimately a rather pathetic figure. However, he does make some revealing observations relating to Hitler and his attempt to command the German Army.

Jodl did not leave any written record of his views regarding Hitler, but there is his testimony from the Nuremburg trials which is located in Volume 15 of the record.

Warlimont, who was not tried as a war criminal, wrote one of the most famous and important works dealing with the way Hitler exercised command through his Fuhrer Headquarters staff at the OKW, where he was based throughout virtually the entire war. He had to leave the OKW on medical grounds as the result of an injury suffered during the unsuccessful assassination of Hitler in July 1944. His book *Inside Hitler's Headquarters, 1939–45* is an invaluable source.

Field Marshal von Manstein masterminded the offensive in the west in 1940 and was an army group commander on the Eastern Front, including the attempt to relieve Stalingrad and the southern pincer of the 1943 Kursk offensive, Operation *Citadel*. He is widely regarded as the most able of the senior German commanders in the Second World War, although this did not save him from being sacked by Hitler. His book *Lost Victories* is an instructive account dealing with his commands, including his pivotal role in the 1940 campaign and those on the Eastern Front until his dismissal on 30 March 1944. It contains his views on Hitler as the supreme commander of the German Army and is all the more important as coming from an expert operational commander and strategist.

Von Bock was one of the most successful of Hitler's generals during the initial campaigns of the war, Hitler regarding him so highly that he promoted him to field marshal on 19 July 1940 and placed him in command of the all-important Army Group Centre during the initial stages of Operation

Barbarossa. He was sacked by Hitler in 1942 – the circumstances of which are extremely important in assessing the Fuhrer's modus operandi – and never used again. His diary, published as *Fedor von Bock, the War Diary 1939–1945* in 1996, does not strictly reflect views on Hitler, but does comment in general on German operations and implies his views on them.

Field Marshal Rommel's papers, collected and analysed by Basil Liddell Hart, were published together with comments by his Chief of Staff, General Fritz Bayerlein. His conclusions and the papers Rommel wrote as Commander-in-Chief of Army Group B in France, especially that of 3 July 1944, are particularly edifying. The documents reveal Rommel as a brave and direct person, out of his depth in dealing with someone such as Hitler. They were published under the title *The Rommel Papers* and are readily available in several editions. Liddell Hart also interviewed Rommel's son, Manfred, whose recollections of his father's comments are particularly important. The biography *Knight's Cross: A Life of Field Marshal Erwin Rommel* by David Fraser is also an invaluable source.

Field Marshal Kesselring, somewhat of a favourite of Hitler, commanded both Army and Luftwaffe formations. He was Chief of Staff of the Luftwaffe before the war and in active commands for the entire war, ending it as Commander-in-Chief of Army Group West at the time of the surrender. He was also Commander-in-Chief South during the time that Rommel was in Africa and commanded the defence of Italy. He wrote a memoir in 1954, which is invaluable as he was involved in so many of the campaigns during the war and was exposed to Hitler's methods of command for a long period at the highest operational level. The memoir, titled *A Soldier's Record*, is an important addition to understanding Nazi Germany and Hitler. He was tried as a war criminal after the war with respect to anti-partisan operations in Italy, his death sentence being commuted to life in prison, although he was subsequently released.

Adolf Galland was one of the most outstanding air aces of the Luftwaffe, being promoted by Goering to be the general in command of the Luftwaffe's fighter forces. He did not want the job and soon became a thorn in Goering's side because of his unvarnished opinions, which did not conform to Goering's expectations. Galland tried to induce rational decision-making at the highest levels, only to be bitterly disappointed. In the course of his duties, he met with Hitler on several occasions concerning the development and use of the Me 262. He was one of the first to pilot the jet aircraft and believed that it presented a real possibility of causing significant damage to the Allied bomber fleets which were pounding Germany day and night. Hitler's decision to use the 262 as a bomber was deeply disappointing to him. During 1944, Galland accumulated large reserves of fighters – numbering thousands – which he wished to use in an all-out attack on the Allied bombers to inflict damage severe enough damage to force the curtailment of their offensive against Germany. However, these reserves were frittered away on two occasions by Hitler to support the ground forces, which ruined all Galland's efforts. He ended the war flying one of the few 262s produced as a fighter, no longer wishing to participate in command positions. After the war, his criticisms of Hitler's actions were made in a trenchant but factual manner.

Albert Speer, Hitler's architect, was appointed to be Minister for Armaments on the death of Dr Todt, who had been an early collaborator with Hitler on Germany's autobahns, among other projects. He rose to become the second most powerful person in the state before falling foul of Hitler's henchmen during 1944. He wrote two books which are of great interest and use as source material, the most instructive being *Inside the Third Reich*. The breadth of the events he covers makes this book invaluable.

Reviewing the information provided by the recollections and opinions of these most senior commanders and personalities of the Third Reich is crucial to understanding the way that the war developed and in attempting to understand what actuated Hitler to make the decisions he did. The information they provide and views they express can hardly be gainsaid, as their authors were witness to the events described and there is enough material from external sources to determine whether their views are consistent with known events and therefore credible.

Interviews

As part of the process undertaken at the time of the Nuremberg trials, interviews with the defendants were carried out by US Army psychiatrist Leon Goldensohn. These included the generals of the OKW, but there were also interviews with the witnesses being called for various reasons for the trials, which included the most important generals of the German supreme commands of the Army, Luftwaffe and Kriegsmarine. Published as *The Nuremberg Interviews*, these provide interesting and important information.

Basil Liddell Hart also interviewed many of the senior German commanders, including Field Marshal von Rundstedt, while they were prisoners of the British in the early post-war period. He collected these interviews and published them together with his own observations in 1949 as *The Other Side of the Hill*, which is an important reference point for any evaluation of Hitler's military decisions.

Government publications

The trial of the major war criminals before the International Military Tribunal at Nuremberg was arguably the most important trial of the twentieth century, running between 14 November 1945 and 1 October 1946. At the time there were many complaints regarding the length of the trials, but in retrospect the timing seems incredibly short having regard to the information produced. The record of the trial extends to forty-two volumes and is now readily available on the internet in several archives. For decades after it was first published, the record could only be obtained from Government printers, and I remember that when I first enquired, the record cost more than £4,000 in the 1970s, a considerable sum at the time. The trials have had many detractors over the years, with allegations of 'victor's justice' and other attempts to impugn its integrity and relevance. However, no-one who reads the record can doubt the fairness of the treatment accorded to the defendants or the integrity of the process involved in determining the veracity and accuracy of both the verbal and documentary evidence. The trial was as fair as it could possibly have been, given both the enormity of the issues involved and the time – straight after the war – when it was conducted. Even its location was notable, Nuremberg being where the Nazis held their annual rallies and the Palace of Justice being where the special court set up to try the conspirators involved in the 20 July 1944 attempt on Hitler's life were tried – no greater contrast could be imagined. The information collected is of first-ranking relevance even today. After their release, there were attempts by some of the defendants to show in published books that their treatment was unfair, but none are convincing or deal with the central issue – the guilt of the senior members of the government and military hierarchy for the appalling war crimes and human rights abuses perpetrated by the Nazi regime. The only defendant to acknowledge this form of guilt was Speer, who also warned in his final statement of the problems for humanity with the increasing power of technology which could be used to entrench dictatorships in the years to come – a timely warning if ever there was one.

Other subsidiary trials for war crimes were conducted against groups of defendants, such as the doctors involved in the appalling Nazi medical experiments on concentration camp inmates and the major industrialists who co-operated with the Nazi state in waging aggressive warfare. There were also trials conducted by governments relating to war crimes within the borders of their countries, some of which were not carried out with the same rigour or regard for evidence as was exhibited by those at Nuremberg.

The influence of the Nuremberg trials has been felt through the enactment of laws relating to war crimes and human rights, both within individual countries and internationally through the United Nations. It can therefore be stated with confidence that no trials in history have had the same influence as those at Nuremberg.

The United States Strategic Bombing Survey (USSBS)

The USSBS is extremely important in understanding the effect of the Allied bombing campaign, the damage it caused to the German war effort and its imperfections. As the Second World War was the first and only occasion on which such a concentrated strategic bombing offensive has been undertaken, the research provides extremely valuable information. While there is no question that the offensive caused significant damage to the German economy and retarded its war effort, the findings of the survey show that a still greater effect could have been obtained through concentration on a relatively small number of crucial industries and their infrastructure, including the oil industry and power-generation infrastructure.

The survey was commenced before the end of the war and was remarkable in its scope, thoroughness and relative speed. It is available through a number of online archives, including Internet Archive at archive.org.

Epilogue

The man who had held the fate of the world in his hands on the night of 31 August 1939 and had conquered much of Europe lay dead by his own hand, partially cremated and then buried in an ignominious ditch in the gardens of the Reich Chancellery in Berlin on 30 April 1945. His 'Thousand Year Reich' was completely shattered and utterly defeated. During the twelve years of his rule, Germany had suffered total military defeat and catastrophic destruction, despite the seemingly overwhelming early victories it had attained under his leadership.

The journey which led from those early triumphs to inglorious defeat was a long, bloody and terrible one, but the starting point must involve the question of how a person such as Hitler could ever have attained the leadership of one of the most advanced and sophisticated societies humanity had ever created. The contrast between the appalling views of the absolute dictator he was, and the ideologies developed through the best examples of Western culture in which Germany had been at the forefront, are so extreme as to make comparisons irrelevant.

The Nazis never obtained a majority of the votes in a free election for the Reichstag, although they were the largest single party, so Hitler's policies obviously had widespread support and were popular, not only in Germany but in Austria as well. The question as to why he was popular with the German electorate can only be understood by reference to the time in which he sought power. The economic distress of the German people was real, as it was real for the people of many countries, in the aftermath of the Great War and during the Great Depression which followed. It is important to remember that during the 1920s and 1930s, many countries in Europe became dictatorships under various names because of the stresses of that time, including Spain, Portugal, Romania, Hungary, Poland, Bulgaria and the greatest of them all, the Soviet Union under Stalin.

The combination of circumstances which determined the political and social environment in Germany was similar but unique to itself. To many in Germany, the governments which preceded Hitler's elevation to the Chancellorship did not appear to have policies which dealt with the impact of unemployment and inflation on the ordinary working man who had dependants whom he could not support. Hitler's proposed programmes and policies seemed to be the only ones which were attuned to the needs of the working man, and which also gave the middle-class some hope that they would be able to improve their situation. Obtaining work and food was the priority for most unemployed people, and that is where Hitler's emphasis was placed. It is therefore no wonder that his policies were popular. It should also be remembered that the second-largest party in the Reichstag was the Communist Party, and many Germans of all classes feared the consequences of the communists taking power. There was a real possibility of civil war if they became the government, and many who had lived through the unrest and violence which occurred following the fall of the German Empire in 1918 understandably dreaded any reoccurrence.

Hitler's beliefs were those of a person of his time. His racial dogma was common throughout Europe, including with the people of the Austro-Hungarian Empire, particularly in Vienna, although there were few who shared his brand of virulent anti-semitism involving the extermination of the Jews. His radical pan-German nationalism was also typical of nationalists of his time, as can be seen through the terms of the Treaty of Brest-Litovsk of March 1918 that the Imperial German government forced on the infant Soviet Union to terminate its involvement in the First World War. What was remarkable was that a person of Hitler's background, who was essentially uneducated and from the backwoods of the Austro-Hungarian Empire, had reached the forefront of those in power in the German state. This would have been extraordinary for anyone with his social and educational disadvantages, but for a person who was not even a citizen of Germany to do so illustrates the conspicuous political achievement behind Hitler's rise to power.

There was also another element in the German environment at the time which is captured by Erich Remarque's brilliant book *All Quiet on the Western Front*, which exemplifies the frustrated nationalism and idealism of an entire generation who went to war between 1914 and 1918, suffered appalling losses and endured violence on an inhumane scale. These men who fought in the trenches were told by some of their leaders that the loss of the war was not their fault, but that it was lost by effete politicians and shirkers on the home front who gave in before the men at the front. None other than Field Marshal President Paul von Hindenburg himself propagated this pernicious lie, which belied the reality of the Allies' hard-won victory but was widely believed. This argument was taken up by many Germans in power during the Weimar Republic period as the 'stab in the back' theory of why Germany lost the Great War. Hitler's identity as one of the 'nameless fighters' from the front was deliberately used by him to identify with this generation, and the fact that he had won the Iron Cross First Class as a lowly enlisted man allowed him to achieve a credibility with them to which most senior officers could never aspire. These themes, together with the supposed injustices of the Treaty of Versailles, formed the favourite leitmotifs for Hitler's speeches. That the Nazis recognized the power of Remarque's book and its anti-war message is exemplified by the fact that they banned it in 1933. Many disgruntled ex-servicemen joined the Nazi SA (Sturmabteilung), which performed numerous roles, from protection squads for Nazi speakers to terrorist attacks on the speakers of other parties and being a quasi-military organization with socialistic aims promoted by the party's programme. Hitler's ruthless murder of the senior leadership of the SA on the night of 30 June 1934, among whom were some of his longest-standing followers, because he believed they would not follow his commands to the letter was an early indication of the unlimited violence he would use and the illegal nature of his regime. It was also a warning to all those who contemplated resisting the new Reich or not obeying his orders.

Because of the complete defeat Germany suffered and the great disparity in the resources of the combatants, it is tempting to see the result of the Second World War as having been inevitable. The truth is, however, that the eventual Allied victory depended on a small number of crucial and climactic battles, each of which was hard-won and involved small margins to achieve victory. These turning points came during 1942, when the Allies won the three vital victories at Stalingrad, El Alamein and Midway. All of them were gained through an interplay of circumstances and chance which could not be foreseen when the campaigns they were part of had begun. Hitler was directly responsible for the German disaster at Stalingrad, where he elected to ignore the virtually unanimous advice of his most senior military commanders who repeatedly warned him of the dangers his offensive was exposing his troops to, imploring him to allow the breakout of the trapped Sixth Army from the city on the banks of the Volga once it became apparent that it would be surrounded. The result of this battle has been widely viewed as the turning point from which the defeat of Germany can be traced. The Fuhrer's actions on this occasion and many others seem inexplicable if one accepts that he wished to win the war he had so impetuously and unnecessarily embarked upon. The result of the war, however, was cumulative, with individual victories by each one of the Allies assisting the situation of them all; thus, the British and Commonwealth victory at Alamein helped the Soviets just as much it did the Americans fighting in the Pacific.

The slide to defeat which ensued for Nazi Germany was not linear in its development, but was accompanied by a pattern of behaviour in Hitler which was remarkably consistent. This behaviour was characterized by his almost complete isolation in decision-making, a pathological and ever-growing distrust of his generals, chronic procrastination, reliance for victory on new weapons which he had brought into existence and the underestimation of the power of the enemies of the Third Reich on a grotesque scale. As part of this pattern, on numerous occasions he ignored intelligence reports which clearly showed that his deductions were not only incorrect but were without any foundation in reality. That this pattern existed is confirmed by, amongst others, the three Chiefs of the Army General Staffs who had to work with him more closely than anyone else during the war years – Colonel Generals Halder, Zeitzler and Guderian – each of whom left written evidence to this effect.

The military campaign in Normandy and the reaction to the Red Army's Operation *Bagration* in summer 1944, the Ardennes offensive in winter 1944 and the operation in Hungary in March 1945 all bear the hallmarks of Hitler's interference, in the same manner as France 1940, Operation *Barbarossa*, the Stalingrad disaster and the last German offensive with any hope of arresting the catastrophe which his leadership had caused in the East, Operation *Citadel* at Kursk in summer 1943. While he was recovering from the effects of the injuries he suffered in July 1944, Rommel told his son that his role in the defence of Normandy could have been performed by any sergeant major, such was the continuous interference by Hitler in the dispositions he proposed to make. The same could have been said by any of the senior commanders who had to work with Hitler.

When his orders no longer led to victories, the Fuhrer interpreted this to mean that they were not being carried out as he required and reacted by insisting even more forcefully that they be followed to the letter, such was his absolute conviction that he could not be at fault. This requirement ensured that the initiative of operational-level commanders, which German officers were trained to exercise and was one of the strengths of the German Army, would be completely stultified. That he did not understand that this was the case, or its importance, is evidenced by Hitler's numerous denunciations of his senior officers concerning adherence to his orders and his determination to destroy this characteristic of the German Army, even though he had benefitted from it on many occasions without apparently realizing that this was the case.

Hitler's decisions relating to new weapons development and production priorities were based on unrealistic expectations and timetables. He never allowed for the actions of enemies in his plans and undertook no independent process to ascertain the practicality of his decisions and expectations. The most expensive new weapons project undertaken by the Third Reich was the Vengeance weapons programme for the development of the V-1 and V-2. These programmes cost over 5 billion Reichsmarks but could never have equalled the effect of the Allies' strategic bombing campaign which they were supposed to avenge. It has been calculated that if the cost of the programme had been used for the production of conventional fighters, it would have enabled the construction of an additional 24,000 aircraft – even if this figure is only half correct, such a reinforcement to the defence of the Reich would certainly have made a difference even if it had not ultimately enabled the Luftwaffe to defeat the Allied bombing offensive. However, such an approach was not consistent with Hitler's unthinking and unvarying commitment to attack in all circumstances rather than rational defensive measures, as evidenced in his orders to all branches of the Wehrmacht throughout the war. He therefore relied upon the Vengeance weapons programme to transform Germany's and his own position and bring about victory.

Hitler's interference in the production and role of the Me 262 jet fighter is a glaring example of his disastrous methods. When the aircraft had been developed to the stage that it was ready for final testing before production, he told Speer not to proceed any further because it would take too long to become operational. However, when the Fuhrer heard three months later that the British were trialling jet aircraft of their own, he suddenly decided the Me 262 must be given the highest priority, but as a bomber rather than a fighter. This was one of the worst manifestations of Hitler's fixation with always wanting to take offensive action. The Me 262 was designed as a fighter, and as such outclassed every Allied aircraft then available. Its armament was formidable and would have enabled it to be very effective against the bombers which were wreaking havoc on German industry and the civilian population. But because Hitler wanted a means to attack the Allied armies, he insisted that it be produced as a bomber, despite the Me 262 not having a bomb rack or sights to help attack targets, it being unsuitable for low-level flight and its pilots not being trained for ground-attack operations. On this occasion, not only the operational experts of the Luftwaffe pleaded with Hitler to change his mind, but Goering, Speer and the Chief of the Army General Staff also tried to have the decision reversed, all to no avail. Even with the late start caused by Hitler's interference, the Germans produced over 1,250 Me 262s. The impact which these could have had as a fighter was considerable – if they had started production a year earlier, the effect could have been significant. However, because of Hitler's inexpert and entirely wrong-headed interference and decisions, the potential of the Me 262 was in practical terms entirely wasted.

Ultimately, Hitler's successes were also the cause of his demise. After his spectacular early victories, he came to believe that he was a tactical and strategic genius and had an historic role to destroy communism, which he saw as part of the 'Jewish-Bolshevik world conspiracy' to destroy Western civilization and its most perfect example and exponents, the Germanic Aryan *Volk*. He therefore undertook Operation *Barbarossa* against the USSR while at the same time being at war with Britain, and then declared war on the United States despite Germany not being obliged to do so under the terms of its treaty with its Axis partner, Japan. These are again acts which cannot be explained on any rational basis or as being consistent with a desire to win a war he had embarked upon.

Ultimately, Hitler was an enigma who can only be understood on bases other than those which apply to all other human beings. His unequalled arrogance, self-absorption and utter disregard for the suffering he inflicted on his fellow human beings, together with the depth of his capacity for deceit, all combined to make him one of the most terrifying examples of humanity in a position of power to have existed in recorded history. However, it is satisfying to realize that along with these appalling characteristics, he also possessed the capacity for mistaken decision-making on a similar scale to his other defects, a nemesis which led to a record of ineptitude rarely equalled in the history of mankind. This weakness was his own unwitting contribution to the demise of his appalling creation, Nazi Germany. For this, the rest of humanity must surely be eternally thankful.

Appendix I

Text of the Memorandum of 3 July 1944 from Field Marshal Rommel to Kluge and forwarded to Hitler

Context

When von Kluge arrived and took over command from von Rundstedt, he met with Rommel on 3rd July and told him that he would have to get used to taking orders, as everyone else had to. This admonishment was made in front of other staff officers and Rommel was extremely displeased by it. He therefore prepared a memorandum which he gave to Kluge setting out the dispositions he recommended and steps he had tried to initiate which had been blocked by OKW (for which read, Hitler). Kluge sent a copy to Hitler.

It is apparent that if these steps had been taken the task of the allies would have been much more difficult than it was on D-Day. For example, Rommel wished to locate the 12th SS Hitler Jugend division to a position which would have allowed it to launch an immediate counterattack against any force landed on either the West or East coast of the Cotentin. The implications for the American landings are immediately apparent. There are many other examples which could be sited, almost all of which would have made the allies' task much more difficult.

The text of this Memorandum is available in full at the as noted on the David Irving website, Real History and Field Marshal Rommel - Index to Papers relating to the Life and Times of Field Marshal Erwin Rommel and is also included in Basil Liddell-Hart's book, The Rommel Papers.

The Memorandum is summarised below.

Rommel stated that the reasons why it was not possible to hold the Normandy positions and the steps he recommended to do so but which were not accepted by OKW as being:

(1) The forces in Normandy were not strong enough. Some of the formations had personnel who were over-age. For example, the 709th

Division average age was 36. In addition, equipment and ammunition stocks were inadequate, and construction work on fortifications and field positions were behind schedule because of the utterly inadequate supply arrangements.

(2) Army Group B had made repeated requests for reinforcements which were not supplied. The most important was locating the 12th SS Hiter Jugend division in position so that it could mount an attack against an enemy landing at the base of the Cotentin. Moving the division from its present location would have taken would have taken 2 days and it was better to do this before enemy air interdiction became a problem as it would be once battle was joined.

(3) Rommel's suggestion to locate the Panzer Lehr Division so that it would be able to intervene rapidly in both Normandy or Brittany was not accepted.

(4) Rommel requested that strong anti-aircraft forces should be deployed at the end of May so that the positions being hardest hit by the allied airforces could be defended. This was not done, and the 3rd A.A. Corps was not stationed between the Orne estuary and Montebourg, but deployed to defend V2 launching sites.

(5) Rommel suggested that the 7th Nebelwefer Brigade be used to strengthen the defences near Carentan prior to the invasion. This was not done and the Brigade was not put under the command of Army Group B until after the invasion had occurred and was therefore not available during the first days of the invasion.

(6) Rommel repeatedly requested that the Bay of the Seine be mined by the Navy and air-force before the invasion began. These waters are particularly appropriate for this type of activity as the bay is shallow. Because the request was not acted upon until after the invasion began, it could not be effective.

(7) During May the Quartermaster-General of Army Group B was ordered to reduce the stocks of ammunition in Normandy in order to build up stocks in depots elsewhere for the army group. If this order had been complied with the stocks of ammunition at the front would have been reduced to unacceptable levels. General Marcks succeeded in resisting this proposal.

(8) Supply conditions in Normandy were already difficult before the invasion due to heavy bombing of the railways by the enemy air-forces.

(9) Army Group B intended to wipe out the enemy's weakest landing north of Carentan and then to attack the other landings around the Orne and Vire. This would have eliminated the threat to Cherbourg. However,

OKW did not agree and ordered concentration on the eastern flank landings which were the strongest landings made by the allies.

(10) Because it was not moved in accordance with the Army Group's request, 12th SS did not arrive at the battlefield north-west of Caen until 9.30 on 7th June and had a 75 mile approach march, during which it sustained substantial losses due to enemy air attacks. Accordingly it could not attack as a complete formation and the attack which was made was not effective.

The Panzer Lehr Division was located 110 miles from Caen and did not begin to arrive at the battlefield until 13.00 hours on 7th June. During the approach march the enemy air-forces attacked and inflicted loss and disorganised the formation. Because of this delay, it was not able to perform its attacking role and became caught up in the defensive battles around Caen. It was unable to support the 352nd Infantry Division which were still fighting at Bayeux.

The 2nd Panzer Division was 160 miles from the battlefield and arrived on 13 June. Because of the disruption caused on the march to the battlefield, it took another 7 days before it could be committed as a division to the defence of Normandy.

3rd Parachute Division was moved to Brittany on orders from OKW and required six days for its approach march to the battle area north east of St Lo, during which time it was under constant attack from the air. When it arrived, strong enemy forces had taken the forest of Cerisy which negated the attack for which it had been intended on Bayeux.

It required 6 days for the 77th Division before it could intervene in the fighting north of the Cotentin peninsula.

Because of the positioning of the reserves they all arrived far too late to intervene on the day of the invasion and the opportunity to defeat it as intended was lost as the enemy had landed strong forces and was attacking himself under cover of powerful air and naval artillery support.

(11) Luftwaffe support did not occur on the scale which had been indicated and the enemy had total command of the airspace over the battlefield to a depth of approximately 60 miles inland. Defence installations and the deployment of reserves were attacked by sorties of immense strength. The supply situation was also made acute by attacks on the railway system.

(12) Naval activity was only a fraction of the level which had been promised. Only 6 U-Boats were committed instead of the 40 promised. No outpost ship was in place on the 5th of June to warn of the approach of the

enemy due to weather conditions. Subsequent activity against the enemy invasion fleet was on a small scale.

(13) The Army Group has no Quartermaster staff of its own and had at first no authority to give instructions to the Quartermaster at Headquarters West.

(14) Channels of command were unsatisfactory, as the Army Group had no control over the mobile formations of Panzer Group West, or the deployment of the Nebelwerfer Brigade or A. A. Corps as previously indicated. Only unified, close-knit command of all services, after the pattern of Montgomery and Eisenhower, will vouchsafe final victory.

Rommel, Generalfeldmarschall

Appendix II

Senior German Military Personnel and their Fate

Reichsmarschall Hermann Goering	Committed suicide 15 October 1946
Field Marshal Werner von Blomberg	Died in prison Nuremberg, 1946
Field Marshal Fedor von Bock	Killed in Allied air attack 4 May 1945
Field Marshal Eduard von Bohm-Ermolli	Died 9 December 1941
Field Marshal Walther von Brauchitsch	Died in prison 18 October 1948
Field Marshal Ernst Busch	Died in British PoW camp 17 July 1945
Field Marshal Robert von Griem	Committed suicide 24 May 1945
Field Marshal Wilhelm Keitel	Convicted of war crimes, executed 16 October 1946
Field Marshal Albert Kesselring	Convicted of war crimes, died 16 July 1960
Field Marshal Ewald von Kleist	Convicted of war crimes, died in Moscow 13 November 1954
Field Marshal Gunther von Kluge	Committed suicide 19 August 1944
Field Marshal Georg von Kuchler	Convicted of war crimes, died 25 May 1968
Field Marshal Wilhelm von Leeb	Convicted of war crimes, died 29 April 1956
Field Marshal Wilhelm List	Convicted of war crimes, died 17 August 1971
Field Marshal Eric von Manstein	Convicted of war crimes, died 9 June 1973
Field Marshal Erhard Milch	Convicted of war crimes, died 25 January 1972
Field Marshal Walter Model	Committed suicide 21 April 1945
Field Marshal Fredrich Paulus	Captured at Stalingrad, died in Dresden 1 February 1957
Field Marshal Walter von Reichenau	Died 17 January 1942
Field Marshal Wolfram von Richthofen	Died 12 July 1945
Field Marshal Erwin Rommel	Forced suicide after *Valkyrie* plot, 14 October 1944
Field Marshal Gerd von Rundstedt	Discharged from custody because of medical reasons, died 24 February 1953
Field Marshal Ferdinand Schorner	Convicted of war crimes, died 2 July 1973
Field Marshal Hugo Sperrle	Charged with war crimes, found not guilty, died 2 April 1953
Field Marshal Maximilian von Weichs	Died 27 September 1954
Field Marshal Erwin von Witzleben	Involved in *Valkyrie* plot – executed 8 August 1944

Notes

Introduction
1. Meaning 'sub-human', which was the description the Nazi race theories assigned to the people of the Soviet Union.
2. Adolf Hitler, *Mein Kampf* (Reynal & Hitchcock Edition, New York, 1941), pp.947–50.
3. See, for example, Albert Speer, *Inside the Third Reich* (Weidenfeld & Nicholson, London, 1995), p.416.
4. Specifically General Ludwig Beck, the Chief of Staff of the Army, and General Werner von Fritsch, who was Commander-in-Chief of the Army, both of whom Hitler sacked.
5. Field Marshal Wilhelm Keitel, Colonel General Alfred Jodl and General Walter Warlimont.
6. Colonel Generals Franz Halder, Kurt Zeitzler and Heinz Guderian.
7. Field Marshals Ewald von Kleist, Gerd von Rundstedt, Erich von Manstein, Erwin Rommel and Albert Kesselring.
8. SS-Colonel General Sepp Dietrich.
9. By virtue of being created Reichsmarschall.

Chapter 1
1. HC Deb, 21 June 1935, vol 303 cc 705–9.
2. David Wragg, *'Plan Z': The Nazi Bid for Naval Dominance* (Pen & Sword Books Ltd, Barnsley, 2008), p.69.
3. *Brassey's Naval Annual, 1948*; *Fuhrer Conferences on Naval Affairs, 1939–1945* (The Macmillan Company, New York, 1948), p.34.
4. Anthony Preston, *Navies of WWII* (PRC Publishing, London, 1998), p.21.
5. Brassey, p.37.
6. Brassey, p.38.
7. Brassey, p.32.
8. Wragg, p.69.
9. Holger Herwig, 'The Failure of German Sea Power, 1914–1945: Mahan, Tirpitz, and Raeder Reconsidered', *The International History Review* (February 1988), Vol 10, no 1. pp.68–105.
10. *The Trial of the Major War Criminals before the International Military Tribunal at Nuremberg* (HMSO), Volume 12, 2 May 1946, p.560.
11. William Garzke and Robert Dulin, *Axis and Neutral Battleships in World War II* (United States Naval Institute, Annapolis, 1990), p.314.
12. Garzke and Dulin, p.290.
13. Garzke and Dulin, p.39.
14. Brassey, p.38.
15. Chesneau, *Aircraft Carriers of the World, 1914 to the Present, An Illustrated Encyclopedia* (Brockhampton Press, London, 1988), p.288.
16. Brassey, p.68.
17. Karl Donitz, *Memoirs: Ten Years and Twenty Days* (The World Publishing Company, Cleveland and New York, 1959), p.21.

18. The *Trial of the Major War Criminals before the International Military Tribunal at Nuremberg*, Volume 13, 8 May 1946, p.249.
19. Albert Speer, *Inside the Third Reich* (Weidenfeld & Nicholson, London, 1995), p.375.
20. See his CV on p.11 of *The Battle of the Atlantic*.
21. Stephen Howarth and Derek Law, *The Battle of The Atlantic* (Greenhill Books, Barnsley, 1994), p.302.
22. Howarth and Law, p.132.
23. Michael Salewski, *Die Seekreisleitung* (The Naval War Command) *1939–1945* (Bernard & Graefe, Munich, 1970–75).
24. Donitz, p.12.
25. Brassey, p.32.
26. Donitz, pp.38, 39.
27. Brassey, p.35.
28. Brassey, 16 October 1939, p.52.
29. Jack Greene and Alessandro Massignani, *Hitler Strikes North* (Frontline Books, Barnsley, 2013), p.66.
30. Greene and Massignani, page 63
31. Churchill, *History of the Second World War*, Volume 1 (Penguin Books, London, 1988), p.592.
32. Brassey, p.201.
33. Brassey, p.217.
34. Brassey, Report to the Fuhrer of 22 January 1942, p.259.
35. Brassey, Report to the Fuhrer of 12 January 1942, pp.258–59.
36. Brassey, Report to the Fuhrer of 12 January 1942, p.257.
37. Brassey, p.260.
38. Brassey, p.117.
39. Brassey, pp.117, 118.
40. Quoted in Brassey, p.118.
41. Brassey, pp.119–20, Fuhrer Naval Conference 21 July 1940.
42. Brassey, p.122.
43. Brassey, p.122.
44. Brassey, p.122.
45. Brassey, p.124.
46. Brassey, p.128.
47. Brassey, p.128.
48. Brassey, p.131.
49. Anchey and Todman, *War Diaries, 1939–1945, Field Marshal Lord Alanbrooke* (Phoenix, London, 2002), p.108.
50. Brassey, p.136.
51. Brassey, p.136.
52. Brassey, p.138.
53. Brassey, p.139.
54. Brassey, p.141.
55. Brassey, p.154.
56. Brassey, p.162.
57. Bob Carruthers, *Stormbird Ascending* (The Bookzine Company Ltd, London, 2012), p.52.
58. Gabriel Gorodetsky, *The Maisky Diaries* (Yale University Press, London, 2016), p.293.
59. Donitz, p.42.
60. Brassey, p.36.
61. Brassey, p.55.
62. Speer, p.375.

63. Speer, p.239.
64. Charles Burdick and Hans-Adolf Jacobsen (eds), *The Halder War Diary, 1939–1942* (Presidio Press, California, 1988), p.227.
65. Howarth and Law, p.7.
66. The Trial of the Major War Criminals before the International Military Tribunal at Nuremberg (HMSO, London, 1947), Volume 12, 9 May 1946, p.279.
67. James V. Forrestal Papers, Box 131, Folders 5 to 6; Public Policy Papers, Department of Rare Books and Special Collections, Princeton University Library.
68. Brassey, p.306.
69. Brassey, Fuhrer Conferences on Naval Affairs, 11 January 1943, p.307.
70. Trial of the Major War Criminals, Volume 14, 18 May 1946, p.128.
71. David C. Isby, *Fighting the Invasion* (Frontline Books, Barnsley, 2016), p.86.

Chapter 2
1. Quoted from Richard Meredith, *Phoenix, A Complete History of The Luftwaffe, 1918–1945*, Volume 2 (Helion & Co, Solihull, UK, 2017), p.107.
2. Richard Overy, *Goering* (Bloomsbury Academic, London, 2012), p.190.
3. A. Nielsen, *The German Air Force General Staff* (USAF Historical Division, Research Studies Institute, Air University, Alabama, 1959).
4. The memorandum was presented in evidence by US Counsel on 20 December 1945 as Exhibit USA 25 and is read into the record of the trial at p.262 of Volume 2.
5. Overy *Goering*, p.97.
6. Overy, *Goering*, p.98.
7. Overy, *Goering*, p.97.
8. Overy, *Goering*, p.190.
9. Cajus Bekker, *The Luftwaffe War Diaries* (Ballantine Books, New York, 1973), p.8.
10. Meredith, p.513.
11. Trial of the Major War Criminals, Volume 9, 14 March 1946, p.281.
12. Meredith, p.587.
13. Albert Kesselring, *A Soldier's Record* (William Morrow and Company, New York, 1954), p.29.
14. Meredith, p.543.
15. Bekker, p.8.
16. Kesselring, pp.41,42.
17. The Trial of the Major War Criminals, Volume 15, 5 June 1946, pp.377–78.
18. Bekker, p.544.
19. Patrick Facon, *L'Armee de l'air* (Economica, Paris, 2005), p.169.
20. E.R. Hooton, *Luftwaffe at War* (Chevron, London, 2007), p.90.
21. Julian Jackson, *The Fall of France* (Oxford University Press, Oxford, 2003), p.48.
22. Bekker, p.152.
23. Hooton, p.90.
24. Galland, p.20.
25. Galland, p.19.
26. Galland, p.22.
27. Galland, p.27.
28. Bekker, p.330.
29. Brassey, p.128.
30. Bekker, p.240.
31. Speech at the Berlin Sportpalast, on the opening of the Kriegswinterhilfswerk.
32. Speer, p.388.

33. Heaton and Lewis, p.130.
34. Williamson Murray, *Strategy for Defeat: The Luftwaffe 1933–1945* (Air University Press, Alabama, 1983), p.40.
35. Bekker, p.556.
36. The Battle of Britain Historical Society website, Document 41.
37. David Stahel, *Operation Barbarossa and Germany's Defeat in the East* (Cambridge University Press, Cambridge, 2009), p.123.
38. Trial of the Major War Criminals, Volume 9, 8 March 1946, p.49.
39. Hugh Trevor-Roper, *Hitler's War Directives 1939–45*, pp.93–94.
40. Galland, p.34.
41. Michael Jones, *The Retreat – Hitler's First Defeat* (John Murray Publishers, London, 2009).
42. Colin D. Heaton and Anne-Marie Lewis, *The German Aces Speak II* (Zenith Press, Minneapolis, 2014), p.152.
43. Heaton and Lewis, p.18.
44. Bekker, p.556.
45. Bekker, p.556.
46. Appendix 1 of Volume 2 of this work.
47. Jonathan Trigg, *The Defeat of the Luftwaffe*, Amberley Publishing, Gloucestershire, 2018, p. 151.
48. Stewart Binns, 'Barbarossa', Wildfire, 2021, p. 146.
49. Trigg, p. 155.
50. Speer, p. 345.
51. Becker, p. 413.
52. Trigg, p. 167.
53. Becker, p. 429.
54. Adolf Galland, *The First and the Last*, Ballantine Books, New York, 1957, p. 182.
55. Galland, p. 183.
56. Speer, 'Inside the Third Reich, p. 489.
57. Speer, note 3, p. 744.
58. Bob Carruthers, *Stombird Ascending*, Pen & Sword Aviation, Yorkshire UK, 2013, p. 108.
59. Becker, p. 536.
60. Galland, p. 182.
61. Richard Overy, *The Bombing War* (Penguin Books, London, 20114), p.379.
62. Giulio Douhet, *Command of the Air*, first published 1921.
63. Prime Minister Stanley Baldwin, in his speech 'A Fear for the Future', 9 November 1932.
64. Overy, *The Bombing War*.
65. This is referred to in Goering's testimony at the Nuremberg Trials, Volume 9, 15 March 1946, p.360 and succeeding.
66. Richard Overy, 'From Uralbomber to Amerikabomber', *Journal of Strategic Studies*, Vol 1 (1978).
67. Speer, p.382.
68. Trigg, p.191.
69. Speer, note 2, p.728.
70. Trigg, p.192.
71. Galland, p.93.
72. Bekker, p.451.
73. Bekker, pp.460–61.
74. Richard Overy, *Why the Allies Won* (Random House, London, 1995), p.111.
75. Speer, p.493.
76. Speer, p.492.

77. Donald Bennett, *Pathfinder* (Crecy Publishing Limited, Manchester, 1998), p.165.
78. William Chorley, *RAF Bomber Command Losses* (Midland Publishing, Hinckley, 2007).
79. Adolf Galland, *The First and the Last* (Ballantine Books, New York, 1957), p.95.
80. Bekker, p.532.
81. Overy, *Why the Allies Won*, p.118.
82. Overy, *The Bombing War*, p.361.
83. Bekker, p.556.
84. Speer, p.473.
85. Speer, p.475.
86. According to the Theatre History of Operations Reports' hosted by the Defense Digital Service WW2 database.
87. Army Air Forces Statistical Digest, World War II, the Office of Statistical Control, December 1945, p.255.
88. *Ibid.*, p.55.
89. Albert Speer, *Spandau: The Secret Diaries* (Collins, London, 1976), pp.339–40.
90. Speer, *Spandau*, p.340.
91. Overy, *Why the Allies Won*, p.131.
92. From a speech 21 March 1922.
93. Overy, *Why the Allies Won*, p.204.
94. *The United States Strategic Bombing Survey – The Effect of Bombing on Health and Medical care in Germany*, p.13.
95. *USSBS*, p.141.
96. *USSBS*, p.290.
97. Speer, *Spandau*, pp.339–40.
98. Bekker, p.533.

Chapter 3
1. Overy, *Why the Allies Won*, p.199.
2. Overy, *Why the Allies Won*, p.204.
3. Overy, p.201.
4. Speer, *Inside the Third Reich*, p.295.
5. Speer, p.323.
6. Speer, p.320.
7. Speer, p.414.
8. Speer, p.321.
9. Speer, p.327.
10. See for example Speer, p.245.
11. Stahel, p.116.
12. Gunther Blumentritt, in Siegfried Westphal, *The Fatal Decisions* (Pen & Sword, Barnsley, 2012), p.56.
13. Heinz Guderian, *Panzer Leader* (Da Capo Press, USA, 2002), p.276.
14. Guderian, p.277.
15. Guderian p.277.
16. Guderian, p.283.
17. Chris Bishop, *The Illustrated Encyclopedia of Weapons of World War 2* (Amber Books, London, 2018), p.15.
18. Bishop, p.15.
19. Bishop, p.16.
20. Speer, p.326.
21. Guderian, p.190.

22. Overy, p.218.
23. Speer, p.493.
24. Speer, p.493.
25. Speer, pp.493–94.
26. R.V. Jones, *The Wizard War* (Coward, McCann and Geoghegan Inc, New York, 1978), p.417.
27. Speer, p.481.
28. R.V. Jones, p.418.
29. R.V. Jones, p.414.
30. R.V. Jones, p.420.
31. R.V. Jones, p.422.
32. R. Atkinson, *The Guns at Last Light: the War in Western Europe, 1944–1945* (Henry Holt, New York, 2013), p.111.
33. Speer, *Inside the Third Reich*, p.496.
34. Speer, p.496.
35. Speer, p.497.
36. Speer, p.499.
37. Speer, note 6, p.744.
38. Speer, p.492.
39. Overy, p.240.
40. Jean Lopez, *World War II Infographics* (Thames and Hudson Books, London, 2019), p.184.
41. Speer, p.317.
42. Speer, p.316.
43. Speer, p.319.
44. Speer, p.319.
45. Speer, p.316.
46. Overy, p.238.
47. Speer, p.318.
48. Speer, p.317.

Chapter 4
1. Speer, p.338.
2. Walter Warlimont, *Inside Hitler's Headquarters, 1939–1945* (Presidio Press, California, 1964), p.13.
3. Zeitzler, p.143.
4. Wilhelm Keitel, *The Memoirs of Field Marshal Wilhelm Keitel*, ed. Walter Gorlitz (Musterschmit-Verlag, Gottingen, 1961), ed. p. 52.
5. Leon Goldensohn, *The Nuremberg Interviews* (Pimlico, London, 2006), p.166.
6. Speer, *Inside the Third Reich*, p.338.
7. Trial of the Major War Criminals, Volume 15, p.302.
8. Friedrich von Mellenthin, *Panzer Battles* (Ballantine Books, New York, 1971), p.248.
9. Warlimont, p.224.
10. Warlimont, p.244.
11. Burdick and Jacobsen, *The Halder War Diary*.
12. Burdick and Jacobsen, p.209.
13. Burdick and Jacobsen, p.211.
14. Warlimont, pp.251–52.
15. Franz Halder, *Hitler as Warlord* (Putnam, London, 1950), p.7.
16. Warlimont, p.605, 'I heard this myself'.
17. See his comments to Goldensohn, p.294.
18. Kurt Zeitzler, in Westphal, *The Fatal Decisions*, page 117

19. Zeitzler, p.118.
20. Zeitzler, p.133.
21. Trial of the Major War Criminals, Volume 15, 3 August 1946, p.300.
22. Zeitzler, *The Fatal Decisions*, p.155.
23. Benoit Lemay, *Manstein: Hitler's Master Strategist* (Casemate Publishers, Pennsylvania, 2017), p.376.
24. Zeitzler, *The Fatal Decisions*, p.165.
25. Guderian, p.431.
26. Guderian, p.439.
27. Guderian, p.441.
28. Guderian, p.441.
29. Guderian, p.443.
30. Basil Liddell Hart, *A History of the Second World War* (Pan Books, London, 2014), page 825
31. Erich von Manstein, *Lost Victories* (Presidio Press, California, 1994), p.124.
32. Manstein, p.275.
33. Manstein, p.287.
34. Manstein, p.544 – a direct quote from his diary made the day after the interview took place.
35. Trial of the Major War Criminals, Volume 20, 10 August 1946, p.625.
36. Goldensohn, p.342.
37. Goldensohn, p.346.
38. Goldensohn, p.346.
39. See David Fraser, *Knight's Cross: A Life of Field Marshal Erwin Rommel* (Harper Collins, London, 1994), quote from a conversation with Manfred Rommel, p.508.
40. See Basil Liddell Hart, *The Rommel Papers* (Da Capo Paperback, New York, 1953), pp.480–84.
41. See for example Speer, *Inside the Third Reich*, p.588.
42. Kesselring, p.339.
43. See *The Fatal Decisions*, p.249.
44. See *The Fatal Decisions*, p.252.
45. Liddell Hart, *The Other Side of the Hill*, p.468.
46. Peter Caddick-Adams, *Snow and Steel* (Arrow Books, London, 2014), p.239.
47. Speer, *Spandau*, p.18.
48. Carruthers, p.49 and following.
49. Goldensohn, p.103.
50. Geyr von Schweppenburg in Isby, *Fighting the Invasion*, p.73.

Chapter 5
1. Adolf Hitler, 'Speech delivered before the German Reichstag on July 13, 1934' (M. Muller & Sohn, Berlin).
2. Liddell Hart, *The Rommel Papers*, p.487.
3. Fraser, p.507.
4. Warlimont, p.500.
5. Warlimont, p.462.

Chapter 6
1. Carl von Clausewitz, *On War*, Kegan Paul, Trench, Trubner & C., 1918. Vol. 1. Chapter I: WHAT IS WAR?
2. Volume 10, 28 March, 1946, p. 207.
3. John Wheeler-Bennett, '*The Nemesis of Power 1918–1945*', Macmillan, London, 1964, p. 447.

4. Andrew Roberts, 'The Holy Fox', Weidenfeld and Nicholson, London, 1991, p. 192.
5. Gibson, p. 120.
6. Warlimont, p. 145.
7. Warlimont, p. 211.
8. Warlimont, p. 208.
9. Had Hitler not declared war on the United States, it is by no means certain that Congress would have agreed to a declaration of war on Germany after the attack on Pearl Harbor. That the German declaration of war simplified the situation for President Roosevelt is confirmed by a poll of the Senate's sentiment concerning the repeal of Part or all of the Neutrality Act which would keep the United States out of the war except in the most blatant circumstances as set out on page 753 of *Undeclared War* by Langer and Gleason, Harper Brothers, New York, 1953 as follows: '...an informal poll of Senate opinion early in October only twenty-nine members were well disposed toward total repeal or the elimination of Sections II, III and VI, and only thirty-five were prepared to vote even for the arming of merchantmen. Twenty were opposed to any change and the remainder expressed themselves as undecided. When one remembers that relatively few Senators were needed to kill the bill by filibuster, one can hardly escape the conclusion that Mr. Roosevelt was well advised in trying to make progress slowly.'
10. Joachim Fest, '*Hitler*', Harcourt Books, Florida, 1974, p. 693.
11. Fest, p. 694.
12. Adolf Hitler, '*Mein Kampf*', Reynal & Hitchcock Edition, New York, 1941, p. 947–50.
13. Ian Kershaw, '*Hitler: 1936-1945, Nemesis*', W. W. Norton & Co, London, 2000, p. 898.
14. Warlimont, p. 452.
15. Warlimont, note 8, p.598.
16. Zeitzler, p.116.
17. Westphal, p.77.
18. Manstein, p.293.
19. Warlimont, p.243.
20. David Stone, *Twilight of the Gods*, Conway Books, London, 2011, p.235.
21. Burdick and Jacobsen, p.646.
22. Warlimont, p.258.
23. Westphal, pp.115–66.
24. Speer, p.345.
25. Zeitzler, *The Fatal Decisions*, p.145.
26. Warlimont, p.243.
27. Stone, p.238.
28. Zeitzler, *The Fatal Decisions*, p.126.
29. Zeitzler, *The Fatal Decisions*, p.149.
30. Speer, p.345.
31. Warlimont, p.428.
32. Omar Bradley, *A General's Life* (Simon & Schuster, New York, 1983), p.255.
33. Warlimont, p.434.
34. Blumentritt, p.238.
35. Liddell Hart, *The Rommel Papers*, p.495.
36. Warlimont, p.449.
37. Zimmerman, *The Fatal Decisions*, p.202.
38. Benoit Lemay, *Manstein, Hitler's Master Strategist* (Casemate Publishers, Pennsylvania, 2017), p.376.
39. Guderian, p.387.
40. Guderian,, p.383.

41. Keitel, p.160.
42. Keitel, p.163.
43. Warlimont, p.246.
44. Warlimont, p.252.
45. Keitel, p.181.
46. William Morrow and Sons, New York, 1954.
47. Kesselring, p.293.
48. Guderian, p.403.
49. Guderian, pp.414–15.

Index

Ardennes offensive Commitment of Luftwaffe on Hitler's orders led to disaster, p 99; Manteuffel states that neither Hitler or Jodl spoke to him in planning the Ardennes offensive of 1944, p 139; Jodl was arrogant, p 139; Hitler did not speak to Rundstedt regarding Ardennes offensive of 1944, p 150; Manteuffel saw that the forces were too weak to achieve the results Hitler wanted, p 157; SS Colonel General Sepp Dietrich on difficulties of Ardennes offensive, p 158; utterly unrealistic, p 162; even after it had failed Jodl continued to contend that the offensive should be continued, p. 199.

Blomberg, Field Marshal Werner Too inclined to praise Hitler's military abilities, p. 135; dismissed by Hitler in 1938, p. 136; how Keitel was chosen, p. 136; was sacked because he resisted Hitler's wishes, p. 200.

Blumentritt, General Gunter Effect of the t-34 on German troops, p. 116.

Bock, Field Marshal Fedor von Sacking of Field Marshal von Bock, p. 202; one of the most successful commanders of the German Army, in command of Army Group Centre, p. 209.

Bormann, Martin Hitler's power crazed secretary's role in Goering's downfall, p. 57.

Bradley, General Omar Hitler's last chance to defeat Normandy landings, p. 191; role in Ardennes offensive, p. 198.

Brauchitsch, Werner von, Field Marshal Command in Chief of the Army dismissed by Hitler as scapegoat for the failure of operation Barbarossa, p. 140; Keitel's recollections on the sacking, p. 201.

Braun, Werner von Headed the entire research programme at Peenemunde and NASA moon project after WW2, p. 123; presentation to Hitler of potential for V-2 on 7 July, 1943 won Hitler's approval to the project, p. 126; Hitler regarded V-2 as war winning, p. 126.

Churchill, Winston Promoted intervention by the western powers in the Russian revolution, p. 43; comments on the U-Boat war, p. 49; Nazi Germany's most implacable foe, p. 67; demands retaliatory raids on Berlin, p. 73; first 'Thousand Bomber' raid on Cologne, p. 94; Lord Cherwell retained to analyse results of bombing campaign, p. 95; quote on war, p. 103; miracle of Dunkirk, p. 151; response to Hitler's peace offer, p. 176.

Dietrich, Colonel General 'Sepp' Attempted to change Hitler's mind relating to role of ME-262, p. 87; impossibility of task in Ardennes offensive, p. 158; Hitler was crazy, p. 159.

Doenitz, Karl, Grand Admiral Recognized before the war that the only chance to defeat Britain was through the U-Boat, p. xiii; appointed Fuhrer U-Boats on 1 October, 1936, p. 9; 'Wolf Pack' strategy, p10; wanted the largest possible number of U-Boats produced, p. 10; evidence at Nuremberg, p. 10; worked with Speer to achieve highest possible number of U-Boats, p. 13; failure of Luftwaffe reconnaissance, p. 13; importance of counter measures, p. 15; evaluation of Plan Z, p. 16; role of U-Boats in operation Sea Lion, p. 28; anxiety over war with Britain, p. 45; Memorandum on outbreak of war regarding build up of U-Boats, p45; new production programme, p. 48; reasons for loss of U-Boat campaign, p. 50; promoted Grand Admiral and head of Kriegsmarine on 30 January, 1943, p. 54.

Eisenhower, General Dwight Reaction to Ardennes offensive, p. 198; Rommel's memorandum of 3 July 1944.

Fortitude Allied deception plan to cover Normandy invasion, p. 189;

Fritsch, Colonel General Werner von Commander in Chief of the Army, sacked in February 1938 as result of plot by Goering and Himmler to discredit the Army supposedly for being homosexual but in reality because he resisted Hitler's wish to increase the size of the army to 36 divisions, p. 200.

Index   235

Goering, Reichsmarschall Hermann   Interview after the war, p. xii; heavy bomber program, p. xiii; naval aviation, p. 12; all aircraft to be developed by the Luftwaffe, p. 13; advice to Hitler to take British Mediterranean empire not USSR, p. 42; Mediterranean strategy much sounder than attacking USSR, p. 44; complained to Hitler that defending heavy naval units were a waste of his aircraft, p. 51; appointed Minister for Aviation, p. 57; decides not to produce HE-177 strategic bomber, p. 58; intended composition of the Luftwaffe, p. 59; role of the Luftwaffe in Spanish Civil War, p. 61; two-thirds of Luftwaffe committed to Polish campaign, p. 64; measure introduced to overcome lack of strategic bombers, p. 72; terror attacks against English population, p. 72; meeting to decide Luftwaffe strategy against England, p. 73; using new incendiary bombs against London, p. 74; advises against attacking USSR, p. 76; assured Hitler that the Sixth Army at Stalingrad could be supplied by the Luftwaffe, p. 81; Goering backs the use of the ME-262 as fighter, p. 84; appoints General Kammhuber to organise defence against RAF strategic campaign against Germany, p. 92; impact of raids on Hamberg, p. 94; appoints General Galland to command all fighters in Luftwaffe, p. 97; did not defend position of Luftwaffe against Hitler, p. 99; disputes with Galland, p. 99; allied tactics in destruction of Luftwaffe over Germany, p. 100; waning influence with Hitler, p. 112; relationship with Manstein, p. 152; interview after the war, p. 160; succession to Hitler, p. 165; intended to be eliminated with Hitler in Operation Valkyrie, p. 166; role in Dunkirk evacuation, p. 181; found guilty of war crimes by Nuremberg Tribunal and committed suicide 15 October 1946, p. 224.
Guderian, Colonel General Heinz   Tried to get Hitler to change role of Me-262, p. 87; quoted by Hitler, p. 114; German tank building programme, p. 117; Hitler's ideas on huge tanks 'without any useful result' and a 'fantasy', p. 117; General Staff production programme, p. 118; Hitler's bizarre ruling regarding spare parts for tanks, p. 120; Manstein states he is most responsible for the success of 1940 France offensive, p. 147; made Chief of the General Staff on 21 July, 1944 succeeding Zeitzler, p. 147; Hitler's ability as commander in Chief of the Army, p. 148 & 149; recommends not to carry out Operation Citadel, p. 196; Ardennes offensive, p. 198; Hitler's and Jodl's incomprehension of situation on Eastern front, 1945, p. 199; comment on Himmler's appointment to command Army Group Vistula, p. 204.
Halder, Colonel General Franz   Hitler puzzled by Britain's continued resistance after fall of France, p. 49; Hitler's choice as Chief of the General Staff of the Army, p. 141; attitude to Hitler's interference in military affairs, p. 141; examples, pa 142; final argument with Hitler, 24 August 1942, p. 142 & 143; gaoled after 20 July plot, p. 143; review of Hitler's capacity, p. 143; warned Hitler of error of Stalingrad offensive, p. 144; Hitler's errors in disposition of 4th Panzer Army in Stalingrad offensive, p. 184; 'no room for any serious work' with Hitler, p. 185; sacking of Field Marshal von Bock, p. 202.
He 177   2,000 to be produced by 1943, p. 58; Goeing decided not to produce them, p. 58; had these existed the outcome of the Battle of Britain would have been unpredictable, p. 58; problems with engines and not reliable, p. 60; used at Stalingrad.
Heisenberg, Werner   Hitler's go to expert on Physics had won the Nobel Prize in 1925, p. 129; had not given any answer on whether nuclear chain reaction could be managed, p129; Europe only had one cyclotron and needed a better one for research, p. 130.
Himmler, Heinrich, Reichsfuhrer SS   Role in sacking of Manstein, p. 152; who would succeed if Hitler was assassinated, p. 165; Stauffenberg intended to assassinate Himmler as well as Hitler, p. 166; Hitler appoints Himmler to command of Army Group Vistula on 24 January, 1945, p. 204.
Hitler, Adolf   War with Poland occurred because of unnecessary brinkmanship with western powers, p. x; treated Generals with contempt, p. xi; wanted to avoid conflict with Great Britain until the Kriegsmarine had been made ready, p. 1; negotiation of Anglo-German Naval agreement enhanced his prestige, p. 2; told Raeder to be ready for war with Great Britain by 1944-45, p. 3; proposed composition of Kriegsmarine and when war occurred, p. 3 & 4; issued order for naval construction to be speeded up, p. 5; ships of Plan Z would have consumed more oil than Germany had, p. 5; changed the law so that the Reichsbank had to supply the government with unlimited credits, p. 6; wanted battleships to be armed with 800mm guns, p. 6; Raeder reports to Hitler on damage to the Graf Spee, p. 8; did not order

U-Boats to highest priority construction until April 1943, p. 11; allowed Goering to take over Naval aviation which was treated as low priority, p. 12; Hitler accepted Plan Z on 27 January, 1939, p. 15; Naval war strategy made redundant by Hitler invading Poland, p. 16; Kriegsmarine was less prepared than other services because of war, p. 17; U-Boat campaign lost by the time Hitler gave it highest production priority, p. 17; discussions regarding strategic value of Norway, p. 18; view of Norway campaign, p. 19; the Bismarck breakout, p. 21; questions Raeder regarding Bismarck's engagement, p. 22; ignorance of naval warfare, p. 23; feared invasion of Norway in 1942, p. 23; orders Kriegsmarine ships to leave Brest and reinforce Norway, p. 24; Raeder points out difficulty of operation Sea Lion to Hitler, p. 27; Hitler's questions to Raeder re Sea Lion, p. 29; Hitler endorses Naval plan for Sea Lion, p. 33; Kriegsmarine's appreciation of Sea Lion more valid than Luftwaffe or Hitler's, p. 35; Sea Lion to be delayed and bombing of London continued, p. 36; Kriegsmarine war strategy to eliminate Britain from the Mediterranean, p. 37; could have been achieved with help of Vichy French and Italians, p. 41 & 42; Hitler believed that the Wehrmacht could knock out USSR within 6 months, p. 43; Doenitz anxiety regarding early war with Britain, p. 45; Despite war coming, Hitler would not allow U-Boat construction to be accorded highest priority, p. 47: Hitler ordered highest priority too late as the U-Boat war was lost, p. 48; Hitler reluctant to destroy the British Empire, p. 49; 'Peace offer' of 19 July 1940, p. 49; had no experience of other countries, p. 49; Hitler orders scrapping of the surface fleet, p. 51; confrontation with Raeder, p. 51-53; Raeder resigns, p. 54; Kriegsmarine could only inflict 'fleabites' on D-Day landings, p. 54; made Goering Minister of Aviation on 30 January, 1933, p. 57; told Goering to have the Luftwaffe ready for war by 1944-45, p. 58; stated that Germany's problems could only be solved by force during Hossbach conference, p. 59; no doubt Hitler intended that the Luftwaffe would have strategic bombers, p. 59 & 60; viewed the Spanish Civil war as an opportunity to upset the status quo in Europe, p. 60; Luftwaffe only fit for a short blitz campaign at the outbreak of war, p. 64; terror attacks against London, p. 72; forbad attacks against London during August 1940, p. 73; changed point of attack against London because of RAF raids during September, 1940, p. 74; diversion of effort gave the RAF breathing space from attacks on airfields etc, p. 74; strategic defeat in Sea Lion led to the attack on USSR, p. 76; Goering advised against attack on USSR until Britain was beaten, p. 76 & 77; Luftwaffe role in Barbarossa, p. 78; expansion of the war in 1942 spread the Luftwaffe beyond its power, p. 80; accepted Goering's advice that the Luftwaffe could supply the 6th Army in Stalingrad, p. 81; Luftwaffe never recovered from the losses at Stalingrad, p. 82; Hitler delays production of the Me-262, p. 84; designates it as a bomber, p. 85 & 86; ensured that the Luftwaffe could not stop the allied bombing campaign, p. 87; Galland's view of Hitler's decision, p. 88; one of the very worst decisions made during the war, p. 88; encouraged the populace to shoot allied crews who were shot down, p. 91; completely incomprehensible strategy against the allied bombing campaign, p. 95; did not order production of Waterfall anti-aircraft missile, p. 96; Hitler's bizarre strategy to defend the Reich, p. 98; Speer and Galland try to change Hitler's mind re role of Me-262, p. 99; squandered reserve of 800 fighters trying to defend Normandy, and 3,000 fighters in Ardennes offensive, p. 99; authorises Speer to use any labour needed to repair oil industry installations after concentrated attacks, p. 101; effect of Hitler's decisions on Luftwaffe's ability to defend the Reich, p. 107; exercised ultimate control over new weapons development, p. 109; effect of German military control over production, p. 110; Hitler not interested in organization of industry, p. 111; Hitler's technical horizon, p. 111; U-Boat construction did not get attention from Hitler, p. 112; amateurishness was one of Hitler's dominant traits, p. 112; made decisions in complete isolation, p. 112; weapons conferences, p. 113; Hitler supported creation of Panzer forces and his attitude to types of tanks needed, p. 114; approved production of the Panther in May 1943, p. 117; fantastic vision of tank types, p. 117; chopped and changed production levels and types, p. 117 7 118; new heavy tank, Tiger, p. 118; bizarre order regarding spare parts for tanks produced, p. 120 & 121; effect of Hitler's decisions on Army's ability to fight, p. 122; genesis and role of the Vengeance Weapons programs, p. 123; intended and actual deployment of the V-1, p. 124; authorisation of V-2 program, p. 126; intended 5,000 V-2s to be sent against London on first day, p. 127; one of the worst mistakes of the war, p. 128; Hitler did not understand the principles of the A bomb, p. 129; considered the basis of the A bomb 'Jewish physics', p. 130; would not have hesitated to use the A-Bomb against London, p. 132; Generals of OKW influenced Hitler's decisions significantly, p. 136; Jodl briefed Hitler separately from the Army Chief of Staff, p. 136; a 'demon like man possessed of inordinate willpower', p. 137; Jodl completely submitted to Hitler's will, p. 138; Hitler's methods of command described, p. 140; did not understand the principle of concentration of forces, p. 141; did not have the time to devote to being Commander in Chief of the Army, p. 141; disputes regarding chopping and changing of orders with Halder, p. 142; refusal to consolidate line leads to Halder's dismissal, p. 141; Halder's view of Hitler's ability, p. 143 & 144; Hitler 'trusted no-one', p. 144; 'I won't go back from the Volga', p. 145; dismissal of Field Marshal List, confrontation with Jodl, p. 145; Army Group 'A' saved despite Hitler, p. 146; role in Operation Citadel, p. 146; Colonel-General Zeitzler's view of Hitler, p. 147; appoints Guderian as Chief of the General Staff on 21 July, 1944, p. 147; Guderian's view of Hitler, p. 148; Hitler's mistaken declaration of war on USA, p. 148; 'lack of consistency, and subject to continual vacillation in its execution', p. 149; Rundstedt's view, p. 150; Manstein's view of Hitler as Supreme Commander, p. 151, 152, & 153; Kleist's view, p. 153 & 154; Rommel's view, p. 154-156; Kesselring's view, p. 156-157; Manteuffel's view, p. 157-158; Dietrich's view, p. 158-159; Goering's view, p. 159-161; the only effective resistance to Hitler could be made through the Army, p. 165; probable disputed succession of Hitler assassinated, p. 165; Valkyrie operation aimed to kill Hitler, Goering and Himmler but had to act against Hitler alone, p. 166; role of Kluge and Rommel, p. 167; immediate effects of failure of plot, p. 168; medium term effects, p. 169; Hitler was great devotee of Clausewitz, p. 172; diplomatic successes, p. 173; western allies lose trust in Hitler, p. 174; Non-aggression pact with USSR, p. 175; attacking Poland was greatest diplomatic error of Hitler's life, p. 176; errors in evaluating motives of other countries, p. 176; did not involve Spain, Vichy France or Japan in his plans, p. 176-177; declaration of war on USA, p. 177; offers of peace from USSR ignored, p. 179; using Manstein's strategy in 1940 offensive best military decision of war, p. 181; operational mistakes in implementing strategy, p. 181; reasons for attack on USSR, p. 182; Hitler's interference with execution of Barbarossa, p. 182-183; errors in planning and execution of Stalingrad offensive, p. 183-188; Defence of Normandy, errors in strategy and operational commands, p. 188-194; Operation Citadel, not the offensive Manstein suggested, p. 194-197; Ardennes offensive, flawed strategy, p. 197-199; last Soviet offensives, p. 199-200; sacking of Blomberg, Beck and Fritsch, p. 200; Sacking of Rundstedt, Brauchitsch, Halder, Leeb, Bock, List, Manstein, Kleist, p. 201; always looking for a scapegoat, p. 201; 'pathological delusion that all his Generals were conspiring against him...' p. 203; argument with Guderian on appointment of Himmler as Commander of Army Group Vistula, p. 204; Guderian final argument with Hitler, p205.

Jodl, Alfred, Colonel General Importance of Norway campaign, p. 65 & 66; Tries to change Hitler's mind regarding Me-262, p. 87; Influence on Hitler's decisions, p. 136; Opinion of Hitler as military leader, p. 138; culpable for mismanagement of Germany's military campaigns, p. 139; Mantueffel's observations concerning, p. 139; defence at Nuremberg Trials, p. 140; dispute with Hitler regarding Field Marshal List, p. 145; state of resigned acquiescence to Hitler's orders, p. 148; failure in achieving any unity of command, p. 155; negligible operational experience, p. 161; role in Ardennes offensive, p. 162; Hitler's decision to declare war on USA, p. 178; role in Normandy defence, p. 190 & 191; Jodl's incomprehension of state of Eastern Front, p. 199; strategic errors regarding Ardennes offensive, p. 199; executed after Nuremberg Trials, p. 209.

Keitel, Field Marshal Wilhelm Speer describes new weapon demonstration to Hitler, p. 113; Hitler's reasons for appointing Keitel, p. 136; Keitel's influence on decisions, p. 136; Stalingrad, p. 136; held in contempt by most senior commanders, p. 137; describes Hitler as 'demon' p. 137; Speer describes as 'servile flatterer', p. 137; Hitler decides to sack, p. 145; Guderian states he was in a state of 'permanent hypnosis', p. 148; Rundstedt tells Keitel to end the war after failure at Normandy, p. 192; Hitler always looking for scapegoat, p. 201; sacking of Brauchitsch, p. 201; Hitler's 'pathological delusion', p. 203; Memoirs, p. 209; executed after Nuremberg Trials, p. 209.

Kesselring, Field Marshal Albert The role of the Condor Legion in Spain, p. 62; Luftwaffe in Polish Campaign, p. 63 & 64; French campaign, p. 69; strategic bomber, p. 71; Kesselring's view of Sea Lion, p. 73; comments re Hitler's system, p. 156; appointed Commander in Chief, West, p. 203.

Kleist, Field Marshal Ewald View of Hitler as Supreme Commander, p. 153-154.

Kluge, Field Marshal Gunther Defense of Normandy, p. 155; suspected of complicity in assassination attempt on Hitler, p. 168; Hitler told Kluge that Rommel and Rundstedt were too pessimistic about Normandy, p. 192.

Lenard, Philipp Won Nobel Prize for physics in 1920, p. 130; told Hitler that nuclear physics was 'Jewish physics' which dissuaded Hitler form committing resources to the potential of a German A bomb, p. 130.

List, Field Marshal, Wilhelm Hitler's confrontation with Jodl when List sacked, p. 145.

Maisky, Ivan Information given to him by British government concerning German attack, p. 43.

Manstein, Field Marshal Eric No evidence of soviet dispositions to attack Germany, p. 43; Zeitzler supportive of Manstein's plan for Operation Citadel, p. 146; Guderian was operationally responsible for success of attack against France 1940, p. 147; view of Hitler as supreme commander, p. 151-153; evidence at Nuremberg Trials, p. 153; attempt to relieve Stalingrad, p. 187; analysis of 'Operation Citadel', p. 194-197; sacked by Hitler as result of machinations by Himmler and Goering, p. 209.

Manteuffel, General Hasso Ardennes offensive, December 1944, view of Hitler as Supreme Commander, p. 139.

Messerschmidt ME-262 First jet propelled fighter to become operational, p. 83; Galland's impressions, p. 83; Goering's enthusiasm for, p. 84; delays caused by Hitler, p. 84; Hitler decides to produce it as a bomber, p. 85; Hitler issues order to produce as a bomber, thus throwing away the best chance the Germans had to defeat the allied bomber offensive, p. 87; Speer's view on potential to affect allied air offensive, p. 88.

Milch, Field Marshal Erhard Goering advised Hitler not to attack the USSR, p. 58; additional bomber program would cost 500 million RM, p. 60; testimony at Nuremberg Trial, p. 77; told Speer that the Luftwaffe had told Goering it could not supply Stalingrad army, p. 81; wanted Me-262 to be given highest production priority as fighter, p. 84; attempted to get Hitler to approve Me-262 as fighter, p. 95.

Model, Field Marshal Walter Attempted to persuade Hitler to change views on use of Me-262, p. 87; Hitler did not consult him on Ardennes attack although he was to command it, p. 150; rescinded Kluge's orders when took over as C-in-C West but changed his mind after a few days, p. 169; role in Operation Citadel, p. 195-196; Ardennes offensive 'didn't have a damned leg to stand on', p. 198; committed suicide on 15 March 1945 and discharged his Army and was denounced as a traitor, p. 204.

Montgomery, Field Marshal Bernard Role in Ardennes defence, p. 198.

Nuremberg Trials Evidence of Schacht, p. 6; evidence of Doenitz, p. 10 & 50; evidence of Raeder, p. 52; evidence of Goeing, p. 61 & 161; evidence of Jodl, p. 65, 138, 140 & 145; evidence of Milch, p. 76; interview with Keitel, p. 137; evidence of Manstein, p. 153; Kleist interview, p. 153.

Panther tank – PzkfwV Approved by Hitler for production in May 1943 at 600 per month, p. 117; effect of chopping and changing priorities, p. 118; characteristics, p. 119; cost and man hours to produce, p. 119; Hitler should have concentrated all resources on Panther production, p. 133; rushed to use in Citadel offensive before ready, p. 195.

Paulus, Field Marshal Friedrich Questions who it was who said the Luftwaffe could supply Stalingrad army, p. 83.

Raeder, Grand Admiral Erich Commander in Chief of the Kriegsmarine, p. xii; Plan Z, p. 3; view of the plight of the Kriegsmarine on outbreak of war, p. 5; not enough oil to fuel ships of Plan Z, p. 5; role of battleships and battlecruisers in Plan Z, p. 6; description of Scharnhorst and Gneisenau on outbreak of war, p. 8; damage to Graf Spee, p. 8; U-Boats in Plan Z, p. 9; War strategy against Royal Navy, p. 14; Plan Z adopted by Hitler on 27 January 1939, p. 15; lack of bases to wage war against Britain, p. 18; weakness of surface fleet meant German

Index 239

plans could not be implemented, p. 19; victory in Norway involved crippling losses, p. 20; Hitler quizzes Raeder relating to loss of Bismarck, p. 22; did not agree with Hitler that the allies were going to invade Norway in 1942, p. 24; operation Cerberus a strategic defeat, p. 25; difficulties of operation Sea Lion, p. 27; meeting with Hitler on 21 July 1940 re Sea Lion, p. 29; eventual plan for Sea Lion landings, p. 34; Kriegsmarine's view of strategic options after defeat of France, p. 37; advocates destruction of British mediterranean positions with Italians, p. 40, 41 & 42; Doenitz recommends concentration on U-Boats, p. 45; Hitler orders scrapping of the surface fleet, P 51, & 52; Raeder resigns 30 January, 1943, p. 54; evidence at Nuremberg, p. 65; found guilty of war crime, Nuremberg Trials sentenced to life imprisonment.

Reichenau, Field Marshal Walter   Replaced Rundstedt as Commander, Army Group South, p. 201.

Ribbentrop, Joachim   Anglo German Naval Agreement, p. 1; Hitler's attitude to USSR, p. 179.

Rommel, Field Marshal Erwin   Afrika Corps showed how vulnerable Britain was in the Mediterranean, p. 41; awarded the Pour le Merite in WW1, p. 154; command of 7th Panzer division in 1940, p. 154; command of Army Group B for defence of France, p. 154; Hitler's flawed strategy, p. 155; agreed with Kluge that political action should be taken if invasion successful, p. 155; Memorandum to Hitler of 3 July 1944, p. 155; injured in strafing attack on 17 July 1944; the troops of the Fifteenth Army had to be committed to the defence of Normandy, p. 192; forced suicide on 14 October, 1944; Appendix I, p. 220.

Rundstedt, Field Marshal, Gerd   No evidence of short term intention to attack Germany, p. 43; request for OKW reserves on 6th June refused by Jodl, p. 139; disagreements with Hitler, p. 150; Hitler did not consult him in planning of Ardennes offensive, p. 150; Hitler's compromise defence strategy in France, p. 155; replaced by Kluge, p. 155; Hitler's orders re BEF in 1940, p. 181; tells Keitel to end the war, p. 192.

Schweppenburg, General Geyr   View of Hitler's command structure, p. 163.

Speer, Albert   Hitler raises naval construction to highest priority, April, 1943, p. 11; Hitler only prepared for the risk of war in 1939, not the actuality, p. 48; Hitler describes destruction of London, p. 74; Goering assures Hitler the Luftwaffe can supply the Sixth Army in Stalingrad, p. 81; Hitler's role in development of the ME-262, p. 86; effect of strategic bombing campaign against Germany, p. 92 & 93; 'Waterfall' anti-aircraft missile, p. 96; 'Vengeance' weapons program one of the worst mistakes of the war, p. 96; Hitler instructs Speer to stop production of all fighter aircraft, p. 99; severe damage to German oil industry, p. 101; effect on German tank production, p. 101; difficulty in defending against allied bombing offensive, p. 102; describes defence against allied bombing offensive as 'lost front', p. 106; Hitler not interested in organisational changes to armaments industries, p. 111; Hitler's technical horizon limited to time of WW1, p. 111; Hitler's amateurism, p. 112; Hitler's decisions made in vacuum, p112; description of weapons conferences with Hitler, p. 113; Hitler's bizarre decision relating to spare parts for tanks, p. 120; description of Waterfall anti-aircraft missile, p. 122 & 123; V weapons program cost RM5 billion, p. 123-126; comparison of effect of V-2 with US B17 bomber, p. 127; the whole notion [of the V weapons program] was absurd, p128; Hitler didn't understand potential of A Bomb, p. 129; only one cyclotron in Europe not suited to atomic research, p. 130; Hitler believed atomic bomb based on 'Jewish physics', p. 130; impossibility of developing A bomb before allies, p. 130; program shut down in 1942 because of lack of resources, p. 131; Hitler would have used the A bomb if he had it, p. 132; Hitler's entourage was partially to blame for his hubris, p. 135; Keitel reduced to 'servile flatterer', p. 137; Sepp Deitrich says Hitler was crazy for a long time, p. 159.

Sperrle, Field Marshal Hugo   Command in French campaign 1940, p. 69; meeting on strategy for Sea Lion, p. 73; tried for war crimes, found not guilty.

Tiger Tank Mk 1 PzkfwVI   Guderian's remarks on tank programme, p. 118; very powerfully armed and armoured, p. 118; disadvantages of weight, p. 118; Zeiss optical systems, p. 119; costly to produce, p. 119; Hitler's bizarre decision regarding spare parts for the Tiger, p. 121; difficult to service, p. 121; used in Operation Citadel, p. 195.

Tiger Tank Mk2 – Sd.Kfz.182 Characteristics, p. 120; used on Normandy and the Ardennes offensive, p. 120; too expensive and time consuming, p. 133.

Vengeance weapons program Most resource intensive program of the war, p. xii; Hitler's enthusiastic support, p. xiv; tonnage of bombs including V weapons dropped by combatants, p. 91; comparison with 'Waterfall' anti-aircraft missile, p. 96; Hitler's involvement in production of, p. 109; intended to counter the allies' strategic bombing campaign, p. 123; V-1 world's first cruise missile, p. 124; first results disappointing and Hitler decides to cancel the program but changes mind, p. 124 & 125; numbers sent to London on 15th June, 1944, p. 125; British knew of the V-1 flight characteristics, p. 125; fed the Germans misleading information, p. 125; use of proximity fuse against, p. 126; damage done by V-1s, p. 126; V-2 prototype of all intercontinental missiles, p. 126; problems with directional system, p. 126; no defence against, p. 127; comparison of effectiveness of V-2 and US B17 bomber, p. 127; V weapons programme a 'spectacular failure', p. 128.

Warlimont, General Walter Appointed as representative of German command to Franco, p. 61; view of Hitler's command methods and decisions, p. 140; dispute between Hitler and Halder resulted in Halder being dismissed, p. 142; atmosphere at Supreme Headquarters after assassination attempt, p. 170; German attitude to Japanese allies, p. 177; decision to declare war on USA, p. 178; Hitler's orders regarding BEF, p. 181.

Zeitzler, Colonel-General Kurt Appointed Chief of the General Staff of the Army after sacking of Halder in September, 1942, p. 81; Keitel's reaction to breakout from Stalingrad, p. 136; Hitler 'trusted no one', p. 144; warned Hitler on many occasions of faulty dispositions in Stalingrad offensive, p. 144; tried repeatedly to obtain Hitler's agreement to breakout of Sixth Army from Stalingrad, p. 144; urged withdrawal of Army Group A from Caucasus, p. 145 & 146; role in Operation Citadel, p. 146; 'Hitler never admitted to a mistake …', p. 147; Hitler was intoxicated by numbers, p. 183; reputation built on work with Kleist's First Panzer Army and as Chief of Staff, OB West, p. 185; Hitler refused to 'shake hands with any General', p. 202.